SOCIAL AND ECONOMIC CONDITIONS UNDER THE IMPERIAL RĀSHṬRAKŪṬAS

Circa A.D. 750-973

Social and Economic Conditions under the Imperial RĀSHTRAKŪTAS

Circa A.D. 750-973

JAYASHRI MISHRA
Reader in History
Magadh Mahila College
Patna University, Patna

Commonwealth Publishers
NEW DELHI-110002
(INDIA)

Published by

AJAY VERMA
for COMMONWEALTH PUBLISHERS
4378/4B, GALI MURARI LAL
ANSARI ROAD, NEW DELHI-110002
INDIA Telephone : 3272541

First Published, 1992

ISBN 81-7169-171-4

Printed at

Gaurav Printers
Maujpur
Delhi-110053

Dedicated to

the loving memory of
my mother
the Late (Smt.) Sushila Devi
[b. 15 April 1931
d. 22 October 1982]

Foreword

Before the dawn of the 8th century A.D., remarkable progress had been achieved in India in the fields of polity, administration, social set-up, philosophy, literature and fine arts. The ancient literature, inscriptions, archaeological relics and foreign accounts bear eloquent testimony to this. From the proto-historic period to *c.* 700 A.D. Indian history and culture are marked by a broad-based ideal of a welfare state, humanitarian emphasis on the administrative system, social justice and cultural advancement.

During the epochs of the Mauryas, the Śuṅgas, the Sātavāhanas and the Guptas, the country witnessed an all-round progress in state administration and socio-economic and cultural growth. Several institutions, with strong foundations for public welfare were established. They contributed to the growth of state-craft, the formation of a strong social system, based on the *varṇāśrama dharma*, the development of education and fine arts. These elements contributed to the growth of political and cultural integration. They had also a congenial impact on the inter-state relations inside the country and on India's inter-relations with several outside countries.

The Maurya empire had paved the way for the formation of a strong country-wide empire. Kauṭilya, the wise preceptor of Chandragupta Maurya, envisaged a strong welfare state. Kauṭilya derived his ideal from the Vedic polity. Kauṭilya was not only a man of vision but also a practical statesman, who guided the Maurya emperor to give concrete form to the Vedic principles, which were elaborated scientifically in the Artha-śāstra. The Śuṅgas, the Sātavāhanas, the Guptas, the Vākāṭakas and the Pallavas largely followed the state-craft of Kauṭilya. By the end of the 7th century A.D. India emerged, both in the North and South, as a great power in the contemporary civilized world.

After the disintegration of the Gupta empire, several kingdoms arose in the country. In the North the Maukharis of Kanauj were succeeded by the Vardhanas. In western India the Maitrakas and in the Deccan and southern India the Chālukyas of Bādāmī and the Pallavas of Kanchī rose to power.

Till almost the middle of the 7th century A.D. the North dominated over the South. But with the rise of the Rāṣṭrakūṭas, who succeeded the Bādāmī Chālukyas, the pendulum of political power turned from the South towards the North. Thus, in a way the Rāṣṭrakūṭas continued the work of the Sātavāhanas, who several centuries ago, had established their hegemony in the North.

The Rāṣṭrakūṭas, like the Kalachuris, had several branches. The chief branch extended its rule not only in the areas of Deccan and Karnataka but also in some parts of the Tamil land. Thus they became a super political power of the country.

The political frame-work of the Rāṣṭrakūṭa dynasty had been very well prepared by Prof. A.S. Altekar in the thirties of this century. The present work supplements, in an admirable manner, the work of Prof. Altekar.

Dr. Jayashri Mishra, in her study of the social and economic conditions under the Imperial Rāṣṭrakūṭas, has fully utilized the source-material. This material is in the form of inscriptions (mostly in Sanskrit and Kannada), coins, monuments and antiquities, literature and foreign accounts, particulary of the Arab writers. The results obtained from the field work at important sites like Bhokardan, have also been utilized.

The analysis of the social set-up, education, literature.

agriculture and industry and trade and commerce has been made judiciously.

The exposition of some of the problems related to the socio-economic history of the period is brilliant and convincing. The causes of the economic growth and later on of its decline have been critically assessed. Along with the archaeological original sources, the evidences obtained from several works, composed during the period, e.g., the *Yaśastilaka* and the *Nītivākyāmṛta* of Somadeva have been duly evaluated.

It has been aptly pointed out in the present work that, in spite of the continuation of the well-defined principles of Indian polity and social order, during the period of the Rāṣṭrakūṭas, necessary changes in the social set-up and economic policy were made. The economic guilds and a broad-based industrial policy of the Rāṣṭrakūṭas were largely responsible for the growth of the State. This is amply borne out from the contemporary inscriptions, literature and the foreign accounts.

The learned author has earned the gratitude of scholars of Indian history by preparing an adequately documented study of the early medieval society.

Sagar
Vijayā-daśamī,
18th October, 1991

K.D. BAJPAI
Tagore Professor and Head
of the Department of Ancient
History, Culture and
Archaeology, Sagar
University (Retd.)

Preface

The Rāshṭrakūṭas occupy an important place in the early history of India because they enjoyed a comparatively large kingdom and ruled for a longer period. It was a super-power of the time too, though only for a limited period. So to do work on 'Social and Economic Conditions under the Imperial Rāshṭrakūṭas' seemed to be more enchanting and challenging for me.

I have taken utmost care of the sources of the period and allowed them to speak in their own way. Nowhere in the present work have I tried to put them forcibly to prove my own hypothesis. Nothing beyond the period and empire of the Rāshṭrakūṭas has been utilised; if there is anything, that is minimal in number and used either for argument-framing or for comparison only.

The whole work has been divided into eight chapters. After introducing the subject, there are two chapters on the social set-up and organisation. The chapter on education and literature has been followed by agriculture and industry. Then I have discussed trade and commerce. Subsequently, means of transport available during those days and important Rāshṭrakūṭa towns have been elaborated to produce a complete picture of the social and economic aspects of the times.

I wish to express my profound gratitude to my revered *guru*, the late Professor B.P. Mazumdar, formerly University Professor and Head of the Department of History, Patna University for his constant help and fatherly encouragement to complete the work. I am beholden to Dr. Ramavatar Shukla, the then Vice-Chancellor of the Patna University, for awarding me a Teacher-Fellowship under the U.G.C. scheme of Faculty Improvement Programme which enabled me to complete the work. Consequently, the Patna University awarded me the degree of Doctor of Philosophy in History in May 1987.

I am humbly grateful to the renowned historian Professor K.D. Bajpai, formerly Tagore Professor and Head of the Department of Ancient Indian History, Culture and Archaeology, University of Sagar, who kindly agreed to write the foreword of this book. I am thankful to Professor U.V. Singh, Professor and Chairman, Department of Ancient Indian History, Culture and Archaeology, Kurukshetra University, who gave valuable suggestions.

I owe much to a number of scholars too for their help, though indirect, but very valuable. Prominent among them are Drs. T.V. Pathy (Marathwada University, Aurangabad, Maharashtra), S.V. Sohoni, Retired I.C.S. (Poona), S.H. Ritti (Karnatak University, Dharwar), M.S. Nagrajrao (Ex-Director-General, Archaeological Survey of India), Amarendra Narayan (Archaeological Survey of India), D.N. Sharma and Y.K. Mishra (both from Institute of Prakrit, Jainology and Ahimsa, Vaishali).

I express my sincere thanks to Dr. Qeyamuddin Ahmad and Dr. Rajendra Ram (both Professors of History, Patna University) for their help. My thanks are due to Dr. Bishwambhar Jha, Reader in History, C.M. Arts College, Darbhanga also for his help extended to me at the initial stage of the work.

I have utilised materials from History Department Library, Patna University; Patna College Library; Patna University Library; Khuda Buksh Oriental Public Library; Archaeological Survey of India, Mid-Eastern Circle Library; Bihar Research Society Library; K.P. Jayaswal Research Institute Library; Sinha Library (all at Patna); Sharada Sadan Pustakalaya, Lalganj (Vaishali); Prakrit Institute Library, Vaishali; Marathwada University Library, Aurangabad; Bombay University Library; Bharatiya Vidya Bhavan Library, Bombay; Bombay Branch of Asiatic Society Library; Poona

University Library; Bhandarkar Oriental Research Institute Library, Poona; Deccan College Library, Poona; Karnataka University Library, Dharwar; Mysore University Library; Library of the Chief Epigraphist, Government of India, Mysore; Mythic Society Library, Bangalore; Osmania University Library, Hyderabad; Library of the State Archaeology Department, Andhra Pradesh, Hyderabad etc. Librarians of the above mentioned Libraries deserve my thanks. But Shri Ram Swarup Prasad Singh, Librarian, Archaeological Survey of India, Patna deserves my special thanks because without his help the work would have been quite difficult for me. Mr. Satish G. Sangle, Librarian, BORI, Poona, also showed a very helpful attitude. I thank him very much.

My father, Dr. Yogendra Mishra, formerly Professor and Head of the Department of History, Patna University has gone through the whole manuscript of the book. Though I am indebted to him by birth, but I shall fail in my duty if I do not thank him at this stage too. I must also thank Dr. Ram Naresh Sharma, my husband, for all his help and co-operation extended to me.

Lastly, I do not wish to miss thanking Mr. Vinay Kumar Pandey (Proprietor, Gaurav Printers, Delhi) and Mr. B.R. Verma, Publisher of this book who virtually forced me to get the book published. I appreciate their role. I also thank them for printing the book in quickest possible time with utmost care and sincerity.

Patna : 18-10-1991

JAYASHRI MISHRA
Reader in History
Magadh Mahila College
Patna University, Patna

Abbreviations

ABORI	*Annals of the Bhandarkar Oriental Research Institute*, Poona
AIOC	*All India Oriental Conference (Proceedings)*
ASI	*Archaeological Survey of India*
ASWI	*Archaeological Survey of Western India*
BDCRI	*Bulletin of the Deccan College Research Institute*, Poona
BG	*Bombay Gazetteer*
BISM	Bharata Itihasa Samsodhaka Mandala, Poona
BKI	*Bombay Karnataka Inscriptions*, Dharwar
CII	*Corpus Inscriptionum Indicarum*
EC	*Epigraphia Carnatica*, Mysore
Ed.	Edited, Editor
EHD	*Early History of the Deccan* by R.G. Bhandarkar
EI	*Epigraphia Indica*, Mysore
HCIP	*History and Culture of Indian People*, Bharatiya Vidya Bhavan Series
HIED	*History of India as told by its own Historian* by Elliot & Dowson
HK	*History of Karnataka*, Ed. by P.B. Desai
IA	*Indian Antiquary*, Bombay
IAP	*Inscriptions of Andhra Pradesh*
IHQ	*Indian Historical Quarterly*, Calcutta

JAHRS	*Journal of the Andhra Historical Research Society*
JAOS	*Journal of the American Oriental Society*
JASB	*Journal of the Asiatic Society of Bengal*, Calcutta
JBBRAS	*Journal of the Bombay Branch of Royal Asiatic Society*
JBORS	*Journal of the Bihar and Orissa Research Society*, Patna
JBRS	*Journal of the Bihar Research Society*, Patna
JIH	*Journal of Indian History*, Trivandrum
JKU	*Journal of the Karnataka University* (Social Sciences), Dharwar
KI	*Karnataka Inscriptions*, Dharwar
KRI	*Kannada Research Institute*, Dharwar
List	*Kielhorn's List*
Mahā.	*Mahāpurāṇa* of Pushpadanta
MAR	*Mysore Archaeological Report*
MUJ	*Marathwada University Journal* (Social Sciences), Aurangabad
NUJ	*Nagpur University Journal*
Periplus	*Periplus of the Erythraean Sea* by Schoff
PIHC	*Proceedings of the Indian History Congress*
QBISM	*Quarterly of the Bharata Itihasa Samsodhaka Mandala*, Poona
RATT	*Rāshṭrakūṭa and Their Times* by A.S. Altekar
SBE	*Sacred Books of the East*
SI	*Studies in Indology* by V.V. Mirashi
SII	*South Indian Inscriptions*
SMHD	*Sources of the Medieval History of the Deccan*
TOI	*Times of India*
tr.	Translated by, Translator
Yaś.	*Yaśastilaka and Indian Culture* by K.K. Handiqui

Scheme of Transliteration

अ	a	आ	ā	इ	i
ई	ī	उ	u	ऊ	ū
ए	e	ऐ	ai	औ	au
ऋ	ṛ	क्	k	ख्	kh
ग्	g	घ्	gh	ङ्	ṅ
च्	ch	छ्	chh	ज्	j
झ्	jh	ञ्	ñ	ट्	ṭ
ठ्	ṭh	ड्	ḍ	ढ्	ḍh
ण्	ṇ	त्	t	थ्	th
द्	d	ध्	dh	न्	n
प्	p	फ्	ph	ब्	b
भ्	bh	म्	m	य्	y
र्	r	ल्	l	व्	v
श्	ś	ष्	sh	स्	s
ह्,	h	क्ष्	ksh	त्र्	tr
		ज्ञ्	jñ		
		अनुस्वार	ṁ (anusvara)		
		विसर्ग	ḥ (visarga)		

Contents

Foreword vii

Preface xi

Abbreviations xiv

Scheme of Transliteration xvii

1. INTRODUCTION 1-24

Section I
Significance and Scope, 1.
Section II
Political Background and Origin, 5; The Founder 6; Epithets of the Rāshṭrakūṭa Emperors, 8; The Royal Emblem, 11; Extent of the Empire, 12; Rāshṭrakūṭa Supremacy, 13; Collapse of the Empire, 16.
Section III
Sources—Inscriptions, 17; Coins; Monuments and Antiquities, 20; Literature: (a) Indigenous Literature, 21; (b) Foreign Notices, 23.

2. SOCIAL SET-UP AND ORGANISATION—I 25-68

Caste System: The Brāhmaṇas, 26; The Kshatriyas, 35; The Vaiśyas, 35; The Śūdras, 36; The Untouchables, 37; The Muslims, 40;

The Navayats, 42; Different Stages of Life, 46; Means of Livelihood, 46; Status of Saints in Society, 47; Mahājanas, 48; Family System, 50; Marriage, 51; Position of Women, 57; Satī System, 62; Purdah System, 67.

3. SOCIAL SET-UP AND ORGANISATION—II 69-108

Dress, 69; Hair Style, 73; Ornaments, 73; Household Articles, 76; Food and Drinks, 79; Festivals, 82; Sports, Games, Pastimes and Amusements, 85; Manners and Customs, 91; Superstitious Beliefs, 96; Astronomy and Astrology, 98; Importance of Regnal Years, 99; Charitable/Meritorious Works, 100; Forced Labour, 102; Corruption, 104; Crime and Punishment, 105; Place Names: an observation, 106.

4. EDUCATION AND LITERATURE 109-139

A. Education, 109
B. Literature, 115
(a) Sanskrit : General Works, 115
(b) Sanskrit : Scientific Works, 127
(c) Apabhraṁśa, 128
(d) Kannada, 131
(e) Telugu, 136
(f) Marathi, 137
(g) Trilingual or Bilingual Inscriptions, 138.

5. AGRICULTURE AND INDUSTRY 140-162

Section I

Agriculture, 140; Types of Land, 140; Ownership and Transfer Right of Land, 141; Unit of Land Measurement, 144; Main Crops, 146;

Fruits and Spices, 147; Garden and Forests, 147; Irrigation Works, 148; Agricultural Taxes, 149; Time of Agricultural Tax Collection, 152; Exemption from Taxation, 152; Love for Cattle, 156.

Section II

Industries, 154; Mineral Resources and Industries, 155; Textile Industry, 157; Leather Industry, 158; Sugarcane Industry, 159; Coir Industry, 160; Boat Industry, 160; Oil-Mill Industry, 161; Bangle Making, 161; Other Industries, 161.

6. TRADE AND COMMERCE 163-191

Arab-Rāshṭrakūṭa Trade Relations, 164; Ports and Indian Coasts, 165; Trade Routes, 167; Indian Commodities and Their Popularity, 170: Slave Trade, 172; Internal Trade, 173; Position of Traders, 176; Coins and Currency System, 178; Weights and Measures, 186; Banking System, 188; Commercial Taxes, 188.

7. MEANS OF TRANSPORT 192-198

(A) Land Transport : (a) Horses, 193; (b) Chariots, 194; (c) Elephants, 195; (d) Bullock Carts, 196; (e) Palanquins, 197

(B) Water-Transport : Boats, 197.

8. IMPORTANT RĀSHṬRAKŪṬA TOWNS 199-222

The early Capitals : Latūr, 199; Elichpur, 200; Mayurkhindi, 201; Elūra, 202; Mānpur, 204; The final Capital : Mānyakheṭa, 204; Religious and other Towns : Aihole, 209: Ajantā, 210;

Aland, 211; Aṇṇigeri, 211 ; Bankāpur, 212; Bhokardan, 212; Jogeśvarī, 212; Kandahār, 213; Kanheri, 214; Karahāṭa, 215; Kolhapur, 215; Mangalore, 216; Melapāti, 216; Panahala, 217; Paṇḍharpur, 217; Paṭṭadakal, 218; Poona, 219; Pratishṭhāna, 220; Rohaṇkheḍ, 220; Sanjan, 220; Saundatti, Śrīpura, 221; Vātāpi, 222.

Bibliography 223-255

Index 257-26

1

Introduction

SECTION 1

Significance and Scope

The need for a detailed and thorough study of the social and economic conditions under the imperial Rāshṭrakūṭas was felt by us due to the conspiracy of situations. No attempt had been made previously to present the socio-economic changes that took place during the period of the Rāshṭrakūṭa rule in the Deccan.

The first and pioneer work on the history of the Rāshṭrakūṭas was done by Dr. A.S. Altekar and published as early as in 1934.[1] Although he has dealt with all the aspects of Rāshṭrakūṭa history, but his main purpose of study was to solve problems of political history. In his attempt to write social and economic history under the Rāshṭrakūṭas he has described, at most of the places, the conditions obtaining prior to the Rāshṭrakūṭas and the conditions that prevailed as late as the seventeenth century A.D.[2] This he did in order to find out the mean. Due to the paucity of materials at the

1. A.S. Altekar, *Rāshṭrakūṭas and their Times*, Poona, 1934.
2. *Ibid.*, pp. 329, 331, 334, 345, 355, 356, 360, 367, 393 etc,

time of his writing, he has based his study on the assumption that "social and religious customs and institutions do not change suddenly,"[1] and in so doing he has utilised the inscriptions of the centuries just preceding and following the Rāshṭrakūṭa period. So far as our own study is concerned, we have restricted ourselves to the period and domain of the Rāshṭrakūṭas as far as practicable.

There are chapters written in several prestigious publications such as *The History and Culture of the Indian People*, Vol. IV edited by R.C. Majumdar, *The Early History of the Deccan* (2 vols.), edited by G. Yazdani, *A Comprehensive History of India*, Vol. III, edited by R.C. Majumdar and K.K. Dasgupta, *A History of Karnataka* edited by P.B. Desai etc. also, but they do not suffice the purpose.

We now take up independent books written on the social-economic history that would show that no independent work had been done on the topic concerned. Broadly we can classify these books into the following categories: (i) books written on south Indian history; (ii) books written on north Indian history; (iii) books written on ancient Indian history in general and (iv) books written on a particular dynasty or period or region. Prominent works under the first category are A. Appadorai, *Economic Conditions in Southern India (1000-1500)*; Deepak Ranjan Das, *Economic History of the Deccan (From the first to the sixth century A.D.)*; G.R. Kuppuswamy, *Economic Conditions in Karnataka (A.D. 973-A.D. 1336)*, etc. Prominent works under the second category are B.P. Mazumdar. *Socio-Economic History of Northern India (1030-1194 A.D.)*; Lallanji Gopal, *The Economic Life of Northern India (c. A.D. 700-1200)*; Pushpa Niyogi, *Contributions to the Economic History of Northern India from the tenth to the twelfth century A.D.*; A. Bose, *Social and Rural Economy of Northern India (c. 600 B.C.—200 A.D.)* etc. Some of the books under the third category are S.A.Q. Hussaini, *The Economic History of India (From the earliest times to the formation of feudalism)*; Haripada Chakraborti, *Trade and Commerce of Ancient India (c. 200 B.C.—c. 600 A.D.)*; Pran

1. *Ibid.*, p, v.

Nath, *A Study in the Economic Conditions of Ancient India*; K.T. Shah, *Ancient Foundation of Economics*; N.C. Bandyopadhyaya, *Economic Life and Progress in Ancient India*; S.K. Das, *Economic History of Ancient India*; J.C. Jain, *Life in Ancient India as depicted in the Jain Canons*; D.C. Jain, *Economic Life in Ancient India as depicted in Jain Canonical Literature*, etc. Mention may be made here of some of the important works under the fourth category also. They are S.K. Maity, *Economic Life in Northern India in the Gupta Period (cir. A.D. 300-550)*; R.N. Saletore, *Life in the Gupta Age*; K. Sundaram, *A Study of Economic and Social Conditions in Medieval Andhra*; A.P. Sah, *Life in Medieval Orissa (c. A.D. 600-1200)*, etc. The above survey clearly shows that no book written on the subject takes up the social and economic conditions under the Rāshṭrakūṭa empire. They all lie either beyond the Rāshṭrakūṭa period or beyond the territory of the Rāshṭrakūṭa empire, and it was this very condition which necessitated the present study by ourselves.

SECTION II

Political Background

The Rāshṭrakūṭas of ancient times, like the Deshpandes and Deshmukhs of modern times, were the heads of territorial divisions. The antiquity of this term may be traced to the Mauryas whose inscriptions mention officers called Rāshṭrika.[1] The expression *Rāshṭrakūṭa* is a combination of two words, *Rāshṭra* and *Kūṭa*. Here *Rāshṭra* denotes a region or district and *Kūṭa* means a chief. Some scholars have tried to argue that Raṭṭa was the original name of the family, which was Sanskritized as Rāshṭrakūṭa. But this view has no justification, because raṭṭa itself seems to be derived from Sanskrit *rāshṭra*.

There were several families of this name flourishing in different parts of the country. Most of the Rāshṭrakūṭa families earlier than the Imperial Rāshṭrakūṭas were ruling in

1. *H.K.*, p. 113.

the adjoining areas of Andhra Pradesh, Madhya Pradesh and Maharashtra. They were the Rāshṭrakūṭas of Betul (*c.* 575-650 A.D.), the Rāshṭrakūṭas of Mānpura (*c.* 650-700 A.D.) and the Rāshṭrakūṭas of Pathari (*c.* 750-875 A.D.).[1] They not be considered as related to one another unless there is sufficient evidence to prove such a connection. But parallel to the Imperial Rāshṭrakūṭas of Mānyakheṭa (*c.* 750-973 A.D.) there was a Rāshṭrakuṭa family ruling in Gujarat (Lāṭa) too. They were definitely connected with each other. The Gujarat branch of the Rāshṭrakūṭas was established by Indra II, the son of Dhruva, the Imperial king. Their rise and fall went together. After the fall of the Imperial Rāshṭrakūṭa dynasty we find different Rāshṭrakūṭa families ruling in different parts of the country.[2] They were the Rāshṭrakūṭas of Hastikundi (*c.* 900-1000 A.D.), the Rāshṭrakūṭas of Dhanop (*c.* 950-1010 A.D.), the Rāshṭrakūṭas of Bithu (*c.* 1200-1310 A.D.) (all in Rajputana or Rajasthan),[3] the Rāshṭrakuṭas of Kathiawar (A.D. 1384), the Rāshṭrakūṭas of Pañchāla (eleventh and twelfth centuries A.D.)[4], the Rāshṭrakūṭas of Kanauj (*c.* 1050-1202 A.D.), the Rāshṭrakūṭas of Bihar (*c.* 1050-1150 A.D.)[5], the Rāshṭrakūṭas of Orissa (the twelfth century A.D.)[6] etc. Discussion about the Rāshṭrakūṭas, other than the Imperial ones, is out of the scope of our studies here.

1. For detailed history of these minor dynasties see H.C. Ray, *The Dynastic History of Northern India*, I, Delhi, second edition, 1973, pp. 550-68.
2. *Ibid.*
3. Even today the lineage of the king of Bikaner is popularly connected with the Rāshṭrakūṭas (*Mirror*, a monthly magazine from Bombay, February 1974, pp. 60-63).
4. *H.C.I.P.*. V, p. 50.
5. *Ibid.*, p. 189. From the writings of Somadeva (959 A.D.) there seems to be a Bodh-Gaya Branch of the Rāshṭrakūṭas also. Mathanadeva (maternal uncle of Rāmapāla) was a ruler of Aṅga in the eleventh century A.D. See also pp. 28, 29, 31, 32, 34, 54 and 68 for Mathanadeva.
6. *Ibid.*, p, 221.

Origin

The original home of the Imperial Rāshṭrakūṭas was Lattur or Lattalur as it is indicated by the significant title *Laṭṭalūra-puravarādhīśvara*, 'the lord of the celebrated city of Laṭṭalūra', occurring in their records. This title was assumed by the Rāshṭrakūṭa princes of both the main line and of the subordinate branches of Gujarat, which can be taken to contain the clue to their original home. Lattalur is identified with modern Latur in Osmanabad district of Maharashtra. This area originally formed part of the Kannada stock which is justified by the Kannada place names, Kannada inscriptions and other cultural relics. The stone inscriptions of this dynasty are almost all in the Kannada script and language.[1]

The signature of Dhruva II, who issued the plates,[2] is engraved in south Indian old-Kanarese characters as is the case with the sign manuals of Karka and Dhruva I of the Gujarat branch in their Nausari and Baroda plates respectively. It is therefore clear that even as late as 884 A.D., the members of the Gujarat Rāshṭrakūṭa royal family were accustomed to write in a script which was current neither in northern India, nor in Gujarat, nor in Maharashtra but in Karnataka. This circumstance is very important for determining the home of the imperial Rāshṭrakūṭas. If the royal family had originally belonged to Maharashtra or to northern India, its members deputed to rule over Gujarat and domiciled there for more than a century, would not have continued to use for their sign manual a script current neither in Rajputana, nor in Maharashtra, nor in Gujarat, but in the far-off Karnataka.

All these above circumstances lead us to conclude that the imperial Rāsṭrakūṭas were of the Kannada origin.

Scholars trace the Rāshṭrakūṭas' descent from the lineage of the Sātyaki branch of the Yaduvaṁśa or of a person called Tuṅga. This latter is obviously an attempt at explaining the suffix *tuṅga* occurring in the names of the members of this family such as *Sāhasatuṅga*, *Śubhatuṅga*,

1. *H.K.*, pp. 115-16.
2. *E.I.*, XXII, pp. 98 and 176.

Nṛpatuṅga and *Jagattuṅga* etc. Thus the Imperial Rāshṭrakūṭas were of the Kannada origin. One of the Rāshṭrakūṭa kings Nṛpatuṅga Amoghavarsha I is credited with the authorship of the earliest classical work on Kannada poetics, the *Kavirājamārga.*

The Founder

Dantidurga, the son of Indra II, was the founder of the Imperial Rāshṭrakūṭa rule in the Deccan. The Samangad plates dated A.D. 754,[1] and the undated Daśāvatāra Cave inscription of Elūra[2] of his reign give a complete description of the victorious career of Dantidurga. He is said to have won the battles against Kāñchī, Kaliṅga, Kosala, Śrī-Śaila, Mālava, Lāṭa and Taṅka. Another record[3] informs us that when Dantidurga performed a *Hiraṇyagarbha* sacrifice at Ujjain, the Gurjara ruler and others acted as his door-keepers which shows his power and strength during his time. These statements leave no doubt that Dantidurga was the real founder of this Imperial family.

Dantidurga first fought and got victories for his feudal lord Vikramāditya II, the Chālukya emperor. The Chālukya emperor appreciated his heroism and conferred the titles such as *Pṛthivīvallabha* and *Khaḍgāvaloka* on him.[4] Dantidurga continued to be a loyal feudatory of Vikramāditya II for some years. But Dantidurga was ambitious. After the death of his lord in 747 A.D. Dantidurga became the master of central and southern Gujarat and the whole of Madhya Pradesh and Berar. Kīrtivarman II, the next Chālukya emperor, could not bear the rising influence of his nominal feudatory, and he challenged Dantidurga. In this battle Dantidurga defeated the Chālukya emperor and as a result became the master of the whole Maharashtra by the end of A.D. 753. He now assumed full imperial titles *Mahārājādhirāja Parameśvara Paramabhaṭṭāraka.* The chart below gives the complete picture of

1. *I.A.*, XI, p, 116.
2. *ASWI*, V, 92.
3. *E I*, XVIII, p. 252.
4. *H.C.I.P.*, IV, p. 2.

the period of the Rāshṭrakuṭa rulers and their order of succession.

The genealogy of the Imperial Rāshṭrakūṭas is shown in the following table:

Dantivarman
|
Indra I
|
Govinda I
|
Karka I

Indra II | 2. KṚSHṆA I (756-774 A.D.)

1. DANTIDURGA (*c.* 735-756 A.D.) (son of Indra II)

3. GOVINDA II (774-780 A.D.) | 4. DHRUVA (780-793 A.D.) (sons of Kṛshṇa I)

Karka | Stambha | 5. GOVINDA III (793-814 A.D.) | Indra (sons of Dhruva)

Karka | Govinda (sons of Indra) — Gujarat Branch

6. AMOGHAVARSH I (814-878 A.D.) | Śaṅkhā (m. Pallava Nandivarman III Nṛpatuṅga) | Chadrobalabbe (m. Gaṅga Būṭuga) (children of Govinda III)

|

7. KṚSHṆA II (878-914 A.D.)

|

Jagattuṅga (m. Govindāmbā and Lakshmī of Chedi)

(*Contd.*)

8. INDRA III (914-929 A.D.)

11. AMOGHAVARSHA III (935-939 A.D.)

9. AMOGHAVARSHA II (929-930 A.D.)

10. GOVINDA IV (930-935 A.D.)

12. KṚSHṆA III *Jagattuṅga* (939-967 A.D.)

(son) Indra IV

13. KHOṬṬIGA *Nirupama* (967-972 A.D.)

14. KARKA II (972-973 A.D.)

Here the names of those who were supreme sovereigns in the Deccan have been given in capitals and the order of succession is represented by the numbers. The names of those who did not ascend the throne at all (either central or provincial, local or of a branch line), have been italicised.

Epithets[1] *of Rāshṭrakūṭa Emperors*

The Rāshṭrakūṭa emperors bore different titles symbolising the achievements of their own:

1. For these epithets see R.C. Majumdar and K.K. Dasgupta (eds.), *Comprehensive History of India*, Vol. III, Pt. I, New Delhi, 1981, pp. 440-81; *H.C.I.P.*, IV, pp. 1-17 and *H.K.*, pp. 113-145. We have arranged the epithets below keeping in view their frequency.

King	Titles
1. Dantidurga	*Sāhasatuṅga* ('one who is high in his outstanding enterprise') *Pṛthivivallabha* ('lord of the earth') *Khaḍgāvaloka* ('one whose mere sight is as effective as sword')
2. Kṛshṇa I	*Akālavarsha* ('yielding showers even when not required') *Śubhatuṅga* ('high in prosperity')
3. Govinda II	*Prabhūtavarsha* ('one yielding showers of plenty') *Prabhutuṅga* ('the eminent lord') *Vikramāvaloka* ('he whose glance was heroic')
4. Dhruva	*Dhārāvarsha* ('one yielding incessant showers') *Kali-Vallabha* ('lord of the Kali age') *Śrī-Vallabha* ('the favourite of the Fortune') *Nirupama* ('unequalled')
5. Govinda III	*Prabhūtavarsha* *Jagattuṅga* ('lofty in the word') *Janavallabha* ('lord of mankind') *Śrīvallabha* *Kirtinārāyaṇa* ('God Nārāyaṇa in renown') *Tribhuvanadhavala* ('of unsullied glory in the three worlds') *Jagadrudra* ('God Rudra of the earth')

	King	Titles
6.	Śarva or Amoghavarsha I	*Amoghavarsha* ('one yielding fruitful showers) *Nṛpatuṅga* ('Paramount King') *Vīra-Nārāyaṇa* ('God Nārāyaṇa the valorous') *Atiśaya-dhavala* ('exceedingly pure') *Mahārājashaṇḍa* ('best of the great kings')
7.	Kṛshṇa II	*Akālavarsha* *Śubhatuṅga*
8.	Indra III	*Nityavarsha* ('one yielding incessant showers') *Kīrttinārāyaṇa* *Raṭṭakandarpa* (Raṭṭa, the handsome) *Rājamārtaṇḍa* ('the Sun among kings')
9.	Amoghavarsha II	x x x
10.	Govinda IV	*Prabhūtavarsha* *Suvarṇavarsha* *Vikrānta-Nārāyaṇa* *Nıyakandarpa* *Nṛpati-Trinetra* *Chāṇakyachaturmukha*
11.	Amogha-varsha III	*Suvarṇavarsha* ('showers of gold')
12.	Kṛshṇa III	*Akālavarsha* *Raṭṭakandarpa* *Kachchiyum-Tañjāiyum-Koṇḍa*
13.	Khoṭṭiga	x x x
14.	Karka II	*Amoghavarsha* *Nṛpatuṅga* *Vira-Nārāyaṇa* *Ahitamārtaṇḍa* ('burner or destroyer of evils') *Rājatrinetra* *Nūtana-Pārtha* ('the new Arjuna')

The Royal Emblem

The royal emblem of the imperial Rāshṭrakūṭas was Garuḍa or the Primeval Eagle, the vehicle of Vishṇu, which was exhibited on the seals of their copper-plate charters. They had both Śiva and Vishṇu as family gods; so the figure on the seals, in certain cases, is identified as Śiva. But, in most cases, the symbol of Garuḍa is prominent and conspicuous. Both Vishṇu and Śiva are invoked in the beginning verses of their charters. The images of Gaṅgā and Yamunā were among their insignia. The Rāshṭrakūṭas were heralded in public by the sound of an instrument called Trivali or Tivali.

The Rāshṭrakūṭas of Mānyakheṭa had the Pālidhvaja banner. This was originally the banner of the Chālukyas of Bādāmi and used as a symbol of their victory against north Indian kings. Thus it was inherited by the Rāshṭrakūṭas, because they were the successors of the Chālukyas of Bādāmi. Thus we see that the great change in Dantidurga's position, by which he rose from the dignity of a feudal lord to that of an emperor, did not affect his seal. And this arrangement continued with the same contents to the time of Amoghavarsha I when new details were incorporated. In the seal of Amoghavarsha[1] we notice several innovations. In each hand of Garuḍa is inserted a snake. On his proper right is a figure of Gaṇapati in the upper corner and a *chauri* and a lamp in the lower corner. On the proper left is Pārvatī standing in front of lion and holding a ladle in her hand. Below her is a *chauri* and near the bottom is a *svastika.* The seal of Kṛshṇa I has a relief on a countersunk surface of an image of Garuḍa above a floral device, seated with the palms of his hands joined together and placed close to his chest and with his wings raised.[2] The seal of Govinda III shows the Garuḍa squatting and facing full front, with his hands joined, palm to palm on the chest and turned upwards. His feet are joined sole to sole and are turned downwards. His wings are raised

1. D.R. Bhandarkar, 'A List of Inscriptions of Northern India written in Brāhmi and its derivative scripts', *E.I.*, Vols. 19-23, List No. 133.
2. *Ibid*, List No. 97.

and below is a floral device.[1] On the seal of Kṛshṇa II,[2] the figure of Pārvatī is omitted whereas on the seal of Indra III[3] a *liṅga* and an *aṅkuśa* are added to the contents. The seal of Govinda IV[4] shows altogether different details around the central Garuḍa, *viz.*, a dagger, a bow and an arrow. Lastly the seal of Kṛshṇa III[5] is very elaborate and shows besides the central Garuḍa who holds a snake in each hand, on the proper right from top to bottom an image of Gaṇapati, a *chauri* and a lamp. On the proper left the goddess Pārvatī is riding on a lion and below her is a *svastika*. Along the margin of the seal passes a border of various indistinct emblems, among which a *liṅga* and an elephant goad are recognisable. Thus we see that the main theme of the seal remained unchanged for ever during the Rāshṭrakūṭa rule.

Extent of the Empire

Under Kṛshṇa I (756-774 A.D.) the newly established Rāshṭrakūṭa power, in spite of the difficulties it faced, expanded in all directions. The Bhāndak plates of A.D. 772[6] show that the whole of the wèstern Madhya Pradesh had come under his rule by the time. The Śilāhāras of the southern Koṅkaṇa were made his feudatory in that part of his empire.[7] The expansion of the empire in the southern direction is attested to by several inscriptions.[8] The ruler of Veṅgī at that time was Vijayāditya I (A.D. 755-72) who had escaped by offering formal submission; there was no invasion of the Veṅgī kingdom and no battle. Thus the Rāshṭrakūṭa empire under him may be taken to have extended over the whole of the modern Maharashtra, a good part of Karnataka, part of

1. *Ibid.*, No. 109.
2. *Ibid.*, No. 147.
3. *Ibid.*, No. 151.
4. *Ibid.*, No. 162.
5. *Ibid.*, No. 164.
6. *E.I*, XIV, pp. 121-30.
7. *B.G.*, I, ii, pp. 392-93.
8. *E.I.*, VI, p. 161; *MAR*, 1910, p. 23.

Andhra Pradesh (practically the whole of the former Hyderabad State) and a good part of Madhya Pradesh.

In the *Kavirājamārga*, Amoghavarsha I Nṛpatuṅga demarcates the boundaries of the Rāshṭrakūṭa empire. The Rāshṭrakūṭa dominions were wider in extent than those of the Chālukyas of Bādāmi. Broadly speaking, the Narmadā[1] and the Kāverī demarcated their northern and southern boundaries respectively, their western boundary stretching as far as the Arabian Sea. It included, though not permanently, parts of Malwa and southern Gujarat in the north, strips of western Andhra Pradesh like the tracts of Warangal and Cuddapah in the east, and the areas of Kāñchī and Tanjore in the south. Roughly speaking, they held sway over the whole of the present Maharashtra and Karnataka States and parts of Madhya Pradesh, Andhra Pradesh and Tamil Nadu.[2]

The Rāshṭrakūṭas penetrated to the extreme south and to the north also, but they did not hold sway permanently over the whole territory which they had won. But the permanent territorial boundary defined on the basis of the Rāshṭrakūṭa inscriptions, monuments and antiquities and the literary evidences has been shown in the map given on page 14.

Rāshṭrakūṭa Supremacy

Till the middle of the seventh century it was the North that was making inroads into the South; the whole thing was but a part of the Aryanisation and Hinduisation of the Deccan and the South. Harshavardhana's unsuccessful encounter with Pulakeśin II on the Narmadā was the last episode in that process. The tide now turned in favour of the Deccan and the South, and by about the third quarter of the eighth century we see the Rāshṭrakūṭa emperor marching his armies into the very heart of the North.

The first great conqueror to emerge on the scene was Dantidurga. With his conquering army he swept over the north and captured Ujjayinī during the time of Nāgabhaṭa I.

1. *E.I.*, XXVI, p. 181.
2. *H.K.*, pp. 147-48.

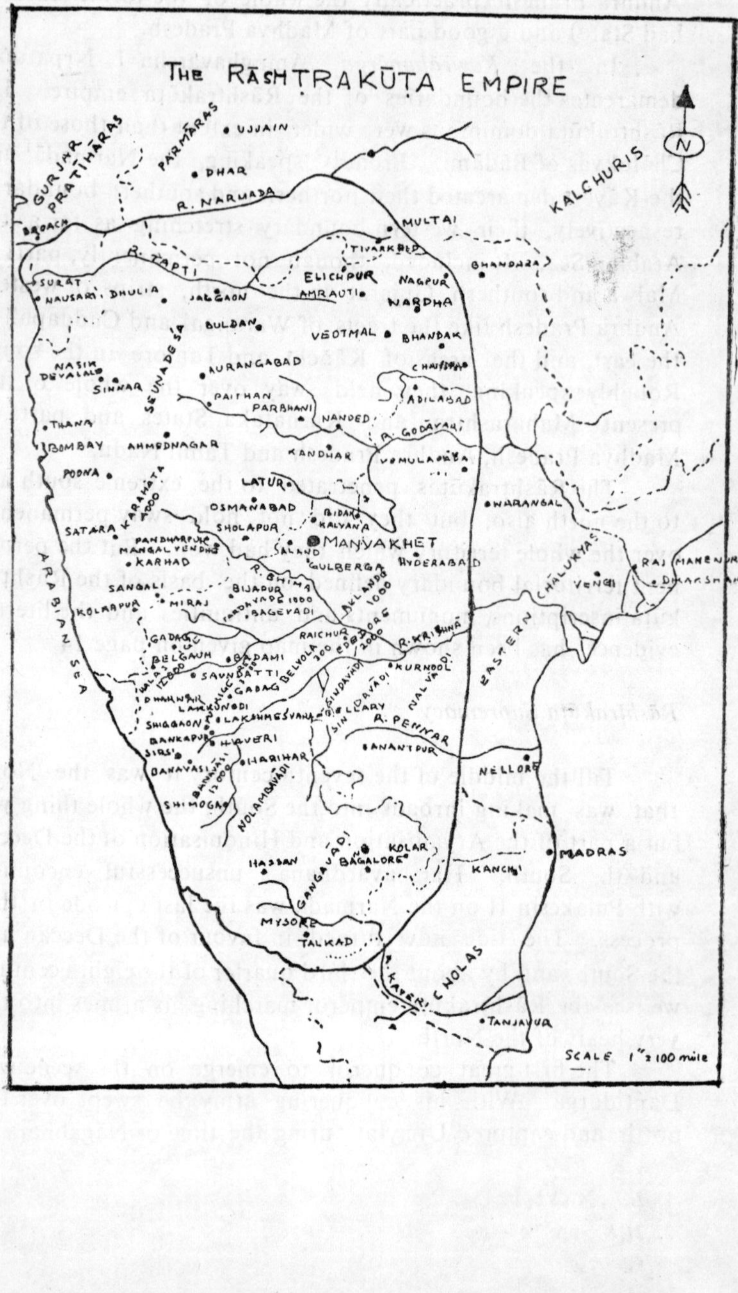
THE RĀSHTRAKŪTA EMPIRE
N
GURJAR PRATIHĀRAS
PARMARAS
UJJAIN
DHAR
R. NARMADA
KALCHURIS
BROACH
MULTAI
TIVARKHED
R. TAPTI
BHANDARA
SURAT
ELICHPUR
NAGPUR
NAUSARI
DHULIA
JALGAON
AMRAUTI
WARDHA
BULDAN
YEOTMAL
BHANDAK
SEUNADESA
NASIK
AURANGABAD
SINNAR
PAITHAN
ADILABAD
PARBHANI
THANA
NANDED
R. GODAVARI
BOMBAY
AHMEDNAGAR
KANDHAR
VEMULAVADA
POONA
LATUR
WARANGAL
OSMANABAD
SATARA
BIDAR
KALYANA
SHOLAPUR
PANDHARPUR
MANGALVEDHE
MANYAKHET
KARHAD
GULBERGA
HYDERABAD
RAJMAHENDRI
SANGALI
R. BHIMA
BIJAPUR
VENGI
KOLHAPUR
MIRAJ
BAGEVADI
EASTERN CHALUKYAS
ARABIAN SEA
GADAG
RAICHUR
R. KRISHNA
BELGAUM
BADAMI
KURNOOL
SAUNDATTI
GABAG
BELVOLA
DHARWAR
LAKKUNDI
BELLARY
SHIGGAON
LAKSHMESVARA
R. PENNAR
BANKAPUR
HAVERI
ANANTPUR
SIRSI
HARIHAR
NELLORE
BANAVASI
SHIMOGA
NOLAMBAVADI
MADRAS
HASSAN
GANGAVADI
KOLAR
BAGALORE
KANCHI
MYSORE
TALKAD
CHOLAS
R. KAVERI
TANJAVUR
SCALE 1" = 100 mile

The grandson of Nāgabhaṭa I, Vatsarāja, also suffered a disastrous defeat at the hands of the Rāshṭrakūṭa king Dhruva (*c.* 786 A.D.), and had to take refuge in some unaccessible region. This was the period of the famous tripartite struggle among the Pālas of Bengal, the Pratīhāras of Madhyadeśa and the Rāshṭrakūṭas of the Deccan. They entered the race for the all-India supremacy. The third Rāshṭrakūṭa conqueror of the North was Govinda III who inflicted a defeat on Nāgabhaṭa II (Pratīhāra) in A.D. 800.[1]

Indra III also marched to the North and occupied Kanauj. But he suddenly died and his army withdrew precipitately to the South. Other kings also had to struggle against the Pratīhāras especially, but they did not allow their enemies to enter the permanent Rāshṭrakūṭa territory.

In this struggle for supremacy India had to suffer great loss. K.M. Munshi writes "The two raids of the Rāshṭrakūṭas (on Kanauj) had unfortunate results for the whole India. Madhyadeśa lay mauled and bleeding."[2] From the tenth century onwards resistance to foreign attacks could not be as strong as it had been in the earlier period. The Rāshṭrakūṭa attack on the Gurjara-Pratīhāra king Mahīpāla in the early part of the tenth century was a great calamity so far as the security of Northern India was concerned, breaking the backbone of his power, and destroying the prestige and reputation on which his family's suzerainty had depended. The decline of the Gurjara-Pratīhāras was hastened as a consequence of the Rāshṭrakūṭa raid.

Stepping in the wake of the Chālukyas of Bādāmi, the Rāshṭrakūṭa age is a lustrous epoch in the history of the Deccan. The achievements of this epoch in the spheres of territorial expansion, political supremacy, military prowess and diplomacy, as well as attainments in the domains of language, literature, religion and art, are shining and substantial, some of them endowed with imperishable merits transcending the barriers of time and space. Thus we see that the Rāshṭrakūṭas, on whom the imperial mantle of the Chālukyas fell continued the imperial traditions and sustained

1. *H.C.I.P.*, II, p. 8.
2. *H.C.I.P.*, IV, p. XXIII.

the glory of the Deccan.

Collapse of the Empire

Kṛshṇa III died without an issue. His younger brother Khoṭṭiga succeeded him in A.D. 967. He was advanced in age and lacked in military capacity and administrative ability. The hostile rulers, who had been molested and provoked in the aggressive wars of Kṛshṇa III, took advantage of this situation to wreak their vengeance. Khoṭṭiga could not repulse the invasion of the Rāshṭrakūṭa dominions by the Paramāra King Sīyaka. Sīyaka crossed the river Narmadā and marched into the Rāshṭrakūṭa territory as far as Mānyakheṭa in the spring of A.D. 972.[1] The capital was plundered completely and the treasury was emptied. The Gaṅga chief Mārasiṁha II, a feudatory of the Rāshṭrakūṭas, succeeded in driving away the enemy, but the blow was serious and fatal which shook the very roots of the Rāshṭrakūṭa empire.

Karka II ascended the throne when the Rāshṭrakūṭa empire was tottering. The officials became insubordinate and the feudatories defied the authority of the crown. Confusion and disorder prevailed; and discontent was widespread among the subjects. A conspiracy was organised under the leadership of Taila II, a scion of the imperial Chālukya house of Bādāmi, for the overthrow of the Rāshṭrakūṭa regime. Taila II had gained vast experience in statecraft and proficiency in military lore by his long service under the Rāshṭrakūṭas in various capacities. He openly revolted against the authority of Karka in the end of 973 A.D. A sanguinary battle was fought somewhere in the northern Karnataka. Karka signally conceded the defeat by escaping from the scene. Thus ended the reign of Karka in 973 A.D. after an ignoble period of eighteen months. However, Karka managed to carve out a small principality for himself in Sorab taluk of Karnataka State, where he continued to rule up to A.D. 991. Others who tried to restore the Rāshṭrakūṭa supremacy were Mārasiṁha, a Gaṅga ruler and Indra, the grandson of Kṛshṇa III. Their

1. *E.I.*, XXVI, p. 181.

efforts failed and they became Jain monks and died by *Sallekhanā*, the former in 975 A.D. and the latter in 982 A.D.

The period of the Rāshṭrakūṭas was the most brilliant chapter in the history of the Deccan, but the "empire crashed like a meteor, its collapse was unexpected, abrupt and dramatic." In 967 A.D. it was at its climax of political power and prestige, but within an inconceivably short period of six years, it vanished like a dream.

SECTION III

SOURCES

1. *Inscriptions*

The density of inscriptions available in India seems to exist more in the Deccan than any other part of the country. A hundred years ago, *The Times of India* wrote[1]: "No authentic work of a definite historical character has been written by the Hindus of Western India. So Mr. J.F. Fleet, of the Bombay Civil Services, asserts, but he adds that in the inscriptions on copper-plates and stone tablets, on monumental stones, on the pedestals of idols, on the walls and pillars of temples, and on rocks, there have come down to us, particularly in the Kanarese country, a large number of original historical records of the most important kind. The first systematic collection of these was made by Sir Walter Elliot, who, when in the Madras Civil Service, was employed for a long time in the Kanarese districts. Subsequent workers in the same field have collected and published a whole mass of such inscriptions, and from these, together with other unpublished inscriptions which Mr. Fleet himself has collected, that gentleman has constructed a history of the dynasties of Kanarese districts of the Bombay Presidency from the earliest historical times to the Mohomedan

1. *T.O.I.*, September 9, 1882. This piece of information is very interesting in the writing of a regional history; so we have attached some value to it by quoting it here.

conquest of A.D. 1318. One has only to glance through the hundred pages of names, dates, genealogies, explanations and references in order to realise the formidable task Mr. Fleet has accomplished, and it will form a valuable feature of a future volume of the *Bombay Gazetteer,* for which work, we notice, it was written. What Mr. Fleet has done is, to trace the history and fortunes of the dynasties that have successively ruled over the country dealt with, thus making the way smooth for others who follow; for the ancient history of the Kanarese country still remains to be worked out in detail—the different territorial divisions and the changes that they underwent, the decay of the Buddhists and Jain religions, the spread of the Śaiva faith, specially in its form of Lingayatism, and similar topics...." Now most of these inscriptions have been deciphered, edited and published in *South Indian Inscriptions, Epigraphia Carnatica, Epigraphia Indica, Inscriptions in Andhra Pradesh, Annual Reports on South Indian Epigraphy, Annual Reports on Epigraphy, Mysore Archaeological Reports, Karnatak Inscriptions, Corpus Inscriptionum Indicarum,* etc. After the publication of Altekar's *Rāshṭrakūṭas and their times,* as many as twenty volumes of *Epigraphia Indica* itself have been published.

A survey of inscriptions in the Deccan by A.V. Naik[1] in 1948 reveals that there were 102 Rāshṭrākūṭa inscriptions discovered by then. Now the number is definitely increased. Out of the 102 inscriptions, the language of 44 inscriptions is Sanskrit, 40 Kannada and 9 Tamil; 9 are bilingual (Sanskrit and Kannada). The find-spots for these inscriptions numbered 56. The Rāshṭrakūṭas evince a decided fancy for stone engraving; and of the total Rāshṭrakūṭa records 3/8th are on copper-plates. Inscriptions on monolithic pillars in the open are rare, but many of them belong to the Rāshṭrakūṭas. Rāshṭrakūṭa copper-plates vary in size also. Their length varies from 12 cm to 46 cm and breadth from 5 cm to 27 cm. The largest copper-plate is from Sanjan of the time of Amoghavarsha I.[2] Rāshṭrakūṭa records speak for the court

1. *BDCRI*, pp. 1-160.

2. *Ibid.*, p. 37.

poets' great acquaintance with the various aspects of Śiva and the *avatāras* of Vishṇu and offer considerable corroboration for the evidence of contemporary sculptures which exhibit a great advance in iconography. The wide-scale propagation of the mythological contents in the Deccan must be attributed to the Rāshṭrakūṭas.

During the Rāshṭrakūṭa rule Nāgarī gradually acquired the status of a ruling script both in Gujarat and the Deccan by deposing the prevailing southern alphabets. The earliest document written throughout in Nāgarī is the Samangad grant of 754 A.D.[1] The find-spots of Rāshṭrakūṭa Nāgarī records are exclusively situated within the confines of the North Deccan, a fact that suggested the recognition of Nāgarī as an official script alongside of the Kanarese. As a living or current script Nāgarī pervaded the major portion of the North Deccan during the late Rāshṭrakūṭa period; and hence all the subsequent records, whose provenance was in the Deccan, had to be written in the Nāgarī script.

Simultaneous use of two court or official languages first effected by Vijayāditya soon became a permanent feature as we see that the practice was followed by the succeeding dynasties, though the exceptional instances are not wanting. Thus the Rāshṭrakūṭa records show the same trend. Their early records up to 780 A.D. which exclusively belong to Maharashtra or the North Deccan are wholly written in Sanskrit. But there is one exception,[2] the Hattimattur record of A.D. 765 which is completely written in Kannada. However, that is not an official record. It only refers to the reign of Kṛshṇa I and records the death of two heroes in a local affray. The Rāshṭrakūṭa records belonging to the Deccan, Gujarat and other parts of North India are in Sanskrit, whereas their Karnataka records are in Kannada and a few found in South India are in Tamil. The use of bilingual records is also not lacking.

Almost all the Rāshṭrakūṭa inscriptions give the date in the Śaka era while some give in addition the regnal years

1. *Ibid*., p. 50.
2. R.G. Bhandarkar's *List* No. 96.

of the reigning king. They contain the full compliment of a precise date, *viz.*, the Śaka year, the *Saṁvatsara*, the month, its fortnight, the lunar day and the weekday. A few of these give in addition the *nakshatra* and the *yoga* which add to the precision of the date. This in itself is one of its special features.

The above discussion gives us the position and nature of the Rāshṭrakūṭa records available to us. They are very useful and valuable materials for the study of any aspects of life and history of the Rāshṭrakūṭas. These inscriptions can be divided into the following categories:

(i) *Viragals*, *satikals* and *niśidhigals*;
(ii) Votive Records;
(iii) Donations or Endowments to gods;
(iv) Secular grants.

2. *Coins*

No definite Rāshṭrakūṭa coins have been discovered so far; but we have concrete evidence to say that the Rāshṭrakūṭas did have their own coins. And also, it is difficult to believe that such a powerful state had no coins in use. Sulaiman writes that the Balharas (the Rāshṭrakūṭas) had silver coins called Tatriya coins which were one and a half times heavier than the Arab coins. After getting this clue, we have tried here to include in the scheme of our discussion all those coins which have been discovered in the places under the Rāshṭrakūṭa empire in case the coins have been assigned a period between the eighth and the tenth centuries A.D. It would show that the Rāshṭrakūṭas did have coins current in their empire.

3. *Monuments and Antiquities*

The existing temples of the Rāshṭrakūṭa period also present a valuable source for the study of the social-economic history of the Rāshṭrakūṭas. The first and foremost of these monuments are the Elūra caves, especially, the Kailāsa temple.

Though the themes or stories depicted in the panels of Elūra by the contemporary artists are from the *Mahābhārata* or the *Rāmāyaṇa*, the expressions evidently represent the current status of the society. Also, the analysis of these sculptures in the light of the social-economic conditions of the time is highly rewarding. The Jain temple at Paṭṭadakal (early part of the ninth century A.D.), the Parameśvara temple at Konnur (860 A.D.), the Nārāyaṇa Temple at Naregal (950 A.D.) (last two belonging to Dharwar district) and several other temples scattered all over Maharashtra and Karnataka have proved to be useful. Even the surface-finds of the Rāshṭrakūṭa period help us in synthesising the evidences. The antiquarian remains at the last and final capital of the Rāshṭrakūṭas, *i.e.*, at Mānyakheṭa (or Malkheḍ), though not numerous, give us an idea of the conditions of Mānyakheṭa during the Rāshṭrakūṭa times.

4. *Literature*

(a) Indigenous Literature

In addition to the *Smṛiti* literature a number of literary works written in Kannada, Sanskrit and Apabhraṁśa during the period offer corroborative evidence on the different aspects of the social and economic life of the people. The first literary treatise on Kannada poetics, the *Kavirājamārga*[1] of Nṛpatuṅga Amoghavarsha I is a singular literary composition in Kannada. Next come the two great poems, the *Ādi-Purāṇa* and the *Vikramārjuna-Vijaya*[2] also called *Pampa-Bhārata* composed in A.D. 941 by the greatest Kannada poet Pampa that offer us immense help.

Among the Sanskrit works the *Yaśastilaka*[3] of Somadevasūri composed in 959 A.D. gives a fair amount of information about Jainism, social customs and beliefs and daily life

1. K.B. Pathak (ed.), *Kavirājamārga*.
2. L. Rice (ed.), *Vikramārjuna-Vijaya or Pampa Bhārata*, Bangalore, 1898.
3. K.K. Handiqui, *Yaśastilaka and Indian Culture*, Sholapur, 1949; Sivadatta and Parab (eds.), *Yaśastilakachampū*, Bombay, 1901-03.

of the people during the period of our study. This literary work written in the *Champū* style during the reign of Kṛshṇa III narrates the story of the legendary king Yaśodhara of Ujjain in seven chapters and shows the great erudition and linguistic attainments of its author. From it again we learn that Somadeva, from his boyhood, had made a deep study of Tarkaśāstra. The last three chapters of this book centre round the Jain dogmas, so much so that this part is often taken to be a manual of Jainism for laymen. Another book of our interest by Somadeva is *Nītivākyāmṛta*,[1] also called *Yaśodhara-mahārāja-charita* which deals with the pathetic story of Prince Yaśodhara. Jinasena's *Ādipurāṇa*, Mahāvīrāchārya's *Gaṇitasārasaṁgraha* and Śākaṭāyana's *Amoghavṛtti* are all important for our study. These books were written under the liberal patronage of Amoghavarsha I.

Pushpadanta was the greatest Apabhraṁśa poet who wrote *Mahāpurāṇa*,[2] *Jasahara-Chariu*[3] and *Nāyakumāra-Chariu*[4] at Mānyakheṭa under the patronage of the ministers of Kṛshṇa III and his successor. In his *Mahāpurāṇa*, he has beautifully delineated the lives of the sixty-three great men while in other two works he has narrated the lives of two other religious heroes. Out of these three literary works of Pushpadant, the *Mahāpurāṇa* throws a flood of light on the social condition of the time too. He narrates the ravages of Mānyakheṭa by the king of Dhārā. This event took place in 972 A.D. and the mention of it by Pushpadanta proves that his literary activity continued for at least seven years after the completion of his *Mahāpurāṇa* in Śaka 887, *i.e.*, A.D. 965.

The *Kuvalayamālākahā*[5] of Uddyotanasūri was written in 779 A D. at Jalore in Rajasthan. Its language is Prakrit. Both

1. *Nītivākyāmṛta of Somadeva*, published by Manikachandra Digambara Jaina Granthamala Series, Bombay.
2. P.L. Vaidya (ed.), *Mahāpurāṇa*, 3 vols., 1937-41.
3. P.L. Vaidya (ed.), *Jasahara-Chariu*, Karanja, 1931.
4. H.L. Jain (ed.), *Nāyakumāra-Chariu*, Karanja, 1933.
5. A N. Upadhye (ed.), *Kuvalayamālā*, Singhi Jain Granthamala, Bombay, 1970 and Prem Suman Jain, *Kuvalayamālākahā kā Sāṁskṛtika Adhyayana* (in Hindi), Vaishali, 1975.

the place of writing and the time are outside the domain and the period of the Rāshṭrakūṭas respectively, but it gives ample information about the cultural contacts between the people of Rajasthan and the Deccan. At places, the narration of economic life of the people has direct bearing on the economic life of the people under the Rāshṭrakūṭas.

(b) Foreign Notices

Another important source of information are the notices of the travellers from the Arab and other Muslim countries. Most of the Arabs visited India between the ninth and twelfth centuries either for pleasure, commerce or adventure. Though they had no clear idea of the topographical division of the country, they have done a great service to historians by mentioning places of commercial importance along the west coast and in the interior, as also the products exported and imported. The most important of these travellers are Ibn Khurdadbeh (A.D. 844-848), Sulaiman (A.D. 851), Yaqubi (A.D. 875-880), Abu Zaid (A.D. 916), Masudi (A.D. 932-956), Al Istakhri, Ibn Hauqal, Maqdisi (between A.D. 951 and 968), Al Beruni (A.D. 973 1048).[1]

Arab writers refer to the kingdom of "Ballah-ray" or "Balahara" (Skt. Vallabharāja) and had great praise for the Rāshṭrakūṭas. They called them "the king of kings". They also say that Banura, who is the king of Kanauj, is an enemy of the Balhara. This is true. The extent of the Rāshṭrakūṭa empire, given by the Arab writers is fully corroborated from other sources such as the Daśāvatāra Cave inscription of Elūra and the Samangad Plates.[2] Thus we see that the accounts of these foreign writers are quite true and clear.

We have taken Alberuni's account into consideration, though its date of writing is slightly beyond the period of the Rāshṭrakūṭas, but it makes little difference for us. The social conditions or economic factors, ordinarily, do not change in such a short period.

1. For a detailed and critical analysis, see S.M.H. Nainar, *Arab Geographers' Knowledge of Southern India*, Madras, 1942.
2. *Archaeological Survey of Western India*, Vol, V, p. 92.

For understanding the Arabic portion of the accounts *History of India as told by its own Historians* (8 Volumes) by Sir H.M. Elliot and John Dowson (London, 1866-77) and its subsequent reprints with introduction by Mohammad Habib, commentary by S.H. Hodiwala and supplement by Khaliq Ahmad Nizami (Aligarh, 1952) serve a useful purpose. Similar is the case with *Arab aur Bharat ke Sambandh* (Hindi translation by Ramchandra Varma) of Sayed Sulaiman Nadvi (Allahabad, 1930). These two works, especially, are of immense help to us.

2

The Social Set-up and Organisation

PART I

Social life in India has not changed much since Vedic times. Many of the customs referred to in the *mantras* of the Vedas can still be found being observed unchanged especially in the villages. Not so the religious life of the people. Luckily, some important details of the social life of the people in the age of the Rāshṭrakūṭas have been preserved in the inscriptions, literature, sculptures and foreigners' accounts of that period.

The *Kavirājamārga* says that even children and dumb persons could teach words of wisdom, though narrated in poetic fancy. It further extols the various good qualities of the people who were martial in nature, had poetic talents; they were self-respecting, noble, fierce (when provoked), wise and beautiful. This gives a clear picture of the people.

The Rāshṭrakūṭa rule witnessed certain changes in religion and social walks of life. Towards the closing period of the Rāshṭrakūṭa rule Buddhist reconversions into Hinduism, inter-caste dinners and marriages and religious congregations having powers to settle socio-religious matters began to fade into the dust of memory. *Vrātas*, tonsure of widows, regional sub-castes, associating dancing girls with temples, the practice of Satī began to enter into the society. However, we find communal harmony and religious tolerance throughout the Rāshṭrakūṭa empire as people of different faiths such as Śaivism, Jainism, Buddhism, Muhammadanism and of several minor sects and cults were living together with mutual understanding and without any known strife.

Caste System

The Hindu society of the early medieval period of Indian history was composed of the usual four Varṇas, namely, Brāhmaṇa, Kshatriya, Vaiśya and Śūdra. These four principal castes are referred to in the records of the period as *nālku-jāti*. Excommunication became an effective deterrent to the flouting of religious injunctions. Besides the four principal castes, the lowest stratum of society consisted of untouchables, referred to as horahinavaru, and those who had been punished with excommunication and expulsion from the *nālku-jāti*.[1]

The Brāhmaṇas

Brāhmaṇas had gained complete ascendancy in the society. It is borne out by the accounts of the Muslim travellers. Al Masūdi[2] who visited India in 915-16 A.D., and Alberuni,[3] who wrote his *Tahkik-i-Hind* in 1030 A.D., inform us that the Brāhmaṇas were honoured by the people as forming the most noble and illustrious caste. The Brāhmaṇas seem to have formed one caste throughout India without any sub-divisions based on provincial or other minor differences. Thus we do not find Brāhmaṇa donees in inscriptions described as Kanaujiā, Gauḍa or Draviḍa etc. The records distinguish

1. K.V. Ramesh, *A History of South Kanara*, Dharwar, 1970, p. 274.
2. Elliot and Dowson, *History of India*, I, p. 19.
3. Sachau, *Alberuni's India*, Vol. I, pp. 100-01. The information from this book can easily be utilized because the Rāshṭrakūṭa empire ended in 973 A.D. and this work was written in 1030 A.D. The collection of material might have started reasonably earlier and thus data of this book are quite relevant for us.

them by their Gotras and Pravaras. Among the former they mention: Agasti, Ātreya, Bandhula, Bhāradvāja, Bhārgava, Chandrātreya, Daksha, Darbha, Dhaumya, Gālava, Garga, Gārgya, Gauṇya, Gautama, Gobhila, Hāridra, Hārīta, Jāukarṇa, Jivantāyana, Kaṇva, Kapisthala, Kāśyapa, Kātyāyana, Kauṇḍinya, Kauśika, Kramaitta, Kṛshṇātreya, Kutimasha, Kūtsa, Maudgalya, Maunya, Moggalu, Parāśara, Pārāvasa, Pippalāda, Sāṁkṛtya, Śāṇḍilya, Sārkara, Śakarāksha, Sauśravasa, Sāvarṇa, Upamanyu, Vājasaneya, Vasishṭha, Vatsa,[1] etc.; and the latter are referred to as follows: Aghamarshaṇa, Aitatha, Ambarīsha, Āṅgirasa, Aurva, Apnavāna, Andalya, Āvatsara, Avitatha, Bandhula, Bārhaspatya, Bhāradvāja, Bhārgava, Bharmyāsva, Chyavana, Devarāta, Dhaumya, Gautama, Gobhila, Jāmadagnya, Kāṅkāyana, Kāśyapa, Kauśika, Maudgalya, Naidhurva, Viśvāmitra, etc.[2]

Besides these Gotras and Pravaras, the Brāhmaṇas seem to have characteristic names according to their occupations and modes of life. Alberuni informs us that "the Brāhmaṇa is in general called by this name as long as he does his work staying at home. When he is busy with the service of one fire, he is called ishṭin; if he serves three fires, he is called agnihotrin; if he besides offers an offering to the fire, he is called dīkshita."[3] In addition, the contemporary records refer to such Brahmanic surnames as Avasthī,[4] Sarman,[5] Dvivedin,[6] Traividya,[7] Tripāṭhī or Tripāṭhin,[8] Chaturvedin[9] or

1. *E.I.*, IV, pp. 10', 132-33; V, pp 118, 212-13; VII, p. 99; VIII, p. 154; XIV, pp. 202-09; XVIII, pp. 12, 222; XIX, pp. 18-19; XXIII, pp. 10, 205; XXXII, pp. 129, 160; XXXIV, p. 123; XXXVI, pp. 257-72.

2. *E.I.*, pp. 101, 112, 130, 13?; VII, pp. 99-100; XVIII, pp. 12, 13, 17, 19, 222, 224; *I A.*, XIV, p. 103.

3. Sachau, *Alberuni's India*, I, p. 102.

4. *I.A*, XVIII, p. ?26.

5. *I.A.*, XVIII, p. 123.

6. *I A*, XIV, p. 207; *E.I.*, XXIII, p. 213.

7. *E.I.*, XXIII, p. 213.

8. *I.A*, XIV, p. 208.

9. *I.A.*, XIV, p. 204.

Chaturvaidya,[1] Miśra[2] and the title Paṇḍita.[3]

We learn from Alberuni that "the life of the Brahman, after seven years of it have passed, is divided into four parts. The first part begins with the eighth year, when the Brahmans come to him to instruct him, to teach him his duties, and to enjoin him to adhere to them and to embrace them as long as he lives. Then they bind a girdle round his waist and invest him with a pair of Yajñopavītas, *i.e.*, one strong cord consisting of nine single cords which are twisted together, and with a third Yajñopavīta, a single one made of cloth. This girdle runs from the left shoulder to the right hip. Further, he is presented with a stick which he has to wear, and with a seal-ring of certain grass, called darbha, which he wears on the ring-finger of the right hand. This seal-ring is called pavitra. The object of his wearing the ring on the ring-finger of his right hand is this, that it should be a good omen and blessing for all those who receive gifts from that hand. The obligation of wearing the ring is not quite so stringent as that of wearing Yajñopavīta, for from the latter he is not to separate himself under any circumstances whatever. If he takes it off while eating or responding to the call of nature, he thereby commits a sin which cannot be wiped off save by some work of expiation, fasting or almsgiving.

"This first period of the Brahman's life extends till the twenty-fifth year of his age, or according to the *Vishṇu-Purāṇa*, till his forty-eighth year. His duty is to practise abstinence, to make the earth his bed, to begin with the learning of the Veda and of its explanation, of the science of theology and law, all this being taught to him by a master whom he serves day and night. He washes himself thrice a day, and performs a sacrifice to the fire both at the beginning and end of the day. After the sacrifice he worships his master. He fasts a day and he breaks fast a day, but he is never allowed to eat meat.

1. *I.A* , XIX, p. 54; *E.I.*, XXIII, p. 205; XXXII, p. 160; XXXIV, p. 123; XXX, p. 270.
2. *I A.*, XIV, p. 207.
3. Some of the titles seem to be on the basis of the knowledge of the number of the Vedas.

He dwells in the house of the master, which he only leaves in order to ask for a gift and to beg in not more than five houses once a day, either at noon or in the evening. Whatever alms he receives he places before his master to choose from it what he likes. Then the master allows him to take the remainder. Thus the pupil nourishes himself from the remains of the dishes of his master. Further, he fetches the wood for the fire, wood of two kinds of trees, palāśa (Buteafrondosa) and darbha, in order to perform sacrifice; for the Hindus highly venerate the fire, and offer flowers to it. It is the same case with all other nations. They always thought that the sacrifice was accepted by the deity if the fire came down upon it, neither the worship of idols nor that of stars, cows, asses, or images....

"The second period of their life extends from the twenty-fifth year till the fiftieth, or, according to the *Vishṇu-Purāṇa*, till the seventieth. The master allows him to marry. He marries, establishe a household, and intends to have descendants, but he cohabits with his wife only once in a month after she has become clear of the menstruation. He is not allowed to marry a woman above twelve years of age. He gains his sustenance either by the fee he obtains for teaching Brahmans and Kshatriyas, not as a payment, but as a present, or by presents which he receives from someone because he performs for him the sacrifices to the fire, or by asking a gift from the kings and nobles, there being no importunate pressing on his part, and no unwillingness on the part of the giver....

"The third period of the life of the Brahman extends from the fiftieth year to the seventy-fifth, or, according to the *Vishṇu-Purāṇa*, till the ninetieth. He practises abstinence, leaves his household, and hands it as well as his wife over to his children, if the latter does not prefer to accompany him into the life in the wilderness. He dwells outside civilization, and leads the same life again which he led in the first period. He does not take shelter under a roof, nor wear any other dress but some bark of a tree, simply sufficient to cover his loins. He sleeps on the earth without any bed, and only nourishes himself by fruit, vegetables, and roots. He lets the hair grow long, and does not anoint himself with oil.

"The fourth period extends till the end of life. He wears a red garment and holds a stick in his hand. He is always given to meditation; he strips the mind of friendship and enmity, and roots out desire, and lust, and wrath. He does not converse with anybody at all. When walking to a place of particular merit, in order to gain a heavenly reward, he does not stop on the road in a village longer than a day. not in a city longer than five days. If anyone gives him something, he does not leave a remainder of it for the following day. He has no other business but that of caring for the path which leads to salvation, and for reaching moksha, whence there is no return to this world."[1]

Alberuni further informs us that "the universal duties of the Brahman throughout his whole life are works of piety, giving alms and receiving them. For that which the Brahman gives reverts to the pitṛs (in reality a benefit to the Fathers). He must continually read, perform sacrifices, take care of the fire which he lights, offer before it, worship it, and preserve from being extinguished, that he may be burned by it after his death."[2]

Perhaps the Brāhmaṇas had the liberty to take to the profession of the lower castes, besides those that were theoretically permitted to them. But there were certain restrictions, for Alberuni says that "every man who takes to some occupation which is not allowed to his caste *e.g*, a Brahman to trade, a Śūdra to agriculture, commits a sin or crime, which they consider only a little less than the crime of theft."[3]

The Brāhmaṇas seem to have filled various offices of the state. They occupied high as well as low ranks. We are told by Abu Zaid that "among the Indians there are men who are devoted to religion and men of science, whom they call Brahmans. They have also their poets who live at the courts

1. Sachau, *Alberuni's India*, II, pp. 130-33.
2. *Ibid.*, p. 133.
3. *Ibid.*, p. 137.

of their kings, astronomers, philosophers, diviners...."[1] The priestly class and the Brāhmaṇas were much respected by the rulers and the people. Many medieval records include the *purohitas* in the list of officials present in the royal audience hall.[2]

The Brāhmaṇas lived in their own *agrahāras* in every village and the Udiyāvara inscription[3] (*c.* A.D. 765-805) considers the destruction of the brahmapura ((*i.e.* brahmins' quarter) of Śivalli as a *mahāpātaka.*

The name of the grantee of Deoli Plates ends in *appa,* or apayya, which shows that he was a southern Brāhmaṇa.[4] The Kolhapur Copper Plate grant mentions the name of the village Rikkaṭi in the district of Alatage with the rows of trees in it which was donated to a celebrated Brāhmaṇa Govindabhaṭṭa, who was conversant in Veda and Vedāṅga, the son of Yautubhaṭṭa, who was the son of Rāmadevabhaṭṭa, of Ātreya *gotra*, and an emigrant from Kuregrāma (Koregaon) in the country of Kakata.[5] The object of the Andura Plates (in Balapur Taluk of the Akola District, Maharashtra) of Govinda IV, dated 930 A,D. is to record the grant of the village Elaurī included in the territorial division of Vadanera—300 to eight Brāhmaṇas on the occasion of *Tulāpurusha Mahādāna*.[6] Here is the list[7] of all the above-mentioned eight Brāhmaṇas each with the name of his father, *Gotra* and *Śākhā* to which they belonged and their original home:

1. Elliot and Dowson, *History of India*, I, p. 10.
2. K V. Ramesh, *A History of South Kanara*, Dharwar, 1970, p. 274.
3. *S.I.I.*, VII, No. 284.
4. R.G Bhandarkar, *Early History of the Deccan*, Poona, 1983, p. 311.
5. *JBBRAS*, X, pp. 2 -37.
6. *E.I.*, XXXVI, pp. 257-272.
7. This list has been rearranged by ourselves keeping in view the common nature of the Gotra, the Śākhā and the original home.

Sl. No.	*Name of the donee*	*Name of his father*	*Gotra*	*Śākhā*	*Original home*
1.	Saṇvai-bhaṭṭa	Madhuva-payya-bhaṭṭa	Bhāradvāja	Ṛgveda	Chandra-pura
2.	Tikke-bhaṭṭa	Viḍapaiya	Bhāradvāja	Ṛgveda	Puri
3.	Vāvaṇaiya	Risiyaṇṇa	Bhāradvāja	Ṛgveda	Chikhali
4.	Prabhā-karabhaṭṭa	Vachu-bhaṭṭa	Kauśika	Ṛgveda	Sīsave
5.	Vāvaṇa	Tikkapayya	Kauśika	Taitti-rīya	Nala-grāma
6.	Śrīdhara-bhaṭṭa	Revaṇai-bhaṭṭa	Hārīta	Taitti-rīya	Nala-grāma
7.	Keśava	Mādhavaiya	Vatsa	Taitti-rīya	Dharma Sellukā
8.	Janni-bhaṭṭa	Viddhapaiya	Gārgya	Taitti-rīya	Vāvī

This list is enough to prove that during our period, Brāhmaṇas were freely migrating from one place to another and they settled at places of their choice. We have some more evidence to show that the Brāhmaṇas in our period were immigrants.[1] The donees of the Alas plates of Yuvarāja Govinda[2] and the Wani-Dindori plates of Govinda III[3] were immigrants from Veṅgī in Kaliṅga. The villages granted were

1. For more details see Swali Datta (*nee* Sen Gupta), *Migrant Brāhmaṇas in Northern India*, Delhi, 1989.
2. *E.I.*, VI, p. 208.
3. *I.A.*, XI, p. 157.

in Maharashtra and so it is clear that they had permanently settled in that province. The donee of the Jambgaon Plates of Indra III[1] was Brāhmaṇa Dāmodara-bhaṭṭa of the Bhāradvāja *gotra* and Vājasaneya Śākhā, the son of Bhīmāśita-bhaṭṭa. He was proficient in the four Vedas and had hailed from the district Veṅgī.

Evidences of Brāhmaṇa's migration removes certain prejudices prevalent in the society. The donees of the Begumra plates of Indra III[2] and the Sangli plates of Govinda IV[3] were immigrants from Pāṭaliputra (Patna) and Puṇḍravardhana (Purneā in Bihar or some part of North Bengal) respectively. The view of the *Atrisaṁhitā* that a Magadha Brāhmaṇa was not to be honoured even if he was as learned as Bṛhaspati[4] is ruled out here, because the donee of Begumra plates was from Magadha. Nāgamārya, the donee of the Cambay plates of Govinda IV,[5] was an immigrant from Kavi in Gujarat settled in Mānyakheṭa. This shows that present-day prejudice in the Deccan that a Brāhmaṇa from Gujarat is inferior did not hold good in our period.

Karhatak Brāhmaṇas are found in the Rāshṭrakūṭa inscriptions of Dantidurga II (810 A.D.) and Govinda IV (930 A.D.).[6] Somadeva Sūri also mentions such Brāhmaṇas in his *Yaśastilaka*.[7] References to Karhāda Brāhmaṇas are found in Bharhut inscriptions also. P.K. Gode has tried to prove that Karhatak Brāhmaṇas, who were migrating in the time of the Rāshṭrakūṭas, are still existing in Maharashtra today and equivalent term for this Brāhmaṇa is Kanhada Brāhmaṇa.[8]

Brāhmaṇa scholars trained at the famous centres of education in the Deccan like Kalas, Mangoli, Salotagi etc., used to proceed to royal courts after their education was over

1. *E.I.*, IX, p. 24.
2. *E.I*, XXXVI, p. 223.
3. *I.A*, XII, p. 248.
4. *RATT.*, p. 335.
5. *E.I.*, VII, p. 26.
6. *E.I.*, XXIII, pp. 101-13.
7. K.K. Handiqui, *op. cit.*, p. 28.
8. P.K. Gode, *op. cit.*, pp. 17 & 21.

in order to show their talents with a view to being appointed to government posts. These scholars used to receive grants of land or government service.[1]

Exemption from taxation and capital punishment are two of the main privileges claimed for the Brāhmaṇas by the Smṛtis and the Purāṇas. This privilege was only applicable to the learned Brāhmaṇas. It is quite clear from the numerous Rāshṭrakūṭa charters that the donees of the *Brahmadeya* grants, who were learned Brāhmaṇas, used to receive all the taxes payable by the inhabitants to the king, they themselves had to pay nothing to the latter. But this privilege for ordinary Brāhmaṇas is doubtful. From the Tuppad Kurahatti inscription of Kṛshṇa III,[2] it is quite clear that even land granted to temple by king was not entirely exempted from taxation. Somadeva, a contemporary writer, lays down that when the king had to make a capital levy, in order to tide over a difficulty, he could take a portion of the property of Brāhmaṇas and temples, taking the only precaution that money absolutely necessary for the performance of the sacrifices and worship was left with them.[3] This would again suggest that not all the Brāhmaṇas could have enjoyed complete exemption from taxation in our period. Although we do not have any epigraphical evidence for capital punishment for Brāhmaṇas, Alberuni states that the Brāhmaṇa was above the death sentence; nevertheless, he could be banished and his property confiscated, and that if he was guilty of stealing a precious and costly article, he was blinded and his right hand and left foot were cut off.[4] Altekar does not support this view because such punishment was worse than the death sentence and he might have been exepted from such punishment.[5] And, moreover, general Brāhmaṇas were intellectually so high that any such low work, for which people deserved punishment was unthinkable for the Brāhmaṇas.

1. *RATT.*, p. 325.
2. *E.I.*, XIV, p. 366.
3. *Nītivākyāmṛta*, XXI, 14.
4. Sachau, *op. cit.*, I, p. 162.
5. *RATT.*, p. 329.

The Kshatriyas

Next to the Brāhmaṇas were the Kshatriyas. They seem to have formed one caste, for we are told by the merchant Sulaiman (851 A.D.) that "in all these kingdoms the nobility is considered to form but one family."[1] The Kshatriyas did not refer to their *Gotras* during the period under consideration. Probably the Kula began itself to be called Gotra.[2] A.S. Altekar suggests that the absence of the mention of their *gotras* by the kings of our period in their copper plates would show that they were getting more and more dissociated from the orthodox Vedic atmosphere[3] and the worship of the Puranic deities became supreme. The former required recital of *gotra* and *pravara,* while the latter did not. Though their usual occupation was that of arms, there was no dearth of the Kshatriyas devoted to letters. According to Alberuni,[4] they could read and learn Vedas, but they were not permitted to teach them. He further informs us that "after the twelfth year of life, Kshatriya girds himself with a single cord of the three-fold *yajñopavita,* and a single other cord of cotton."[5] It appears from the *Parāśara Smṛti* that like the Brāhmaṇas the Kshatriyas also had taken to agriculture.[6]

The Vaiśyas

The Vaiśyas ranked third in the society. It may be presumed that they too yet formed one caste throughout India, for we do not come across the names of their modern sub-divisions. Perhaps they had lost touch with the Vedic rituals and forgotten their *gotras.* Alberuni tells us that the duty of the Vaiśyas was "to practise agriculture and to cultivate land, to tend cattle and to remove the needs of the

1. Elliot and Dowson, *History of India*, I, p. 6,
2. *E.I.*, IX, p. 200.
3. *RATT.*, p. 332.
4. Sachau, *op. cit*, II, p. 136.
5. *Ibid.*
6. *ABORI*, XXXVII, p. 195.

Brāhmaṇas."[1] But the Vaiśyas had probably long given up agriculture under the influence of Buddhism. The Buddhists believe that 'agriculture is sinful because it required the cutting of the ground and this involves the killing of various insects'.[2] The Vaiśyas were generally described as artificers and domestics.[3] They were losing their position among the Traivarṇikas, for Alberuni says that the Vaiśyas were not allowed to hear Vedas, much less to pronounce and recite them. If such a thing could be proved against one of them, the Brāhmaṇas dragged him before the magistrate, and he was punished by having his tongue cut off.[4]

The social status of a Vaiśya was much better than what has been painted by Alberuni. The Rāshṭrakūṭa inscriptions, as noted by V.V. Mirashi, refer to a section of Vaiśya community known as Mahājanas who were recipients of concessions from the rulers for certain religious pursuits.[5] It would thus appear that the Vaiśya community still held an honoured position in the framework of society.

Like Brāhmaṇas we find people of this community also migrating from one place to another. The Chinchani Plates of Kṛshṇa III[6] state that there was a well-organised settlement of merchants of Bhimal origin (Rajasthan) at Sanjan and that they had installed a Vaishnavite deity of their own and named it after their home town as Bhillamaladeva. They further mention the assembly of learned Brāhmaṇas 'Aryadeśīya-Mahā-Parishad'. The Kandhar inscription of Kṛshṇa III[7] records a Gujjara Apana. It throws a welcome light on the early settlement of Gurjara traders in Maharashtra.

The Śūdras

The lowest among the Varṇas were the Śūdras. Alberuni gives the following account of their life: "The Śūdra is like a

1. Sachau, *op. cit.*, II, p. 136.
2. C.V. Vaidya, *History of Medieval Hindu India*, II, p. 182.
3. Elliot and Dowson, *op. cit.*, I, p. 16.
4. Sachau, *op. cit.*, I, p. 125.
5. V.V. Mirashi, *Saṁśodhanamuktāvalī*, III, pp. 145-47.
6. *E.I.*, XXXII, p. 57.
7. *E.I.*, XXXV, p. 105.

servant to the Brāhmaṇa, taking care of his affairs and serving him. If, though being poor in the extreme, he still desires not to be without a *Yajñopavīta*, he girds himself only with the linen one. Every action which is considered as the privilege of a Brāhmaṇa, such as saying prayers, the recitation of the Veda, and offering sacrifices to the fire, is forbidden to him."[1] He further informs us that if a Śūdra was proved to have recited the Veda, he was punished like the Vaiśyas.[2] According to Medhātithi, who lived sometimes in the ninth century A.D.,[3] a Śūdra was entitled to perform pākayajña and religious sacrifices like Prakaraṇaśrāddha, Ashṭaka and Vaiśvadeva.[4] Somadeva, a Jaina writer of the Deccan of our period, observes that internal and external purity qualified even a Śūdra for spiritual duties connected with gods, Brāhmaṇas, and ascetic life.[5] There is no epigraphical evidence to show that these privileges were actually enjoyed by the Śūdras of our period.

The Untouchables

Alberuni refers to one more class of people called Antyaja after the Śūdras. He says that the Antyajas rendered 'various kinds of services', and were 'not reckoned among the castes, but only as members of certain craft or profession'. There were eight classes of them, who freely intermarried with each other, except the fuller (washerman), shoemaker, and weaver, for no others condescended to have anything to do with them'. The eight guilds were the fuller, the shoemaker, the juggler, the basket and shield maker, the sailor, the fisherman, the hunter of wild animals and birds, and the weaver. The four varṇas did not 'live with them in one and the same place'. 'These guilds lived near the villages and towns of the

1. Sachau, *op. cit.*, II, p. 136.
2. *Ibid.*
3. P.V. Kane, *History of Dharmaśāstra*, I, p. 261.
4. *Medhātithi on Manu*, III. 67.
5. *Nītivākyāmṛta*, VII, 12.

four castes, but just outside them'.[1]

Alberuni further informs us that 'the people called Hāḍi, Doma (Domba), Chaṇḍāla and Badhtan (sic) were not reckoned among any class or guild'. They were occupied with dirty work, like the cleansing of the villages and other services. 'They were considered as one sole class, distinguished only by their occupations'. 'In fact, they were considered like illegitimate children; for according to general opinion they descended from a Śūdra father and a Brāhmaṇa mother as the children of fornication, therefore they were degraded outcastes'.[2]

Ibn Khurdādba, who died in 912 A.D., refers to seven classes of the Hindus, namely, "Sābkufria, among whom were men of high castes, and from among whom kings were chosen; Brahma, who totally abstained from wine and fermented liquors; Kataria, who drank not more than three cups of wine; the daughters of the class of Brahma were not given marriage to sons of this class, but the Brahma took their daughters; Sūdariā, who were by profession husbandmen; Baisurā, who were artificers and domestics; Sandālia, who performed menial offices; and Lahūd, who were fond of amusements and games of skill."[3] It is quite obvious from these details that Brahma, Kataria, Sūdariā, Baisurā, Sandālia and Lahūd are the same as Brāhmaṇas, Kshatriyas, Śūdras, Vaiśyas, Chaṇḍālas and Bāzigars and itinerant jugglers. The term Sābkufria is unintelligible. Perhaps it also stands for the Kshatriyas, for kings were generally chosen from this caste.[4] Alberuni, however, differs from him and maintains that there were sixteen castes, the four well-known ones, five semi-untouchables and seven untouchables.[5]

The contemporary records make reference to the Buddhists and the Jains. We may conclude that the members of these sects had their customs and manners and led a life

1. Sachau, *Alberuni's India*, I, p. 101; see also *RATT.*, pp. 319-20.
2. Sachau, pp. 101-02.
3. Elliot and Dowson, *History of India*, I, pp. 16-17.
4. *RATT.*, pp. 318-19.
5. *Ibid*, p. 319.

of their own. The Arab traveller Sulaiman refers to one class of people who wandered in the woods and mountains and rarely communicated with the rest of mankind. Some of them went naked. Others stood naked with the face turned to the Sun, having on but a panther's skin.[1]

Somadeva in his writings vehemently opposes the privileges of other castes belonging to different faiths other than Jainism. He advises against the appointment of Brāhmaṇa and Kshatriya *amātyas*. He seems to be suspicious of the caste privileges of the Brāhmaṇas and the military character of the Kshatriyas.[2] He also distinctly says that 'those who do not possess the Three Jewels, that is, do not believe in the fundamental Jain dogmas of Right Faith, Right Knowledge and Right Conduct, are not eligible for gifts; and that charity practised in favour of those who hold wrong views and indulge in wrong conduct, that is, all who are outside the pale of Jainism, leads only to evil consequences, like the feeding of serpents with milk. Hospitality towards such people should be limited to a residual portion of food to be taken away, as a Jain layman is forbidden to entertain them in his house. He is also asked to keep at arm's length members of other communities such as the Buddhists, the Śaivas, and the Brāhmaṇas who perform sacrifices lest familiarity with them should lead to friction and disputes ending in violence. Isolation rather than amity based on free social intercourse was the object aimed at in inter-communal relations.'[3] But it is very doubtful whether the advice of Somadeva was actually followed in any part of the Deccan at any time.

These various classes of people appear to have begun to entertain the feelings of distinction in their social intercourse. We learn from Alberuni that each of the four principal varṇas or castes, when they ate together, formed a group for themselves, one group not being allowed to compromise two

1. Elliot and Dowson, *History of India*, I, p. 6.
2. *Nītivākyāmṛta*, 18.22-24.
3. K.K. Handiqui. *Yaśastilaka and Indian Culture*, Sholapur, 1949, p. 331.

men of different castes.[1] He further informs us that if a Brāhmaṇa ate in the house of a Śūdra for sundry days, he was expelled from his caste and could never regain it.[2] As regards social relations between the Muslims and the Hindus, Alberuni says that no drinking or eating with Mlechchha was permitted in his time.[3] He was repeatedly told that when the Hindu slaves in Muslim countries escaped and returned to their country and religion, they were admitted after an expiation; but when he enquired from the Brāhmaṇas whether this was true, they denied it, maintaining that there was no expiation possible for such individuals.[4] It is thus clear that 'the masses were for reconversion, but the orthodoxy had begun to frown on the practice'.

The Muslims

The process of Muslim infiltration continued without any positive counter-steps from the Hindu states which were too busy in their own feuds and bickerings However, their advance towards the fertile plains of Gujarat was checked by Avanijanāśraya Pulakeśin and the Pratīhāra Nāgabhaṭa of Avantī.[5] The Nausāri grant vividly portrays the onslaught of the Tājikas or the Muslims into Western India.[6] Despite these facts the Hindus allowed them to settle down in the areas occupied by them and live in freedom.[7] A Rāshṭrakūṭa king had even a feudatory chief who was an Arab Muslim by faith.[8] This fact is clear from the statement of Ibn-Asir according to whom "there were Musalmans in that country since the days of Mahmud bin Sabuktigin, who continued to be

1. Sachau, *Alberuni's India*, I, p. 102.
2. *Ibid.*, II, p. 163.
3. *Ibid.*, I, pp. 10-20.
4. *Ibid* , II, pp. 162-63.
5. *HCIP*, V, pp. 155, 248; *ABORI*, X, p. 31; *HIED*, I, (1955 ed.), p. 72.
6. *ABORI*, *X*, p. 30; *E.I.*, XVIII, p. 107.
7. V.V. Mirashi, *Saṁśodhanamuktāvalī*, Pt. III, pp. 149-70.
8. *HIED*, II, p. 251 (New ed.).

faithful to the law of Islam, and constant in prayers and good works."[1] It is interesting to note that Sulaiman, another Muslim traveller, praises the Rāshṭrakūṭas for extending their patronage to Muslim settlers.[2]

The Arab authors, Sulaiman (851 A.D.), Ibn Khurdābda (died in 912 A.D.), Abū Zaid (before 916 A.D.), Al Masūdī (932-56 A.D.), Ibn Haukal (between 943 and 968 A.D.) and Al Istakhrī,[3] have written about the partial attitude of the Rāshṭrakūṭa kings towards the Muslim community. Altekar[4] regarded it unreliable but the Chinchini Plates of Indra III[5] have proved the veracity of the statement of Arab writers. The inscription records how Madhumati, the Arab governor, associated himself with the construction of a Hindu monastery, the installation of an image therein and the creation of a permanent endowment in its favour, establishment of free ferry, free meals, which throws welcome light on the outlook of the Arab governor. This might be indicative of the Rāshṭrakūṭa rulers reciprocating similar attitude towards Muslims.

The name of the above-mentioned Tajika governor of Sammayan *Vishaya* is given as Madhumati-Sugatipa. The first part of this name is no doubt the Sanskritized form of the Arabic name "Muhammad" or "Muhammadi" (the second part is not yet explained).[6] This governor ruled over his co-religionists living in the empire very successfully. This is interpreted to mean that the Rāshṭrakūṭas appointed Qazis to look after the religious and judicial affairs of the Muslim subjects who were mostly Arabs. Muhammad was naturally grateful for the confidence placed in him by the emperor.

1. *Ibid.*, I, p. 4.
2. *Ibid.*
3. Elliot and Dowson, *History of India as told by its own Historians*, Vol. I, pp. 3ff., 9f , 13ff., 21ff., 27ff. 34.
4. A S. Altekar, *Rāshṭrakūṭas and their Times*, Poona, 1934, pp. 187, 276-77.
5. *E.I.*, XXXII, p. 50.
6. H.D. Sankalia, *T.O.I.*, September 19, 1982.

This governor conquered all the harbours (*Vetakula*) of the neighbourhood, evidently for the Rāshṭrakūṭas. Further, Muhammad placed (or was permitted or ordered to place) his own officials in these ports.[1]

The Navayats

The Arabs who came to India were not motivated either by political ambitions or missionary zeal, and their main business was trade handed down to them by their forefathers from pre-Islamic times. Later on, the establishment of Muslim settlements, particularly on the west coast of India, was due mainly to the encouragement to trade given by the Hindu rulers. Of these rulers Rāshṭrakūṭas and the Zamindars of the Malabar coast were known to be the most partial to Muslims.[2] Several Muhammadan traders, encouraged by this kindly attitude of the Rāshṭrakūṭas took up their abodes at so many places. They were treated with great consideration, allowed to build mosques and permitted to practise their religion without hindrance, with the result that these early Muslim settlers established themselves all along the coast, intermarried with the Hindu population, and thus gave rise to the various Muslim communities on the coast that are found even today.

History has recorded that from ancient times settlements have been formed in various parts of the world by ship wrecked crew. There have been cases also where traders have settled in various parts of the world either for purposes of trade and contracted marriage or have settled in the land of their adoption and married local women.

1. *Ibid.*
2. The relationship between the Balhara and the Arabs and the Muslims has been spoken of very highly by various Muslim merchants and travellers such as Sulaiman (851 A.D.), Masudi (932-56 A.D.), Istakhri (950 A.D.) and Ibn Hauqal (between 943 and 968 A.D.). Cf. S. Muhammad Husyan Nainar, *Arab Geographers' Knowledge of Southern India*, Madras, 1942, pp. 162-64.

The nature of the voyages in early medieval times could not but have encouraged the Arab mariners to have marital connections with Indian women. The boats of the Arabs used to come to Malabar and other coastal areas of India sometime in July or August and after four months of business returned in December or January. In those days the voyage used to take about thirty to forty days.[1] So, even if the Arab sailers and merchants had any settled home life in Arabia, they were away from their homes for the greater part of the year. Thus they were in India for about four months in union, temporary or permanent, with the Indian women, for there is no evidence to show that they brought along with them their own womenfolk. At least in Malabar it was extremely easy for Arabs to have such unions with the local women, due to the peculiar nature of the social organisation of both the early Arabs and the people of Malabar.

The society in early Arabia was organised on the basis of mother-right. By tribal rule, the woman was not allowed to leave her own kid but could entertain a stranger as her husband at her own place. The man either settled down permanently with his wife's tribe or visited his wife occasionally. There was also present a Nair polyandry, the woman receiving more than one suitor even though they belonged to different tribes. The children born of such unions belonged to the mother's stock and remained with the mother's tribe.[2] The type of marriage in which the husband goes to settle in his wife's tribe is called *beena* marriage.[3]

Another special institution of the early Arabia which has survived even today and which needs to be mentioned in this connection is known as *muta* marriage. It is the marriage of a temporary nature in which the contracting parties agree to live together in the house of the woman (wife) for a stipulated period of time, and for which the man has to pay an amount mutually agreed upon. The contract may be either

1. Hakim Sayyad Shamsulla Qadri, *Malabar* (in Urdu), Aligarh, 1928, p. 15.
2. W. Robertson Smith, *Kinship and Marriage in Early Arabia*, London, 1907, pp. 77-79.
3. *Ibid.*, p. 87.

terminated before the stipulated period or extended by mutual consent and on terms agreeable to both the parties. But the main purpose of *muta* marriage is to provide a man with a wife when he is away from home.

The Arab mariners must have also practised a sort of *muta* marriage while they were in the ports of India. It was not possible for them to settle down for a long time in one particular place attaching themselves to the same wife or wives. Much of their time was spent in the sea and the remaining period was distributed over their stay in different ports. In different ports of anchor they were required to stay for periods of varying durations and during such periods it was customary for them to marry local women wherever possible, for they did not voyage with their wives. When it was time for them to leave the port they would also leave their wives behind and establish fresh marital connections in a new port.

There are various opinions regarding the origin and meaning of the term Navayat and these could be broadly divided into two categories:[1] those which hold that the term is of Arabic origin and others which ascribe to it an Indian origin.

In the Arabic language Nāyaṭ means backbone which signifies unity. So according to one opinion the community originally derived its name from the remarkable unity among its members under the leadership of one man. Consequently the community is called Nāyaṭ.

Another view about Navayat is that they are the progeny of an Arab called Abdullah Wayat.

According to *Qāmus*, the Arabic dictionary, the Navayats are a tribe of sailors, the term is being derived from *Nawwātī*, the plural of *Nuti*, which means sailor. The view is further supported by the Muslim historian Syed Sulaiman Nadvi who states that the Arab sailors of the Mediterranean Sea were known as *Nuti* and Nawwātī. He is of the opinion that the

1. Victor S. D'Souza, *The Navayats of Kanara: A Study in Cultural Contact*, Dharwar, 1955, pp. 12-34.

Navayats living in Southern India are descendants of Arab sailors called Navayats.

Next, the opinions ascribing to the term Navayats an Indian origin are:

Wilks says that Navayat is generally supposed to be a corruption of the Hindi and Marathi terms for new comer. In the Sanskrit language the word Navayata can be split up into nava (new) and āyata (come) meaning new comer.

Another opinion gives the term the meaning of those who came by boat, *nāva* or *nāo* meaning boat in Sanskrit and some other Indian languages.

According to yet another opinion the term is apparently a Konkani word connected with Sanskrit *nava* (new), and implying new convert.

The author of Tarikh-un-Nawayat[1] has one more to suggest. He states that Navayat means master or lord.

Tipu Sultan[2] of Mysore (r. A.D. 1782-1799) is reported to have given a most obnoxious interpretation of the term Navayat. On one occasion when several of his noblemen belonging to this tribe were present, he reprimanded them saying that they were an abominable lot because they were the descendants of a woman who had connections with nine men. When a child was born to that woman each of the nine men would have it named after himself as being father. But the court decreed that since all the nine men had connections with her, the child should receive the name of Now-A-ay-thay (or nine came). The progeny of this child were consequently called Navayats.

There are also ather Muslim communities on the coast such as the Moplas of Malabar and the Konkani Muslims of the Konkan coast with similar Indo-Arab origins. All these communitics had occupational contacts with one another in the past[3] and their history goes as back as to the eighth century A.D.

1. Nawab Aziz Jung Bahadur, *Tarikh-un-Nawayat*, Hyderabad, 1901.
2. Victor S D'Souza, *op. cit.*, p. 16.
3. *Ibid.*, p. VIII.

Different Stages of Life

We have discussed four stages of life while dealing with the Brāhmaṇas under the sub-heading 'Caste System'. But Pushpadanta, while mentioning different castes in society has given the list of four castes only[1] and he has given importance to *varṇas* on the basis of duty they perform and not on the basis of birth.[2] He advocates that under this system people get liberty to choose profession of their choice and opportunity to show their merit.

The *Mahāpurāṇa* accepts only *Gṛhasthāśrama* (*Sāgāradharma*) and *Sannyāsāśrama* (*Ahāgāradharma*) under different *āśramas* in life. But under these two above mentioned *āśramas* he has incorporated all the important stages and duties of human life.[3]

Means of Livelihood

In society means of livelihood has got an important position. Society cannot be imagined without it. Different means of livelihood are always available in all times. But only useful works in society are the ideal means which is helpful in establishing peace and prosperity in society. In the *Mahāpurāṇa* important means of livelihood are mentioned as employment in army (*asi*), job of teaching (*maṣi*), agriculture, trade, employment in building and temple construction and fine arts such as painting etc.[4]

1. *Mahā.*, 93.4.10-13; 96.2.17-18.
2. *Ibid.*, 5.20.4.
3. *Kavirājamārga*, 1-91.
4. असि मसि सिप्पु वि जं जिह जेहउ,
   अक्खिउ लोयहुं तं तिह तेहउ ।
   —*Mahāpurāṇa*, 5.19.13.

   अवर वि भणिय वणियवर हलहर सुयरियकं हिय कुलवहा ।
   जड पखिडियधम्म चंडाल वि पयडियवि वियपसुवहा ॥
   —*Mahā.*, 5.20.1-2.

Pushpadanta has fixed the maximum limit of taxes to one-sixth (   ) of the wealth and not beyond that.[1]

Individual bravery as displayed in battlefields was held in great respect and the rulers were wont to commemorate the heroic death of their warriors and even to make compensatory grants for the benefit of the dependants of the deceased.[2]

Status of Saints in Society

In ancient times Indian society was religion-oriented, and saints were considered to be the life of religion. Hence saints had the highest position in society. The great poet Pushpadanta, a contemporary of the Rāshṭrakūṭas, also has given them the highest position. They were free to go anywhere they liked. Their entrance either to the emperor's court[3] or poorman's hut[4] was not forbidden.[5] The king always rushed to welcome saints as soon as he got information about their arrival. He attended the preachings of saints along with his whole family and managed everything for their maintenance. Insulting a saint was treated as the greatest sin of the earth.[6]

According to Somadeva, another literary luminary of the time, it was the duty of householders to remedy the ills of monks and saints, which might have been of three kinds: physical ailments, mental worries and external troubles such as the rigorous cold and wind. While the monks were engaged in expounding and studying the sacred texts, they were to be comforted with lodging, food, books and other amenities.[7]

These evidences from two contemporary works are sufficient to prove the high status of saints in the society of the period of our study.

1. *Mahā*, 5.9.3.
2. *S.I.I.*, IX, No. 392.
3. *Mahā.*, 9.5.6-11; 38.21.5; 46.9.3. etc.
4. *Ibid.*, 98.13.4.
5. *Ibid* , 1.18.10-13; 11.35.7-15; 57.27.4. etc.
6. *Ibid.*, 22.17.9-22.18.4 and 90.3.15-90.4.4.
7. K.K. Handiqui, *op. cit.*, p. 286.

Mahājanas

The Mahājanas held a very high position in the society. It would be all the more clear when we see that in several cases of grants made, the donor, either a private individual, or an official or a royal personage or even the king himself, required their presence and even they sought formal permission and approval of the Mahājanas. For example, a gift of gosāsa, a tank and a garden made by an individual after washing the feet of fifty-six Mahājanas of Chiṁchila is mentioned in a record, dated about 873 A.D.[1]

A record dated 868 A.D. from Nīlagunda in Gadag taluk of Dharwar district refers to the assignment of tax levied on clarified butter or ghee made over to the 120 Mahājanas of Nīlgunda *Agrahāra.*[2] Several records speak of similar remission of taxes by the government officials. They, obviously, were doing so in their official capacity. We may further note in this connection that the Mahājanas were also concerned with the collection of taxes. Also in the matter of fixing or charging the taxes, rent etc., they had a voice. We have ample instances to show that when fresh taxes were levied or the rates were fixed, the Mahājanas of the Agrahāra were consulted. In such matters there used to be concord between them as is suggested by the following example. It is recorded in an inscription of 918 A.D. that agreement was reached between an officer mahāśrīmanta and the Mahājanas of Baṭṭakere regarding the revenue of that place.[3]

There is sufficient ground to say that the Mahājanas were Brāhmaṇas. Records eulogise them as learned in various branches of learning. For instance, a record from Kalas, dated 929 A.D. of Govinda IV, while describing the qualities of the residents of the place, refers to *vipras*, *i.e.*, Brāhmaṇas and at the end of the inscription, we find them being referred to as Mahājanas.[4]

1. *B.K.I.*, I, No. 15; see also *E.I.*, XXI, p. 207. Here the gift is made in the presence of fifty Mahājanas.
2. *E.I.*, VI, pp. 98ff.
3. *ARSIE*, 32-33, No. 184.
4. *E.I.*, XIV, pp. 332ff.

Dr. A.S. Altekar[1] holds the view that in some cases at least, the Mahājanas included persons other than Brāhmaṇas. In support of this view, he refers to the following statement in the Radhānpur plate of Govinda III[2] which mentions forty Mahājanas. Among them, according to him, ten named in the record were Brāhmaṇas. Another record from Hatti-Mattur in Dharwar district, dated 917 A.D.,[3] refers to an assembly of fifty cultivators headed by an oilman Jayasingayyasetti and Jummisetti, Malisetti, Namisetti and Kamyisetti. Here the assembly as well as its leader are perhaps all non-Brāhmaṇas. Dr. Fleet is of the view that Mahājanas were a collective body of the Brāhmaṇas.[4] Dr. R.C. Majumdar takes the term Mahājanas to mean merchants.[5] He took Mahājana in the modern sense.

Mahājanas included all the adults of a place. This is the view of Dr. Altekar who based it on the following information in an inscription dated 866 A.D. of Sirur in Dharwar district[6] that refers to 230 Mahājanas of the place. Another inscription from Nargund in Dharwar district refers to 220 Mahājanas of the locality. Yet another inscription dated 916 A.D. of the village of Pattiya-Maltavur mentions 220 Mahājanas of the village. It is thus clear from the above instances that village Mahājanas included practically the heads of all the families of the village.

Under the Rāshṭrakūṭas the basis of rural administration continued to be the same as earlier under the Chālukyas of Bādāmi. The inscriptions give ample evidence of the presence of gāmuṇḍas and mahājanas in each important village and township, and of the diligence and regularity with which they attended to the numerous local affairs.[7]

1. *RATT.*, p. 201.
2. *Ibid.*, VI, p. 246.
3. *I.A.*, XII, p. 125.
4. *E.I.*, V, p. 10.
5. A R. Wadia (ed.), *Social Work in Ancient & Medieval India*, p. 32.
6. *E.I.*, VII, p. 203; also *RATT.*, p. 201.
7. R.C. Majumdar and K.K. Dasgupta (eds.), *Comprehensive History of India*, Vol. III, Pt. I, pp. 738-39.

The Manor plate gives a very interesting piece of information that the grant was made not by a king or a royal official, but by the mahājana. Here V.V. Mirashi terms Mahājanas as a corporation which consisted of the representatives of the city and managed the civic affairs including charitable endowments of the city.[1]

Numerous hero-stones scattered throughout the region speak of the heroic deeds of the Deccan youth on the one hand and the responsible role played by the Mahājanas on the other. The Belber inscription of a Gaṅga feudatory dated 800 A.D. refers to one Āla, who is mentioned as having died in a fight, while rescuing the cattle; this pleased the Mahājanas who made a grant of five Kolagas of wet land for his family.[2]

The above discussion gives a clear picture of the role played by the Mahājanas and their position in the society. As the Brāhmaṇas enjoyed a good status in comparison to other castes, so the Mahājanas included mostly the Brāhmaṇas. It seems that the Mahājanas were the village assembly and the chief person was the headman called grāmakūṭa in Maharashtra and gāvuṇḍa in Karnataka. The most important duty of the Mahājanas was to defend the village from the enemies from within and outside.[3] In order to discharge their duty properly they sometimes used to maintain a militia.[4] They were connected with revenue collection and enjoyed rent-free land. Such organisation was essential because peace of the villages was disturbed not so much by thieves and dacoits as by the rebellions of feudatories and the rivals of the adjacent villages. Thus whatever might have been the caste or castes of the Mahājanas, there can be no doubt that they played an important role in the Rāshṭrakūṭa empire.

Family System

Each family was a closely knit unit of the social structure and it was customary for men, as in the earlier period, to

1. *P.I.H.C.*, Twenty-first Session, Trivandrum, p. 51.
2. *MAR*, 1913, p. 38.
3. *P.I.H C.*, XXXI, p. 84.
4. *Ibid.*

associate their names with the names of their elders and predecessors. Thus the head of the family was much respected at the family level even as the king was acknowledged as their master by the citizens.[1] In many of the early inscriptions, donees as well as deceased heroes are mentioned with names of their respective fathers prefixed to their own.[2]

Though joint families were the order of the day, cases of separation in our period were not as rare as is sometimes supposed. Some of our records, which mention the specific shares of the cosharers of *agrahāra* villages, prove that in many cases fathers and sons were living separately. In the Torkhede inscription of Govinda III,[3] separate shares are assigned to two brothers, showing that they were no longer members of a joint family.

In the *Mahāpurāṇa* of Pushpadanta also the status of each member in a family has been described vividly.[4] It presents ideal relations between wife and husband, father and son, mother and son, brother and brother, father and daughter, mother and daughter, brother and sister, uncle and nephew, woman and younger brother of her husband etc.

Marriage

Marriage is the most important *saṁskāra*, being the base of the whole structure of the society. It is a sacrament regulating one of the primary instincts and providing a proper way for the social recognition of the biological function. The earlier Smṛtis as well as the contemporary ones mention the traditional eight forms of marriage, and each has been discussed in detail.[5] These are the ***Brāhma***, ***Daiva***, ***Ārsha***, ***Prājāpatya***, ***Gāndharva***, ***Āsura***, ***Rākshasa*** and ***Raiśācha***. But the exact source of our period and region, i.e., the *Mahāpurāṇa*

1. K.V. Ramesh, *op. cit.*, pp. 270, 274.
2. *E.I.*, IX, pp. 17-23.
3. *E.I.*, III, p. 54.
4. Sudarshan Mishra, *Mahākavi Pushpadanta aur unkā Mahāpurāṇa* (in Hindi), Vaishali. 1987, pp. 192-99.
5. *Manu*, III.21; *Yājña.*, I.58-61; *Nārada*, XIII.38-39; *Agni*, CLIII. 8-11, pp. 593-94.

of Pushpadanta has mentioned only some of them showing the trend of the time.[1]

We find here marriage through selection of bride or bridegroom by the father of bridegroom or bride. In this form father can give the hands of son or daughter of marriageable age to a suitable bride or bridegroom.[2] It may also involve giving away a daughter after fulfilling the terms and conditions by her father.[3] It may also happen that the father of a bride may marry his daughter to a person with whom he is satisfied.[4] In the support of above-mentioned systems of marriage the poet has supplied us legendary examples.

The *Rākshasa* form of marriage, though not common, was more to the liking of the martial clans who forcibly carried away girls and married them. Pushpadanta gives examples of such marriages,[5] but in this act there are possibilities of humiliation, fear and delicacy; and so he has taken it as an exception. We are aware of such marriages even amongst the royal families. Indra I, the Rāshṭrakuṭā chieftain and father of Dantidurga, had carried away the Chālukyan princess Bhavanāgā from a *Svayaṁvara*-hall and married her forcibly.[6]

References to the practice of *Svayaṁvara* are very few in number, but literary evidences, however, tend to suggest its prevalence. In this system the girl selects her groom by herself. The *Mahāpurāṇa* furnishes two varieties of it. In its first kind the father himself announces for *Svayaṁvara* for his daughter, where people from different parts assemble and the daughter selects one of them by herself.[7] Or otherwise the

1. *Mahā.*, 4.6.16.
2. *Ibid.*, 4.8.13-4.8.9.3; 24.11.9-24.13.15; 25.1.11-12; 51.14.1-51.15.7.
3. *Ibid.*, 84.9.2; 99.5.1-6.
4. *Ibid.*, 99.4.4-10; 101.14.20-22.
5. *bid.*, 65.14.13-65.15.7; 69 16.11-69.21.4; 90.9.15-90.10.11.
6. *E.I.*, XIV, p. 124; XVIII, p. 252; *I.A.* (Third Series), I, p. 10 and V.V. Mirashi, *Indological Studies*, IV, pp. 210f.
7. *Mahā* , 28.12.3-28.21.4; 83 21.6-83.22.15; and 92.8 2-92.9.8.

girl lays down certain condition and she marries the man who fulfils that.[1]

In addition to this, the poet has given us details of different acts at the time of the marriage ceremony. He describes the departure of the groom with the persons of equal age sitting in a palanquin studded with gems. Beating of drums,[2] erection of grand *vivāha-maṇḍapa*,[3] bride-groom sitting with the hand of the bride in his hand on the marriage platform,[4] blessing the couple by the relatives,[5] dance and music,[6] these are some of the things which are done at the time of marriage ceremony as described by Pushpadanta. Pre-nuptial relation is quite unbearable to the poet, and he informs that there was provision for banishment in such cases.[7] Sulaiman informs us that before marriage both the parties used to send messenger to each other. They also used to send gifts and presents to each other and offer money and materials according to capacity.

The caste does not appear to have been so rigid as it is at present. Alberuni informs us that every man of a caste might marry a woman of his own caste or one of the castes or caste below his.[8] Thus *anuloma* marriages *i.e.*, marriages of males of higher castes with females of lower castes was common in society, and even orthodox Smṛti and Nibandha writers regarded them as legal, though not commendable.[9] The *pratiloma* marriages were not allowed, for Alberuni tells us that nobody was allowed to marry a woman of a caste superior to his own.[10] The *Yaśastilaka* also informs about the

1. *Mahā.*, 83.13.8-83.21 2.
2. *Ibid.*, 88.23.12-14; 4.11.1-4.13.8.
3. *Ibid.*, 4.9.8-4.10.7; 24.12.9-13; 51.15.1-3.
4. *Ibid.*, 24.13.10-11.
5. *Ibid.*, 24.13.12-13.
6. *Ibid.*, 4.10 8; 51.15.4; also see S.S. Nadvi, *op. cit.*, p. 26.
7. *Ibid.*, 98.15.14-16.
8. S.S. Nadvi, *op. cit.*, p. 26.
9. A.S. Altekar, *The Position of Women in Hindu Civilization*, Delhi, 3rd Ed., 1962, p. 75.
10. Sachau, *op. cit.*, II, pp. 155-56.

inter-caste marriage.[1] The Pālas were devout Buddhists but they married amongst the Rāshṭrakūṭas and the Kalachuris, who were followers of Brahmanical faiths.[2]

Marriage alliances between political rivals and rulers of neighbouring kingdoms became more common during the time of the Rāshṭrakūṭas of Mānyakheṭa. For instance, Kṛshṇa II (878-914 A.D.) married a Chedi princess, the daughter of Kokalla I. Kṛshṇa's son Jagattuṅga espoused Lakshmī and Govindāmbā, daughters of the Kalachuri dynasty. Amoghavarsha III (935-39 A.D.) and Kṛshṇa III (939-67 A.D.) had taken Kalachuri princesses for their wives.[3] These alliances were sometimes mutually beneficial to the two houses and peace to the society thereof.

It was from about the tenth century A.D. that intercaste marriages began to go out of fashion. Alberuni observes that the Brāhmaṇas of his day no longer availed themselves of the permission to take wives from the three lower castes.[4]

Astrology played no further part in the marriage ceremony. The subject, however, made rapid progress during our period; it then began to play an important part in the making and breaking of matches. Horoscope came into vogue at this time and began to be consulted at the settlement of marriage.[5]

The prevalence of early marriage is attested to both in the *Yaśastilaka* and the *Nītivākyāmṛta*. A speaker in a story in the *Yaśastilaka* identifies heaven with the mutual love of a maiden, twelve years of age, and a youth of sixteen. In the *Nītivākyāmṛta* also, it is clearly stated that a maiden and a youth of the age specified above are fit for marital relations.[6] Alberuni too informs us that the Hindus married at a very young age.[7] He further says that a Brāhmaṇa was not allowed

1. K.K Handiqui, *op. cit.*, p. 30.
2. *I.A* , XV, p. 305 and XXI, p. 255.
3. P.B. Desai, *Basavesvara and His Times*, Dharwar, 1968, p. 6.
4. A.S Altekar, *Position of Women*, p. 77,
5. *Ibid.*, p. 72.
6. K.K. Handiqui, *op.* cit., p. 122.
7. Sachau, *op. cit.*, II, p. 154.

to marry a woman above twelve years of age. But at another place he informs that a Brāhmaṇa boy married after the completion of his education which was at the age of twenty-five.[1]

We learn from Alberuni that, "it was absolutely forbidden to marry related women both of the direct descending line, *viz.*, a granddaughter, or great-granddaughter, and of direct ascending line, *viz.*, a mother, a grandmother, or great-grandmother. It was also forbidden to marry collateral relations, *viz.*, a sister, a niece, a maternal or paternal aunt and their daughters, except in case the couple of relations who wanted to marry each other were removed from each other by five consecutive generations. In that case the prohibition was waived, but, nevertheless, such a marriage was an object of dislike to them."[2] The Wardha Plates tell us that Jagattuṅga was a beautiful person, and that he died without having ascended the throne. He married Lakshmī, the daughter of his maternal uncle Śaṅkaragaṇa, the brother-in-law of Kṛshṇa II.[3] The same was the case with Indra IV.[4] Such marriages are recognized as valid by the Dharmaśāstra literature for the Deccanese and are still not unknown. They may have been fairly in vogue in our period. The marriage with the daughter of maternal uncle is also attested by Pushpadanta in his *Mahāpurāṇa* at several places.[5]

Polygamy also seems to have been prevalent, for we are told by Alberuni that a man might marry one to four wives.[6] This might have been possible in our period too. Jagattuṅga, the son of Kṛshṇa II, married Lakshmī and Govindāmbā,

1. *Ibid* , p. 131.
2. *Ibid.*, p. 155; see also *Medhātithi on Manu*, tr. by Ganganatha Jha, I, Pt. I, p. 232; II, Pt. I, pp. 23 & 27.
3. R G. Bhandarkar, *The Early History of the Deccan*, Poona, 1983, p. 97. Also *I A.*, XII, p. 265.
4. *RATT.*, p. 343.
5. *Mahā.*, 65.14.14-65.15.8; 82.16.4, 92.14.6-7 etc.
6. Sachau, *op, cit.*, II, p. 155.

daughters of Śaṅkaragaṇa of the Kalachuri family.[1] It is reasonable to assume that polygamy was practised by the rich and ruling sections of society, and the poor found it beyond their means. The reverse may also be true. The low origin of Pāmarodāra is described in the *Yaśastilaka* as the cause of his overweening pride. His father was an oilman and mother a low-born woman, while his wife had five husbands.[2] Such might have been the case in the poor section of the society.

An interesting feature of marriages in our period was the marriage-tax. The rate of levy varied from caste to caste and from community to community. The Daṇḍapur inscription[3] of the Rāshṭrakūṭa king Govinda IV, dated 918 A.D. and another one of the time of Kṛshṇa III, dated 929 A.D.[4] differentiate between the rate of taxes on marriages of the *Brāhmaṇas* on the one hand and those of the *Śūdras* on the other. According to these inscriptions the *Brāhmaṇas* were to pay three *drammas* on each marriage whereas it was only one *dramma* on each marriage of the *Śūdras*. From these two examples it is evident that the *Brāhmaṇas* who enjoyed general immunity from taxes were expected to pay social and religious taxes.

There is no doubt that the later Dharmaśāstra literature as a whole (200-1200 A.D.), while liberally permitting the husband to remarry during the life-time of the first wife, refuses the remedy of divorce to the wife even when completely forsaken by the husband.[5] Ties of wedlock were held sacred and indissoluble by the Hindus. We learn from Alberuni that husband and wife could only be separated by death, as they had no divorce.[6] He further says that a widow could not remarry.

1. P.B. Desai, *H.K.*, p. 135.
2. K.K. Handiqui, *op. cit.*, p. 30.
3. *K.I.*, II, pp. 11-14.
4. *I.A.*, XII, pp. 222-24; also R.S. Panchmukhi, *Digest of Annual Report on Kannada Research in Bombay Province for the year 1940-41*, Dharwar, 1945, p. 11.
5. A.S. Altekar, *Women*, p. 83.
6. Sachau, *op. cit.*, II, p. 154.

Position of Women

Somadeva, as a practical thinker, writes that women are neither good nor bad, and compares them to the ocean of milk, the source of poison as well as nectar, adding that they have neither any innate merit nor blemish, and that they become just like their husbands, as rivers assume the character of the ocean when they are merged therein. There was a class of thinkers who considered women superior to men intellectually. Thus Somadeva Sūri thought that discrimination between men and women was valid in respect of physical activity, but considered women superior to men in intellectual activity.[1]

Interestingly enough, the epigraphs of our period contain a good deal of information about many high ranked women. We come across some of the queens and other women holding administrative charge of different regions. This was particularly the case with our period. In 786 A.D. we find Śīlamahādevī or Śīlabhaṭṭārikā, the crowned queen of Dhruva, as an accomplished lady.[2] Grants issued in her name without reference to her husband suggest that she enjoyed sovereign authorities along with her husband. She was one of the few women administrators of early India. She might have felt that being the crowned queen, she had an inherent right to issue routine administrative orders without any reference to her husband; or, the latter may have expressly invested her with certain ruling powers, including the important power of making land grants.[3]

Under the Rāshṭrakūṭa administration princesses are rarely seen occupying government posts. The only known instance is that of Revakanimmadi, a daughter of Amoghavarsha I and wife of Ereyanga, a member of the Gaṅga family, who was associated with the administration of Eḍatore *Vishaya* in 837 A.D.[4] From this situation it is tempting to

1. K.K. Handiqui, *op. cit.*, p. 106.
2. *E.I.*. XXII, p. 98.
3. A.S. Altekar, *Women*, p. 189; also P.B. Desai (ed.), *H.K.*, p. 123.
4. P.B. Desai (ed.), *H.K.*, p. 132.

suggest that the later Chālukyas felt encouraged to follow this practice of giving responsibilities to women and the practice of appointing princesses to high government posts became very common. Mailādevī, one of the queens of Someśvara I, Akādevī, an elder sister of Jayasiṁha III, and Lakshmīdevī, the chief queen of Vikramāditya IV, were holding important administrative charges.[1] Imitating those who are higher in status is a natural process in society.

Women were held in high respect and every care was taken to fulfil their wishes. The Javakheḍa grant was made by Amoghavarsha I at the request of one *Bhaṭṭārikā* (noble lady) in A.D. 829.[2] Another example for showing respect to Rāshṭrakūṭa queen is by Govinda IV. He made some Mahādāna such as Hiraṇyagarbha, Ubhayamukhī, Gosahasra and Kalpavṛksha for the religious merit of his queen, the illustrious Bhāgiyavvā, the *paṭṭa* on whose forehead was caused to be tied by twelve mahāsāmantas (chief Feudatories). The grant of the village was made by Govinda IV without getting down from the pan of the *Tulā* in which he was seated for the Tulādāna in the courtyard of Govindeśvara which was situated in the capital Mānyakheṭa.[3]

The object of the Hulgur inscription of Khoṭṭiga[4] was to record the renewal of a grant by the daughter of Dānapa, *i.e.*, Aṅkabharsi, to the temple of the goddess Pulluṅgūrabbe. The gift consisted of six gardens, twenty-four *mattars* of Kisukhāḍu, 'red-land' and the cess realised on the occasion of fairs (*jārāmukhaṁ*). This gift, we are told in lines 13-16, was made at the request of Mārasinghayya of the Maṇalara family who was the headman (nāl-gāvuṇḍa). Here also we find a princess using her power vested in her.

The religious independence given to Jain women had its repercussion in other spheres of society. There is epigraphic

1. A.S. Altekar, *State and Government in Ancient India*, Delhi, 195?, pp. 357-58.
2. *E.I.*, XXXII, p. 129.
3. *E I.*, XXXVI, p. 259.
4. *E.I.* XXXIV, pp. 61-64.

evidence to show that a Jain woman named Jakkiyabbe successfully discharged administrative duties in the Nagara-khaṇḍe-70 during the reign of Krshṇa III. We have also some Jain women who distinguished themselves in literary work.[1]

In the ninth century A.D., higher education of women was confined to royal, official, rich and well-to-do families and to the class of dancing girls.[2] It may be pointed out that most of the heroines of Sanskrit dramas written in our period, who are represented as fairly educated, belong to the class mentioned above.[3] In one of the concluding verses of *Yaśastilaka* Somadeva tells us that there was a celebrated scribe named Rachchhuka, who was called Lekhaka-Śikhāmaṇi. It seems that his writings have been utilized by the fair sex for writing their love-letters.[4] This information indicates lack of education among general women.

The *Strīdhana* rights, we may presume, were also recognised. They have been conceded in the Hindu society since very early times and even the early writers, who refuse to recognise the widow as an heir, permit women to have undisputed proprietary rights over certain varieties of *Strīdhana* property.[5] That a widow in the Deccan could inherit her husband's property is made clear from the case of a country Gāvuṇḍa, who was succeeded in his office by his widow.[6] That the daughters were heirs on the failure of sons is further proved by a Saundati record.[7]

1. R.B.P. Singh, *Jainism in Early Medieval Karnataka* (*c. A.D. 500-1200*), Delhi, 1975, p. 130.
2. पुरुषवद्योषितोपि कवि भवेषु । श्रूयन्ते दृश्यन्ते च राजपुन्यो महामात्र-दुहितरो गणिकाः कौटिम्बकभार्याश्च शास्त्रप्रहित बुद्धयः कवयश्च ।
3. A.S. Altekar, *Women*, p. 19.
4. K.K. Handiqui, *op. cit.*, p. 1.
5. *Vasishṭha*, XVII.43; *Baudhāyana*, II.2, 49; *Āpastamba*, II, 6, 14, 9.
6. *E.C.*, VII, No. 219.
7. *J B.B.R.A.S.*, X, p. 177.

In the *Mahāpurāṇa* of Pushpadanta the position of the woman has been shown very high in the society. She used to roam in disguise of an acrobat for searching a groom for her.[1] She used to encourage her husband for going to the battle-field.[2] She was very happy to get information of having become pregnant[3] and she used to celebrate her son's birth-day.[4] She used to be very sad in case of separation from her son.[5] She helped those who were denied justice.[6] She accompanied her husband in his amusements, visit to saints and in almost all the affairs of life. But in case of her husband not maintaining his high family traditions she was ready to get rid of her husband for its protection.[7] For this the poet is unable to bear the slave-like and pitiable condition of women.[8] In the case of humiliation of women, the poet suggests even death sentence to the culprit.[9] Though the feelings shown by the poet here seem to be universal in nature, but at the same time it also gives us a clear hint towards the position of women in the eyes of society. Alberuni informs us that at the time of abstinence of her husband she had choice to accompany her husband into the life of wilderness.[10]

A.S. Altekar opines that widow remarriages were getting unpopular in our period. But the question of widow remarriage never troubled the lower classes, among whom they were fairly common.[11] It is, therefore, difficult to say whether virgin widows in the higher classes were remarried or not in

1. *Mahā.*, 32.2.10-32.4.5.
2. *Ibid.*, 52.13.
3. *Ibid.*, 5.3.5, 40.4.15, 41.5.3 etc.
4. *Ibid.*, 4.1 etc.
5. *Ibid.*, 91.9.9.
6. *Ibid.*, 57.9.1-57.10.5.
7. *Ibid.*, 60.26.10.
8. *Ibid*, 71.20.5.
9. *Ibid.*, 69.6.5.
10. Sachau, *Alberuni's India*, II, pp. 130-33.
11. *RATT.*, p. 346.

our period. Tonsuring of the widow in our period is confirmed by the *Mahāpurāṇa* and she used to put on red-cloth,[1] and the use of ornaments and cosmetics was prohibited for her.[2]

Pushpadanta informs us that a mother has great love and affection for her daughter, because who will have less love for a child born out of her womb.[3] Father is also shown training her daughter in different subjects and arts.[4] He brings materials for worship to be performed by his daughter.[5] He also consoles his daughter in case of failure in love.[6]

We get information about the sacred relations between brother and sister too from the *Mahāpurāṇa.* Anantavīrya, the husband of Kanakaśrī kills her two brothers in the battle-field. Hearing this she is unable to bear this pain and she starts living the life of an ascetic in her house with the permission of her husband.[7] There are several stories in this literary work which focus towards the sacrifices made by each other.

The relation between sister and sister has also been depicted here which is a unique one. A Vaiśya couple had seven daughters. All except Śrīdattā, the eldest one, were lepers, deaf, dumb, handicapped etc. Unfortunately the couple died, and all these children became helpless. Śrīdattā alone took the burden of all her six sisters who were suffering from diseases, and looked after them with every care.[8]

Affection for husband's younger brother in the heart of a woman and vice-versa was not lacking as described in the *Mahāpurāṇa.* It was necessary for the peaceful and strong family. The poet elucidates this point with several examples.[9]

1. *Mahā.*, 71.20.1, 73.2.3-4.
2. *Ibid.*, 87.1.9-10.
3. *Ibid.*, 73.23.5.
4. *Ibid* , 5.6.5-5.12.13 and 5.18.3-9.
5. *Ibid* , 61.19.10.
6. *Ibid.*, 22.9.13-22.12.11 and 24.8.1.
7. *Ibid.*, 61.11.5-8.
8. *Ibid* , 61.9.9-61.10.4.
9. *Ibid.*, 83.7.2-12.

In the above discussion we are in a position to say that women in our period enjoyed a good position everywhere, in administration, in society or in family of their own.

Another social feature concerning women was a class of theirs which may be denoted as that of courtesans.[1] Society, since remote past, has had women of easy virtue, many of whom were elevated to a better status at the royal courts. The courtesans seem to have enjoyed a much better status than the ordinary prostitutes and slave girls because of their associations with the elite of the society and the royal courts. In the *Yaśastilaka* they are shown as preceding the queen and the queen dowager to the temple of Chaṇḍikā. The sound of music accompanying the dance of courtesans in the streets announced to the citizens that queen Chandramatī and her retinue were on their way.[2]

Satī System

Sati or *Sahagamana* is vividly described by the authors of our period. They do not, however, hold it as an ideal for the widow : they allow it only as a second alternative and regard ascetic life as preferable to it. Down to *c*. 1000 A.D. Satis were rare in the Deccan. If the immolation of Mādrī is set in its Puranic framework by Pampa, Ranna brings it nearer to its historicity when describing the end of Guṇḍamabbe. Janna[3] distinguishes himself by dwelling on the psychology of the wives parting from their possessions and passions. The following extracts are noteworthy :

(a) Hugging her husband's dead body, Mādrī decides to end her life. Noticing her face lit up with determination, Kuntī falls to the ground, rolls in sorrow, and declares : "Forsaking me and your children, what if you have parted from me ? I shall follow you—oh king, how can I live without you?"

1. P.V Kane, *HDS.*, Vol. II, Pt. I, p. 637.
2. K.K. Handiqui, *op. cit.*, pp. 198-99.
3. Janna, *Anantanāthapurāṇam*, eds., H. Deveerappa and P.C.M. Sharma, Mysore, 1972.

Turning towards Mādrī, she says,

"Accept the care of these children. Give me his body. I shall be what he has become."

To this, Mādrī says in reply,

"I have been blessed with this occasion by my husband; I shall not forgo it for you. Tend my children, and please do not plead further with me."

Thus saying, while the saints and the sylvan deities praised her courage and conviction, Mādrī plunged into the pyre clinging to the body of Pāṇḍurāja. She thus attained an unequalled status of heroine among those of her conviction, the blemishless Mādrī.[1]

(b) Guṇḍamabbe, sister of Attimabbe (two celebrated Jain sisters in Karnataka history), pleaded in terms similar to those of Mādrī :

"Sister, you have a son, the forehead jewel of the world. Remain here and rear him up to adolescence, I shall follow Nāgadeva". Begging thus, she clung to her all husband's body, observed all the rites, and adorned with the (auspicious symbols) ornaments, she plunged into the pyre with unswerving courage. While the congregation acclaimed the noble act of this *mahāsatī*, she ended her mortal life to the great discomfort of the nymphs in heaven.

"Our dream of uniting with Nāgadeva has been shattered" burst the celestial nymphs steeped in jealousy, "the chaste Guṇḍamabbe has rejoined her handsome hero in death and has become his beloved in Heaven too".[2]

1. Pampa, *Vikramārjuna-Vijayam*, ed., K.V. Puttapa, Mysore, 1973, V. 24 (*vacana*) and V. 26.

2. Ranna, *Ajit-Tīrthakara-Purāṇa-Tilakam*, I, vv. 47-48.

(c) In the story of Chaṇḍaśāsana, depicted by Janna, the pathos and passions of the parting women, her psychological tumult and the conflicts in her convictions surface boldly. Chaṇḍaśāsana's obsession for queen Sunandā, his friend's wife, results in her death, and in sorrow at the result of his guile, he throws himself into the pyre, hoping to unite with his love at least in the next life. This evokes mixed reaction from the queens wedded to him, though they are all united in following him by the rite of *sahagamana*. One obdurate queen, as recklessly challenging as the rancorous mounds on her bosom, questions the validity of their obligations to a husband, who has betrayed them all by falling for another's wife.

In her words :

"Shamelessly ignoring the sarcastic grins of others, forsaking all of us, he fell for another's wife; learning of her death, now the king is preparing to end his life, behold this sister !

"Like the jasmine creeper we hugged the mango tree, but the tree is enamoured of the goddess of spring; for his shameless act, we are to pay with our lives. What a fate, oh sister!" This protest provokes reactions from other wives who reiterate traditional social values. One of the dedicated wives has the following reply :

"Should we find fault with our lord, his sins and weakness ? He knows the laws of life, of sins, and of passions; he is the lord of this earth. Come what may, we shall follow him like his shadow wherever he goes, and in all that happens to him. Why protest against it?—are we the judges of his acts?"

Saying this, the queens rushed, each anxious to secure a place ahead of the other.

"Deciding to win the grace of their lord, to abide by the rule, to perform their duty, to return their debt to their protector, the queens rushed forward, vying with each other, to take the vow. They parted with their wealth; they consoled their dependants; they bade farewell to all they had tended birds and creepers, plants and animals.[1] They received honour and reciprocated love. Ruffled in the sea of sorrow, they reached their destination."[2]

Many a brave wife followed her heroic husband in death, but it was not a universal practice. This is evident not only from the examples cited above, but also from a comparatively smaller number of references to this practice in inscriptions and literature. Mādrī followed her husband, but bade Kuntī remain—so did Guṇḍamabbe and convinced Attimabbe to stay and live. Those who plunged into the pyre that consumed the body of the husband, were considered to be following the *sahagamana* rite; but those who plunged into the pyre, after receiving news of their husband's death, are described to have followed the *anugamana* rite. However, both these terms are used rarely in the literature of our period.

Despite sectarian and religious differences, medieval society nourished certain social values, and *sahagamana* appears to be one of them. Among the social groups which observed this practice, we do not seem to meet Brāhmaṇas; of the other three *varṇas*, the Kshatriyas and Vaiśyas observed it occasionally, while among the Śūdras—who incidentally, formed the bulk of the army—this practice appears to have been very popular.[3] Though not in conformity with their religious observances, the Jains seem to have approved of the *sahagamana* (as in the instance of Guṇḍamabbe); but more discriminating of them took to *samādhi-maraṇa,* a process of

1. Here Janna's depiction comes close to the parting scene of Śakuntalā in Kālidāsa's classic.
2. Janna, *op. cit.*, XI, vv. 91 and 93.
3. S. Settar and Gunther D. Sontheimer, *Memorial Stones*, Dharwar, 1982, p. 25.

fast unto death. Despite their criticism of Brahmanical values the Vīraśaivas appear to have generally approved of this, if they did not openly advocate it. In the *Vacana* literature of this period, we come across a casual, and very occasional, reference to the details of this ritual. From the sayings of Basava and Mādara Dhūlamayya, we learn that when the *satī* was taken in procession to the pyre, the heroes of the village begged blessings from her, obtained flowers from her hair and limes held in her hands. By this symbolic act the heroes honoured her, and their conviction was reinforced by the blessings of one who was on her way to attain 'divinity'.[1]

Sulaiman, an Arab merchant who had spent sometime on the western coast of India in the middle of the ninth century, states that it was only sometimes that queens used to mount the funeral pyres of their consorts; it was entirely left to them to choose.[2] It will, therefore, appear that the Satī custom was not so common in the Deccan of our period even in the royal families as it was in Kashmir, where we find even unchaste queens like Jayamatī compelled to ascend the funeral pyre by the force of the public opinion.[3]

Alberuni tells us that the wives of the dead kings were burnt with them whether they wished it or not. An exception was made only for women of advanced years and for those who had children.[4] This statement seems to be based on the condition prevailing in contemporary Kashmir and does not hold good of the Deccan. Perhaps, 'the custom was still confined to the royal families and it had not yet spread to the masses, as was the case in the later centuries.'[5]

The inference that the *sati* system was not so common in the Deccan as it was in the north, is further supported by

1. R.C. Hiremath (ed.), *Sakala-Purātanara-Vacangalu*, Dharwar, 1972, V. 1761.
2. Elliot and Dowson, *History of India*, Vol. I, p. 6; S.S. Nadvi, *Arab aur Bharat ke Sambandh* (in Hindi), Prayag, 1930, p. 26.
3. *Rājataraṅgiṇī*, VIII, p. 366.
4. Sachau, *Alberuni's India*, II, p. 155.
5. *RATT*, p. 344. Also see Marco Polo, II, p. 341; Ibn Batuta, p. 191; Bernier, p. 30; Tavernier, p. 414.

the fact that though there are innumerable inscribed or uninscribed memorial stones *i.e.*, *viragals*, of our period, scattered mostly in Karnataka state which commemorate the deaths of village heroes who had died for their communities, mention or elaboration of *satis* in these memorials is nowhere found so far. The only known case of *sati* belonging to our period is that of Guṇḍamabbe, one of the wives of Nāgadeva, a minister of Satyāśraya, who had no issue and who is known to have burnt herself with her husband when the latter had died in war.

Pushpadanta (959 A.D.) while giving the narration of wife-husband relation hints at the *sati* custom. He says that life becomes unbearable for the woman after the death of her husband and she chooses either to become an ascetic[1] or to burn herself[2] because she feels that no basis is left for her so that she might continue her life.[3] The wife always prefers to die during her husband's life-time.[4]

The Maser inscription[5] gives a detailed account of the Sulki Chief, Narasiṁha, who was under the command of Kṛshṇa III. His son, Kesarin, is said to have destroyed in a battle at Paṭṭaṇaka a large army consisting of horses, elephants and infantry sent by Lolikya. After the description of this battle, the plight of enemy women has been given who were resolved to put themselves to death. This account also gives the example of women being *satīs* but this, too, holds good for the enemy camp who were outsiders. Thus the phenomenon of the *satī* custom was very rare in the Deccan of Rāshṭrakūṭa times.

Purdah System

We may now take up the question of the prevalence of the purdah system.

1. *Mahā.*, 30.9.11, 90.15.1 etc.
2. *Ibid.*, 90.11.6 and 98.15.21.
3. *Ibid.*, 7.24.17.
4. *Ibid* , 78. 21.9.
5. *E.I.*, XXIX, p. 20.

It is remarkable to note that Abu Zaid, an Arab traveller of the early tenth century, records that "most of the princes of India, when they hold a court, allow their wives to be seen by the men who attend it whether they be natives or foreigners"[1] We can nowhere get any references to the purdah in the *Rājataraṅgiṇī* too.[2] The statement in the Kadba plates that the moon-faced damsels in the court of Kṛshṇa I who were skilful in exhibiting internal sentiments by means of the movements of their hands, used to give delight to the ladies of the capital, would support the testimony of Abu Zaid that no purdah was observed in the Deccan of our period.[3] There is no purdah system even today in the Deccan, except in the case of a few royal families that are known to have imitated it from the north. It is therefore clear that the purdah was unknown to our period and there was no bar to women appearing in public.[4]

1. Elliot and Dowson, *History of India*, I, p. 11.
2. A S. Altekar, *Position of Women in Hindu Civilization*, Delhi, second edition, 1956, p. 172.
3. *RATT*, p. 343.
4. *ABORI*, Vol. 37, 1957, p. 200.

3

The Social Set-up and Organisation

PART II

Dress

Costumes, coiffure and ornaments constitute an important aspect of social life. Because of the advent of Islam after the tenth century, and concomitantly the inroads made by its culture, alien, totally different and unfamiliar, the homogeneous character of the Indian society was subjected to radical changes in the succeeding centuries. It may, however, be noted that there are certain traces of foreign elements noticeable in the paintings of Elūra. This was probably due to the Arab settlements in the Rāshṭrakūṭa domain. But this is insignificant when compared to the later phenomenon of the impact of Muslim rule on the social and cultural dynamics of India.

Here an attempt is being made to analyse and interpret the various patterns of dress. Personal equipment such as dress, ornaments and hair styles is a continuous process and the view of Dr. Motichandra[1] that after the seventh century

1. Motichandra, *Costumes, Textiles, Cosmetics and Coiffure in Ancient and Medieval India*, Delhi, 1973, p. 2.

the paintings and sculptures become more conventionalised seems to be untenable. The paintings, mostly in traces, and the sculptures at Elūra clearly show that the changing patterns of styles are not altogether conventionalised.[1] These sculptural depictions are substantially supplemented by the literary descriptions found in the contemporary works such as Jinasena's *Mahāpurāṇa* (A.D. 848) and Somadeva's *Yaśastilaka* (A.D. 959) whose authors were associated with the court of the Rāshṭrakūṭa kings. Descriptions given by the Arab travellers, Al-Masudi and others, further testify to the rich variety of textiles in which Indians traded with Arab countries.

The clothing both of men and women consisted of cloth bound about the loins, and taken up above one shoulder in the case of men and above both in that of women. The *uttarīya* or the second or upper piece of cloth seems to have been used by both men and women.[2] Thus the Hindu dress in our period does not seem to have required much tailoring. Towards the end of the seventh century A.D., the Hindu made dress usually consisted of two unstitched cloths, one worn round like the present *dhotī*, and the other used as an upper garment.[3] The paintings in the Kailāsa temple provide us with a fairly clear picture of the upper garments.[4]

Throughout the history of world civilization, there has been a manifest attempt to glorify womanhood in all possible ways. Ancient Indian people were no exception to this tendency. Poets, dramatists, painters and sculptors have bestowed utmost attention of highlighting the charms of women and the costumes, coiffures and personal ornaments with which they were embellished. Thus Rājaśekhara, a contemporary of the Rāshṭrakūṭas. who lived in the court of the Gurjara-Pratīhāras, gives an interesting description of the dress of a woman in the following words: "With

1. T.V. Pathy, *Elūra* : *Art and Culture*, New Delhi, 1980, p. 75.
2 *ABORI*, 37, p. 200.
3. I-tsing, p. 68.
4. T.V. Pathy, *op. cit.*, p. 78.

ear-rings dancing on the cheeks and with the long necklace moving, down to the navel, the dress of the women of Kanauj deserves to be honoured, their upper cloth going completely round the waist down to the anklet."[1] She is also said to have attired her body with a pair of silken clothes which were as green as the tail of a king parrot.[2]

The lady figures carved in high relief on the pillars of the Yajñaśālā and the seated figure on the eastern side, generally identified as a Rāshṭrakūṭa princess, display a gorgeous *sakachchha* form of *ardhovastra*.[3] This form is very well represented in some sculptures such as the maidservant in the panel of Rāvaṇa shaking Kailāsa and the amorous scenes in Laṅkeśvara and the side pillared porches of Rang Maṇḍapa. The frightened maidservant due to the seismic vibrations that were produced by the titanic strength of Rāvaṇa, turned her back and took to heels. Thus the roll of *ardhovastra* is seen tucked in the *mekhalā* at the back. Similarly the ladies in the love scenes are in this dress. It is interesting to note that this mode of attiring the lower garment is still prevalent in Maharashtra and also some parts of northern Karnataka especially among the village folks and the working classes.[4]

Women were using stitched clothes also. We are told by Alberuni that "the lappets of the kurtakas (short shirts from the shoulders to the middle of the body with sleeves, a female dress) had slashes both on the right and left sides."[5] We further learn from him that "people used turbans for trousers. Those who wanted little dress were content to dress in a rag of two fingers' breadth, which they bound over their loins with two cords; but those who liked much dress, wore trousers lined with so much cotton as would suffice to make a number of counterpanes and saddle-rugs. These trousers had no (visible) openings, and they were so huge that the feet were

1. C.D. Dalal and R.A.K. Shastri (eds.), *Rājaśekhara* : *Kāvyamīmāṁsā*, p. 8.
2. T.V. Pathy, *op. cit.*, p. 78.
3. *Ibid.*, p. 80.
4. *Ibid.*
5. Sachau, *Alberuni's India*, I, pp. 180-81.

not visible. The string by which the trousers were fastened was at the back. Their sidār (a piece of dress covering the head and the upper part of breast and neck) was similar to the trousers, being also fastened at back by buttons."[1]

Flowers had an important place in the everyday life of the people, from worship of the deity to the decoration of the person. Men and women were equally fond of them. No make-up was complete without a garland round the neck or in the hair.

The *Yaśastilaka* refers to shop-fronts of garland-sellers (*sragājīvī*), who must be having brisk business in those times. The flower-sellers (*mālegatiyar*) in the *Pārśvanātha-Purāṇa* are described as holding the long white garlands of jasmine in such a way that they resembled the folds of white cloth.[2]

Yajñopavītas (sacred threads) were put on by the people. They are illustrated in the sculptures of Elūra. A *Chaurī*-bearer on the entrance pillar to Yajñaśālā, Kailāsa temple, is shown wearing a *Yajñopavīta* with rows of beads alternated by plain lines which have the general effect of a twisted thread.[3] The Gajāsura-Vadhamūrti in the Kailāsa temple is shown wearing a *Yajñopavīta* of skulls which is befitting his ferocious nature.

The *Yaśastilaka* refers to stalls of perfume dealers (*saugandhika*), along with those of garland-sellers.[4] In the trade-emporium at Belgaum, various stalls of caterers of perfumes existed (*gandhavaṇa vasara*) as also shops *gandhavaṇigara angaḍi*.[5] All these show that the perfumes and their ingredients were much in demand. As these were required in large quantities, for the worship of the deity, and also for the daily use of the king, the nobility and those who could afford, there was an unceasing supply of articles in demand. Women painted beautiful designs on their cheeks, on foreheads, and on breasts, with sandal paste. An inscription of

1. *Ibid.*, p. 180.
2. *Yaśastilaka*, p. 122.
3. T.V. Pathy, *op. cit.*, Figure IV, 1.
4. *Yaś*, p. 122.
5. *E.I.*, XIII, p 18.

915 A.D. refers to the expression "*Sundarivadanachandana-patrabhañga*."[1] The use of *tilaka* appears much earlier in the *Yaśastilaka*.[2]

Hair Style

Coiffure is one of the important sociological aspects of the ancient Indian society. It is interesting to note that during the Rāshṭrakūṭa period both men and women elaborately dressed their hair. They normally maintained long hair as the sculptures at Elūra show; and women, however, surpassed menfolk in the art of dressing hair in varied and variegated fashions. Hair dressing was considered as a part and parcel of the elaborate application of cosmetics which received sanction from the contemporary *śāstras* and many other books.[3] Therefore, highly sophisticated classes took special care in elaborately trimming their hair and as a prerequisite the tresses were washed with various oils and unguents. Examples of ladies applying cosmetics, looking into mirrors are not wanting in sculptures.[4] It is not unlikely that the people in those days employed false hair and doughnuts in order to obtain the required effect and shape of their coiffures. The use of pearl strings and ribbons was very common and it enhanced the aesthetic effect of a well-turned hairdo. A large number of male and female figures are shown wearing gorgeous diamonds and other varieties of head dresses. The royal personages are shown having long tresses of hair resting on the back and the shoulders.[5] The hair of soldiers was tied up with cloth bands around their foreheads.[6]

Ornaments

People were fond of ornaments. The sculptures at Elūra

1. *E.I.*, IX. pp. 9ff. and *E.C.*, VIII, Sb. 28.
2. P. 82.
3. *E.g.*, Suśruta, *Chikitsāsthāna*, XXIV, 4. Trans. by Kunjlal.
4. T.V. Pathy, *op. cit.*, p. 82.
5. *Ibid.*
6. *Yaś.*, p. 59.

represent an encyclopaedic list of personal ornaments, which defies any systematic analysis. To cite a few examples we are going to take samples from the Kailāsa temple.

Ear ornaments are illustrated in the Kailāsa temple. Here the pendants are shown fixed with hooks but they vary in design. One of them appears to be in conical shape with its bottom more pointed and its top member solidly moulded. The other one is fixed to a crescent-shaped hook and the middle object seems to be a gem with a small ring hanging below.[1] The figures of Pārvatī and Śiva in the Kailāsa temple are depicted with ornaments having geometrical designs and floral patterns. Here the circular-shaped rings are shown with wire volutes and conventionalised petal-shaped motifs.[2] Some ear ornaments are shown with animal motifs. Sometimes the figures are depicted with two different types of ear ornaments. For instance, in Kailāsa temple, a lady figure is shown wearing in her left ear a sort of oblong solid member and a disc-like pulley in her right ear.[3] In one of the Yakshīs found in Goa of our period, the jewllery consists of small round ear-rings, studded with beads around the edge.[4]

The artists of Elūra were at their best in carving an amazing variety of neck ornaments. The execution of these ornaments with meticulous details and geometrical precision is incredible. Their wide ranging types and designs suggest the extent to which they were in use. Perhaps wealthy and prosperous conditions of an advanced and sophisticated society, that Rāshṭrakūṭa power brought about in the Deccan, is faithfully reflected in these sculptures.

Kṛshṇa in the Kāliyamardana panel of the Kailāsa is shown wearing a four-stringed necklace whose beads or gems are of different shapes, such as circles, squares, rectangles of varying sizes.[5] The arrangement of festoons alternated by

1. B. Patankar, *Kailāsa : A Cultural Study*, unpublished thesis, Nagpur, 19 3, Figure VII, D1 and D2.
2. *Ibid.*, Figure VII, A1, A2, B1-B4.
3. T.V. Pathy, *op.cit.*, Figure VII, 1.
4. Information gathered from Mythic Society Seminar Paper on the Rāshṭrakūṭas.
5. B. Patankar, *op. cit.*, Figure V, D4 and D5.

tassels is more frequently delineated. A fine example of this is illustrated in the figure of Śiva in the Kailāsa temple. It is the multi-stringed necklace which contains in its central row a series of round and rectangular stones and the outer rim is provided with festoons alternated by tassels with knob-terminals.[1] Another interesting necklace is shown worn by a door keeper in this temple. Here the lower edge is shown fixed with small jingling bells.[2]

The *Yaśastilaka* gives a beautiful pen-picture of soldiers of different regiments, who were in the employ of the king of that time. The Kannadiga soldiers wore triple necklaces made of many-coloured beads.[3] This is in conformity with sculptural details given above. A contemporary of Kṛshṇa III, Beta, who ruled with the grace of Kṛshṇa III, was anointed as a mere child, being invested with a *Kaṇṭhikā* (necklace).[4] The Yakshī image, found in the village Cottombi, Bicholin Taluka in Goa, wears a broad *hāra* around her neck, which continues between her full and round breasts. Below them it bifurcates into three strands, two passing below the breasts and one serving as a tassel in the centre. This chest decoration is called *suvarṇa-Vaikakshaka.*[5]

Another ornament in great use seems to be the armlet. In the case of Pārvatī in the Kailāsa temple, her upper arm is covered by a coiled armlet.[6] A Rasika figure in this temple is shown wearing an armlet of four rows of beadings and occupies a larger portion of the arm.[7] Next in importance is *mekhalā*, the waist ornament. The figure of the Gaṅgā here adorns girdles of a beaded belt[8] and a *dvārapāla* wears a

1. *Ibid.*, Figure V, B.
2. G.B. Deglurkar, *Cultural History of Marathwara*, Ph.D. Thesis, Aurangabad, Figure XVII, 13.
3. *Yaś.*, p. 59.
4. *E.I.*, XXXI, p. 38. For the significance of the *Kaṇṭhikā* as a juvenile ornament, see *E.I.*, V, p. 138, n. 2.
5. C. Sivaramamurti, *Indian Bronzes*, New Delhi, 1963, p. 33.
6. Patankar, *op. cit.*, Figure A3 and A4.
7. *Ibid.*, Fig. VIII, B2.
8. T.V. Pathy, *op. cit.*, Fig. IV, 3.

girdle of slightly bigger bells.[1]

Household Articles

An affluent society during the Rāshṭrakūṭa rule had equipped itself with well-developed and sophisticated household articles. The household appliances are such as furniture and domestic vessels etc. In furnishing houses, it is obvious that wood was predominantly used because of its aesthetic quality and appeal, its abundant growth, its easy workability into intricate designs etc. The basis of our studies here is sculptures available at Elūra, because they are the idealised versions of human beings translated through the medium of rock.

The bedsteads are represented in the reliefs. It consists of a wooden frame of four beams, the shorter two placed breadthwise, and the longer two lengthwise. The wooden frame is supported by four legs. The *Mahābhārata* panel in the Kailāsa temple provides a fine example of a bedstead. Here the lower portion of the legs is shown slightly bulbous and then taking a cylindrical shape. The wooden frame seems to have been placed above the pillars.[2]

There is a solitary example of a cradle depicted in the *Mahābhārata* panel of the temple. The little child, Kṛshṇa, is shown fighting against the demon. The leg portion of the cradle is divided into two parts, slightly rounded, and then the frame, consisting of four long bars and four short bars, is fixed above the legs. The sides of the cradle are filled by double wavy lines which form into a trellis.[3]

The pottery is the matrix and the ABC of culture. The varied shapes of vessels depicted in the reliefs give some idea of the prevailing pottery types during the Rāshṭrakūṭa period. The surface collection of potsherds made in the vicinity of Elūra and Malkhed, the Rāshṭrakūṭa capital, also give some idea about the pottery used at that time. The common wares

1. Deglurkar, *op. cit*, Fig. XXI, 9.
2. T.V. Pathy, *op. cit.*, Fig. IX, 13.
3. *Ibid.*, Fig. IX, 8.

such as black and red, micaceous and tan were available during the excavation of the Elūra caves. Interestingly enough, the counterparts of the vessels depicted in the reliefs, especially the jars, the bowls, etc. can be easily detected among the surface finds.[1] The principal types represented in the sculptures are described below.

Jars : A jar with elongated body, ring base and a flared rim with a lid is shown held by Brahmā in the Kailāsa temple.[2] Another jar with pedestalled base and elongated body and having a wide mouth and bevelled rim[3] is shown in the *Mahābhārata* panel. In the relief depicting the Vāmanāvatāra scene there is a jar with ring base, bulbous sides and constricted neck.[4]

Basins : A basin with flat circular base and sides slightly flared with thick out-turned rim is depicted in cave XVI. A bucket-shaped basin with flat circular base and elongated body is shown in a relief depicting Rāvaṇa offering his heads to Śiva in the cloister of the Kailāsa temple.[5]

Pots : The pots illustrated in the reliefs are of two types, *viz.*, miniature pots and *haṇḍi* type used for storage purposes. A miniature pot with slightly pointed bottom and globular body has been represented in the Sūrya panel in cave XVI (Kailāsa). The storage jar depicted in a pounding scene in the *Mahābhārata* panel is yet another interesting variety of a *haṇḍi*.[6] The lower portion of the pounding trough is shown in the shape of a jar. Its sides are slightly tapering with a thick clubbed out rim. The other one placed above the former is circular in its base, spherical and with a broad mouth, while the top one has flared sides.

Baskets : One may also visualise the daily rituals performed in the Hindu temples which required large quantities of worshipping material. In this connection it is

1. *Ibid.*, p. 102.
2. *Ibid.*, Fig. XI, 2.
3. *Ibid.*, Fig. X, 16.
4. *Ibid.*, Figs. X, 12 and XI, 11.
5. *Ibid.*, Figs. X, 11 and XI, 16.
6. *Ibid.*, Fig. X. 7 and Plate XXVIII, 3.

worthwhile to mention that an elephant-load of *naivedya* is said to have been provided for ritualistic purposes in the Kailāsa temple alone.[1] Baskets were probably knit from reed or spoiled bamboo. An interesting example of a basket is shown, in the panel of Rāvaṇa offering his heads to Śiva. It has a reference to the morning prayers offered by him to Lord Śiva. The basket is shown overloaded with flowers and other materials for worshipping. It has a circular base with slightly flared sides and elongated body.[2] The other example, illustrated in the Kailāsa temple, resembles a bucket with a handle.[3] It appears to have been used for carrying fruits and flowers. There is a striking resemblance between these types and those used in temples by the modern priests.

Trays : Trays also were an important item of household articles. But we do not have any representation in the reliefs of the Kailāsa temple. However, it may be presumed on the basis of different varieties of trays depicted in the Ajantā paintings, that they too may have existed during the period of our study.

Fans : In a tropical country like India, the fan was an absolute necessity and must have been in use from the earliest times. Fans were probably made of cloth, peacock feathers, bamboo, palm leaves etc. They seem to have been used by the royalty and the well-to-do persons as they are invariably handled by the maids or attendants. The paintings at Ajantā have several varieties of fans.[4]

Mirrors : The lady looking into the mirror is one of the most fascinating themes represented in the art works of ancient India. The convex nature of the mirror, with the handle fixed to it is depicted in the antechamber of the Kailāsa temple. Here the figure of the body is shown adjusting the *Simanta* by looking into the mirror. It may also be stated that toilet articles such as cosmetics, shampoos and cosmetic containers must have been present in the highly

1. S.G. Tulpule (ed.), *Līlācharitra*, Nagpur, 1964, p. 44.
2. T V. Pathy, *op. cit* , Fig. XI, 16.
3. *Ibid.*, Fig. X, 11.
4. M.K. Dhavalikar, *Ajantā : A Cultural Study*, Poona, 1973, Figs. XXIII, 1, 2 and 4.

sophisticated families. But it is difficult to say if some small boxes and trays represented in the reliefs contained cosmetics.

Jewel Boxes: The representation of jewel boxes and vanity purses in the reliefs bespeak the aesthetic consciousness of the society. They are generally shown in the reliefs being held by the dwarfs. These boxes can be seen in the paintings at Ajantā. They are more artistically designed.[1]

The reliefs portray some scenes of the domestic routine providing a glimpse into the contemporary social life by means of which to judge the changing patterns in subsequent periods. The technique of churning of butter-milk as depicted in the *Mahābhārata* panel in the Kailāsa temple is very much the same as obtaining today in the countryside.[2] The churning stick is shown suspended by means of two rings to a pole, and is placed in the pot and piled with the help of a rope.

The second domestic scene depicts the pounding of grains in a mortar. It is illustrated in the same *Mahābhārata* panel. On the basis of certain forest scenes, one might also form an idea about the life of a hermit. A forest hut of reeds and leaves (*parṇa kuṭira*) is depicted on one of the pilasters in the Rangamaṇḍapa of the Kailāsa temple.[3] The inmates are shown with flowing beards and matted hair. The presence of a deer in the vicinity of the hut indicated a sylvan recluse away from the din of the material world.

Food and Drinks

As regards food and drink of the people, the first thing that strikes us is that the Indians were little addicted to drink. We learn from the Arab traveller Sulaiman that the Indians "did not take wine, nor did they take vinegar which was made of wine. This did not arise from religious scruples, but from their disdain of it. They said, 'the prince who drank wine was no true king."[4] His observations may be further supplemented

1. *Ibid.*, Figs. XXIV, 8 and 9.
2. T.V. Pathy, *op. cit.*, Fig. X, 1.
3. *Ibid.*, Plate XXVIII.
4. Elliot and Dowson, *History of India*, I, p. 7.

by the account of Al Masūdi who says that "the Hindus abstained from drinking wine, and censured those who consumed it; not because their religion forbade it, but in the dread of its clouding their reason and depriving them of its powers. If it could be proved of one of their kings, that he had drunk (wine), he forfeited the crown; for he was (not considered to be) able to rule and govern (the empire) if his mind was affected."[1] Ibn Khurdādba tells us that the kings and people of Hind regarded fornication as lawful and wine as unlawful.[2] Whatever may be said of the first part of the observation, the second is indeed creditable to the Indians.[3] He further informs us that the members of the Kshatriya class drank not more than three cups of wine.[4] It may safely be concluded that Kshatriyas were not the total abstainers like the Brāhmaṇas.[5] Alberuni, however, tells us that the Indians of his time drank wine before having eaten anything, then they took their meal.[6]

The Brāhmaṇas seem to have abstained from taking flesh, though not quite completely. We are told by Al Masūdi that they did not eat the flesh of any animal.[7] According to Alberuni,[8] the Brāhmaṇas had the privilege of eating the flesh of the gaṇḍa. It was forbidden to the Brāhmaṇas to take five vegetables such as 'onions, garlic, a kind of gourd, the root of a plant like the carrots called Krnch (?), and another vegetable which grew round their tanks called nālī."[9]

We may safely presume that the usual food of the people in general consisted of grain, milk, sugar and clarified butter and ghee. Alberuni tells us that "the Hindus ate singly, one by one, on a table-cloth of dung. They did not make use of the

1. *Ibid.*, p. 20.
2. *Ibid.*, p. 13.
3. See also *RATT*, p. 346.
4. Elliot and Dowson, *op. cit.*, p. 16.
5. *Ibid.*, p. 196.
6. Sachau, *op. cit.*, I, p. 180.
7. Elliot and Dowson, *op. cit.*, p. 19.
8. Sachau, *op. cit.*, I, p. 204.
9. *Ibid*, II, p. 135.

remainder of a meal, and the plates from which they had eaten were thrown away if they were earthen. They had red teeth in consequence of chewing arecanuts with betel-leaves and chalk."[1]

We get some information about food and drinks of the time from the *Yaśastilaka* too. Gold-coloured broths were used with rice.[2] Here we get some idea of non-vegetarian meal also. It narrates an episode in which fish was caught and ordered by the king to be made over to the cook of a rest-house for the Brāhmaṇas.[3]

The primary drink, of course, was water. Somadeva discusses properties of water at length and says that if properly used, it is amṛta and used without proper care, it is *visha*.[4] He recommends that water, other than specified by him, *i.e.*, transparent water without any taste and smell, and swept by wind and sunshine is beneficial; and in all other cases water should be boiled before drinking. Water exposed to the sun and the moon was not to be used longer than a day and a night; water boiled in day time was not to be taken at night, and water boiled at night was not to be taken in day time.[5]

The *Yaśastilaka* recommends different kinds of food for different seasons. In the autumn, one was to take sweet, bitter and astringent things; in the rainy season and the winter sweet, salty and sour things; in the spring pungent, bitter and astringent things; and in the summer mild preparations.[6] In another verse it is stated that in the winter one was to take fresh food, preparations of milk, pulses, and sugarcane, curds and things prepared with ghee and oil. In the spring one was to take food consisting chiefly of barley and wheat, and containing little ghee, and to avoid heavy, cold and sweet dishes. On hot days one was to take Śāli rice, moong soup containing ghee, lotus stalks, fresh shoots and bulbs, fried

1. *Ibid.*, I, p. 180; also see II, p. 135.
2. *Yaś.*, p. 29.
3. *Ibid.*, p. 38.
4. *Ibid.*, p. 113.
5. *Ibid.*
6. *Ibid.*, pp. 112-13.

barley flour, sherbets, curd mixed with sugar and spices, coconut-milk, and water or milk with plenty of sugar. In the rainy season the food was dry, light, oily and warm; and preparations of old Śāli rice, wheat and barley were to be taken. In the autumn the diet consisted of ghee, moong, Śāli rice, powdered wheat, preparations of milk, grapes, Āmalakī fruits, sugar, and sweet bulbs and leaves. A number of vegetables including slices of fresh ginger are praised and the properties of ghee, curd, butter and milk are described.[1]

They had a good idea of quality and quantity of food intake. They knew that the constant eating of over-sweet dishes led to indigestion, too much of salty food was to cause weakening of vision, extremely sour and pungent dishes was to lead to physical decay, and any unhygienic food was to cause loss of strength.[2]

Somadeva mentions certain kinds of food forbidden under given circumstances like germinating paddy and ghee kept in a brass vessel for a period of ten days. Bananas were not to be taken with curd and butter milk, nor milk with salt, nor broth of pulses with radishes; fried barley powder was not to be taken when it became compact like curd. Similarly, all sesamum preparations were prohibited at night.[3]

Somadeva refers to the entertainment of a miserly, penniless and greedy person named Kaliñjaka. The meal consisted of boiled rice grown stale and full of husk and gravel, some rotten beans, a few drops of rancid Atasī oil, slices of half-cooked gourds and certain badly cooked vegetables as well as some gruel mixed with plenty of mustard and the beverage was some alkaline fluid with a taste like that of the water of a salt-mine.[4] This is how miserly people led their life.

Festivals

Some of the festivals were being celebrated with great

1, *Ibid.*
2. *Ibid.*
3. *Ibld.*, p. 114.
4. *Ibid.*, p. 29.

festivities and pomp and grandeur, a glance of which is available in the sources of our period.

Durga Puja :[1] We learn from the *Yaśastilaka* that the worship of Aparājitā took place on the Mahānavamī day, and the occasion, in fact, was more important than the name of the goddess. The Mahānawamī festival is mentioned by Somadeva in Books I and III. It was usual to celebrate the festival on the ninth day of the bright half of Āśvina. In the Purānas, its popularity is shown as a court festival and the sacrifice of buffaloes on the occasion is referred to. But Somadeva does not speak of animal sacrifices in connection with Mahānavamī; and it is quite possible that they were sometimes omitted, especially when the festival was celebrated under the auspices of a court like that of the Rāshṭrakūṭas, susceptible to the influence of Jain ideals.

Kaumudī :[2] It was a festival of moonlight. Somadeva mentions the Kaumudī festival in his *Yaśastilaka* (ch. VII,27) where the queen Rāmadattā is described as witnessing the celebration of the Kaumudī festival by the women of the city from a high pavilion. The *Kuvalayamālākahā* of Uddyotanasūri assigns this festival to the full moon of the autumn.

Dīpotsava :[3] The festival of lights corresponding to modern Diwali, followed the Mahānavamī and Kaumudī festivals. The *Yaśastilaka* speaks of the whitewashed palaces and the white flags and the rows of lights on the lofty terraces of the edifices of the city, and 'the women excited by gambling,' the gaiety of courtesans, and the sweet notes of music that constituted the special features of the occasion. A bard recites a few verses describing to the king the Festival of Lights :

> 'May the Festival of Lights bring delight to thee, whose desires are fulfilled !
>
> It is enlivened by the flattering words of lovers, defeated in gambling, and held fast by their mistresses, excited by the game. It is charming with the varied adornment of

1. K.K. Handiqui, *op. cit.*, pp. 397-401.
2. *Ibid.*, pp. 402-03.
3. *Ibid.*, pp. 401-02.

the courtesans, engaged in sports. The regions of the sky resound with the deep auspicious notes of instrumenta music."[1]

Somadeva depicts the Dīpotsava as a secular festival, but the details given in the Purāṇic literature indicate its religious aspects also which it has not entirely lost even today.

In the Chinchini Plates of Kṛshṇa III[2] we find that 'srotaka' probably a kind of rent, was to be paid at the end of the festival of lights in the 'Maṭhikā' of the goddess Daśamī. This also gives a clear hint at the celebration of Dīpotsava.

Saṁkrānti : We find royal gifts being donated on the occasion of the *Saṁkrānti* in a festive mood.[3]

Sarasvatī Festival : The cult of Sarasvatī seems to be prevalent in the age of Somadeva, the author of the *Yaśastilaka*. In one of the verses of Book III, he refers to dramatic performances :[4]

> "Let this handful of flowers, radiant with beautiful colours, offered to Sarasvatī, abiding on the white lotus beds emerging on the Mānasa lake, serve the purpose of raṅgapūjā or ceremonial worship preceding a dramatic performance."

Sarasvatī is described by Somadeva as white and seated on a white lotus. She is shown with an extra eye at her forehead with matted hair and ornaments. She has four hands : one hand in *dhyānamudrā*, another with a book, the third with Rudrāksha beads and the fourth in the *varad-mudrā*. There is an old temple of Sarasvatī at Gadag and another at Aihole, the home of early temples in the Deccan.

In the *Mahāpurāṇa* of Pushpadanta we find mention of

1. *Ibid.*, p. 157.
2. *E.I.*, XXXII, p. 55.
3. *E.I.*, XXXIV, p. 123.
4. K.K. Handiqui, *op. cit.*, pp. 403f.

vanakrīḍā at several places in festive moods.[1]

Paṭṭabandha : It was probably the coronation festival. We find its mention in the Rāshṭrakūṭa inscriptions. Two sets of Copper Plates[2] were found from the Navasari district belonging to the reign of Nityavarsha, *i.e.*, Indra. He usually resided at his capital Mānyakheṭa, but when he made these grants he had gone to Kurundaka for the festival of *Paṭṭabandha*. On this occasion he weighed against gold and gave away twenty-one lakhs and a half of *drammas*, and granted Kurundaka and other villages, and restored four hundred and others, which had been confiscated by previous kings. On such joyous occasions the people of the capital Mānyakheṭa which was decorated with flags and buntings, congregated to wish glory and happiness to their king.[3]

Sports, Games, Pastimes and Amusements

The importance of athletics was well recognised in the period of our study. Somadeva Sūri stressed the importance of physical exercises when he wrote:

> "Just as food is not well cooked in a vessel that is neither covered nor stirred so a man who has neither sleep nor exercise cannot digest what he eats."[4]

Games and pastimes are the necessary requirements of any materially advanced society. Man has an urge to have some moments of pleasure and to be free from the drudgery of routine life. The Rāshṭrakūṭa society, so prosperous and contented, seems to have a variety of pastimes and enjoyments. The important among them as depicted in the sculptures of

1. *Mahā.*, 89.10.1; 99.7.3 etc.
2. *JBBRAS.*, XVIII, pp. 253ff. Navasari grant I, l. 46 (श्रीपट्टबन्धोत्सवाये) and II, l. 55 (श्रीपट्टबन्धोत्सवे). Also see R. G. Bhandarkar, *Early History of the Deccan and Miscellaneous Historical Essays*, Poona, 1983, pp. 324, 329 and 332. Also *E I.*, XXXVI, pp. 223-38.
3. *Kavirājamārga*, 2-10.
4. K.K. Handiqui, *op. cit.*, p. 112.

the Kailāsa temple are such as hunting, animal fights, wrestling, playing dice, dance and music etc.

Hunting : The growth of trade and commerce during the period of our study resulted in the emergence of wealthy class in the society. The mercantile community along with the nobility followed the example of the king and the court in their everyday life of sophisticated enjoyments and pursuits of pleasure.[1] Hunting was one of the favourite pastimes of the Rāshṭrakūṭa rulers. One of the inscriptions of Govinda III[2] informs us how he speared the boars preserved for his sport when he returned to Rāmeśvaram on the Tuṅgabhadrā after victory over Kāñchī in 804 A.D. He built a memorial stone in the memory of this event in Ātākur and a 'Gorava' was appointed for worshipping and maintenance of this memorial. It was not considered sufficient only to build a memorial but the rulers were anxious to keep it in a good condition as well. This inscription would show that there were game preserves in the various centres of the empire for the use of the emperors and courtiers.

Hunting scenes are depicted in the Kailāsa temple.[3] On the architrave of the outside screen-wall, and to the left of the entrance gate, are depicted some elephant and horse riders carrying bows presumbly on their way for the hunt. The *Mahābhārata* and the *Rāmāyaṇa* panels, depicted on the northern and the southern walls of the main shrine respectively, contain some hunting scenes. The famous epic story of the *Kirātārjunīya*, which constituted the main theme of Bhāravi's *mahākāvya*, is carved on the top frieze. Here Śiva in the guise of a Kirāta and Arjuna the Pāṇḍava are shown shooting at the wild boar. The scene is intensely action-bound, with the animal in the centre and the two bowmen aiming at their target. Likewise, the chase of the deceptive golden deer (māyā-mṛga) by Rāma is graphically represented in the third frieze of the *Rāmāyaṇa* scene. Yet another hunting

1. Michael Edwards, *Everyday Life in Early India*, London, 1969, p. 95.
2. *I A*, XI, p. 126.
3. T V. Pathy, *op cit*, pl XX

scene is depicted on the pilaster to the right side of the antechamber of the main temple.

Animal Fights : In the *Yaśastilaka*, the king himself is shown as taking part in the training and arming of elephants, and one of favourite recreations is the witnessing of elephant races (*Karivinoda*) in the race courses (*pradhāvadharaṇī*).[1] Thus animal fights were also not unknown in our age. One of the Gaṅga records refers to a fight between a boar and a favourite hound of Būṭuga II wherein both the animals were killed.[2] From the description of a dairy farm at Karhata we come to know that it was famous for excellent buffaloes, and Saurāshtra is even today a breeder of good buffaloes.[3]

In the Kailāsa temple also the scenes of animal combats are depicted in the form of decorative friezes on the plinth portions. The fights are usually between two elephants and elephant and lion. The idea in presenting these two combinations was perhaps the notion that elephant being the mightiest among all wild animals and the lion the most ferocious, made this confrontation spectacular and sensational. A fight among such archetypally powerful animals naturally evoked maximum sensation among the spectators. The lower portion of the Nandīmaṇḍapa and the entire lower portion of the podium in the Kailāsa temple have such lively scenes of animal fight.[4]

Amusements with Birds : Cocks (*tāmrachūḍa*), *quails* (tāvaka), pigeons (*pārāvata*) and falcons (*śyena*) were trained for entertainments in medieval times. In the *Yaśastilaka*, the king Yaśodhara asks Chaṇḍa Karman to take the birds to the scene of the festival and give an exhibition of cock-fighting.[5]

Wrestling : Most of the entertainments were performed during festivals. Professional entertainers travelled long distances to perform their plays, dances and wrestling bouts.

1. K.K. Handiqui, *op. cit.*, p. 90.
2. *E I.*, VI, p. 56.
3. K.K. Handiqui, *op. cit.*, pp. 71-72.
4. T.V. Pathy, *op. cit.*, p. 121.
5. K.K. Handiqui, *op. cit.*, p, 39.

The panels depicting wrestling scenes suggest that the wrestlers were adept in their job. Two wrestling scenes are depicted on the pilaster to the right side of the northern door in the Rangamaṇḍapa of the Kailāsa temple. On the front side of the pilaster is shown one of the wrestlers holding the other's left hand while his left hand is thrown around the neck. Their poses, with one's body bent and the other's aslant, suggest that they were trying to break each other's hold or force a fall. The scenes on the right side of the pilaster is more interesting. Here one of the wrestlers (*malla*) held the calves of the other in order to effect a direct fall. The wrestlers seemed to have been governed by certain rules and regulations and the match proceeded on certain "permitted holds."[1] There is yet another wrestling scene illustrated in the *Mahābhārata* panel. Though it is of a religious nature, one would notice a clear-cut fall effected in the scene with the loser's back falling on the ground and the victor overriding him. The *Rāmāyaṇa* panel also depicts some wrestling scenes. The wrestlers in all the scenes are shown very muscular with well-shaped bodies. They are devoid of any dress except the *laṅgoṭi*.

Dice : Another popular and extremely absorbing pastime as revealed in the sculptural reliefs of the Kailāsa temple is the dice play. As an indoor game, it seems to have been very popular among the people of Deccan during the period under review. It is a game played with various types of dice and on different types of boards. The dice are made either of wood or of ivory. They are oblong in shape with four well-marked sides. The dice board represented in the antechamber of the temple is oblong in shape and consists of eight rows having eight squares in each row.[2] The boards depicted here suggest that the game played by the people at that time was possibly similar to that of *Chaturaṅga* (four corps).

The game of cowries, another similar indoor game, was played on Āśvina Chaturdaśī with the women of the harem, with sons and grandsons. The *Yaśastilaka* corroborates the

1. Michael Edwards, *op. cit.*, p. 97.
2. T.V. Pathy, *op. cit.*, Pl. XXIX.

fact that this game of dice (also called *dyūta* or gambling) was played during the festival of lights (*pradīpotsava*), and gives a nice description. "May the festival of lights bring delight to thee, whose desires are fulfilled! It is enlivened by the flattering words of lovers, defeated in gambling, and held fast by their mistresses, excited by the game. It is charming with the varied adornment of the courtesans, engaged in sports. The regions of the sky resound with the deep auspicious notes of instrumental music."[1]

Other Sports : In Somadeva's time, sport of swings was part of the spring festivities, and he gives a nice description of the play of lovers.

"May the swings, O best of kings, fulfil thy desires! They are beautiful with poles of areca trees with fresh young leaves, and fitted with branching Aśoka creepers with camphor wood boards attached to the ends. Charming they are with canopies and banners of silk set with flower shaped gems. Who is not delighted by the oscillation of the swings, the women adding their weight? During the sport, mouth comes near mouth; eyes meet eyes; the heart is enraptured at the contact of the partner's high projecting bosom; hands more close to hands; and legs are entwined with legs."[2]

Another equally popular sport was watersport or *Jalakrīḍā*. Here also there is the unavoidable conventional description in literature. But of special interest, is the existence of *dhārāgṛhas* or shower houses which are described in the *Yaśastilaka* and other contemporary literature.[3] The *Yaśastilaka* describes that King Yaśodhara passed the hours of noon in the hot summer days in amorous sports in his garden and indulged in watersports with his palace ladies in the hall of mechanical showers (*Yantradhārāgṛha*), cooler than the Himālayas. Various waterfalls, mechanical clouds, streams of water gushing from the mouths of the statues of various wild animals, of fountains from artificial alligators are

1. K.K. Handiqui, *op. cit.*, p. 157.
2. *Ibid.*, pp. 156-57.
3. *Ibid.*, p. 37.

mentioned.[1] At one place in the *Yaśastilaka* we find the king witnessing elephant-races in the race-courses.[2] Like Polo, a play with ball while riding on horse was a favourite of Indra IV.[3]

Dance and Music : Some of our inscriptions supply us with interesting information about dance and music. Dancing was a favourite amusement. The Kadba plates support the inference in this respect to be derived from the contemporary dramas, when they observe that the ladies of the capital used to be charmed by the skilful dance of the dancing girls in the court of Kṛshṇa I.[4] While describing the court life of King Yaśodhara, Somedeva speaks of dance exhibitions held in the court theatre, and the king is described as witnessing these performances in the company of expert dancers and well-trained exponents.[5]

Music and dance programmes held on social and religious occasions also provided a major source of entertainment. Music and dance are sister disciplines and are mutually complementary. It is through music and dance that the human emotions, *bhāva* and *rasa*, are fully expressed. In a procession after the coronation of Yaśodhara in the *Yaśastilaka* we find the elders reciting congratulatory verses, and women singing to the flute and the lyre. The neighing of horses and the trumpeting of elephants mingled with the sound of drums.[6]

There are several musical instruments available in the Elūra complex but in the Kailāsa temple we find a small drum depicted above the right side door of the main shrine in the Kailāsa temple.[7] A gaṇa (dwarf) is shown squatting, holding the drum under his arm. It appears that he takes the support

1. *Ibid.*, p. 33.
2. *Ibid.*, p. 28.
3. K.A. Nilakantha Sastri, *A History of South India* (Hindi), Patna, 1978, p. 282.
4. *I.A.*, XII, p. 13.
5. K.K. Handiqui, *op. cit.*, p. 97.
6. *Ibid.*, p. 28.
7. T.V. Pathy, *op. cit.*, Fig. XI, 17.

of his right knee while playing on it. The instrument has only one face, while the other side is cylindrical. Its face is tied with leather and fastened by vertical braces. The entire instrument is probably made of wood. The percussion instrument 'Karade', so popular in Karnataka, was in use during those days. 'Pagarana' a type of folk drama, seems to have been dominated by vulgar and obscene jokes with the sole purpose of entertaining the audience.

Manners and Customs

People of our period appear to have led a simple and healthy life. We are told in the *Karpūramañjarī* that when persons met, they saluted and hugged each other.[1] Alberuni informs us that "they did not ask permission to enter a house, but when they left it, they asked permission to do so. In shaking hands they grasped the hand of a man from the convex side. In their meetings they sat cross-legged."[2] On festive days they besmeared their bodies with dung instead of perfumes. In washing they began with the feet, and then washed the face.[3] We are further told in the *Bālabhārata* of Rājaśekhara that when a man introduced himself to the other, he took the name of his father.[4]

From Alberuni we learn that "it was the duty (of the Brahman), if he wanted to cohabit with a wife to get a child, to perform a sacrifice to the fire called *garbhādhāṇa*; but he did not perform it, because it required the presence of the woman, and therefore he felt ashamed to do so. In consequence he postponed the sacrifice and united it with the next following one, which was due in the fourth month of the pregnancy, called *Sīmantonnayanam*. After the wife had given birth to a child, a third sacrifice was performed between the birth and the moment when the mother began to nourish

1. Durga Prasad and K.P. Parab (eds.), *Rājaśekhara*: *Karpūramañjarī*, p. 35.
2. Sachau, *Alberuni's India*, I, p. 182.
3. *Ibid* , p. 181.
4. Durga Prasad and K.P. Parab (eds.), *op. cit*., p. 4.

the child. It was called Jātakarman. The child received a name after the days of the childhood had elapsed. The sacrifice for the occasion of the name-giving was called nāmakaraṇam. As long as the woman was in childbed, she did not touch any vessel, and nothing was eaten in her house nor did the Brahman light there a fire. These days were eight for the Brahman, twelve for the Kshatriya, fifteen for the Vaiśya, and thirty for the Śūdra. For the low caste people who were not reckoned among any caste, no term was fixed. The sacrifice on the occasion of the first cutting of the child's hair was offered in the third, the perforation of the ear took place in the seventh and eighth years."[1]

The tonsure ceremony also served as an occasion for the levy of some small tax. This is evident from Śālotagi inscription of the Rāshṭrakūṭa King Kṛshṇa III, dated A.D. 945 which mentions a tax levied on the occasion of the tonsure ceremony.[2] References to tonsure of a widow are available in the *Mahāpurāna* of Pushpadanta.[3]

Among popular customs as mentioned in the *Yaśastilaka*[4] was *ājayāvekshaṇa* or looking into clarified butter in the morning to counteract the evil dreams and obtain other salutary results. The well-known custom of *nīrājana* or ceremonial waving of lights was observed as part of the evening rites to ensure the well-being. It was also customary to perform the *nīrājana* ceremony in honour of the royal horses and elephants on the special occasions like the coronation of the king.[5] A quantity of salt, thrown into the fire, after whirling it over the head, was supposed to counteract the evil eye, and this was also accompanied by the ceremony of offering boiled rice to the goblins on the roadside.

Our records prescribe a tax of five flowers of good money

1. Sachau, *Alberuni's India*, II, pp. 156-57.
2. *I.A.*, I, pp. 210-21.
3. 71.20.1, 73.2.3-4.
4. K.K. Handiqui, *op. cit.*, p. 407.
5. 'आचरितराजवाजिनीराजनैः', Book II.

to be given to the congregation of scholars at the college of Śālotagi at the time of the sacred thread ceremony.[1] A grant of Kṛshṇa III, dated A.D. 929 records the allotment of *drammas* on each *māṇi* on the occasion of the Upanayana ceremony.[2] The levy of such tax proves the existence of the Upanayana ceremony in our period. We find references of *Śāntikarma* for bringing peace over bad dreams.[3]

Another custom was that the dead were usually burnt on the pyre,[4] except perhaps in the case of hermits whose dead bodies were buried. Alberuni says that those who could not afford to burn their dead, threw them either somewhere on the open field or into running water.[5] The bodies of children under three years were not burnt.[6] He further informs us that the body of the dead had a claim upon his heirs to wash, embalm, wrap it in a shroud, and then to burn it with as much sandal and other wood as they could get.[7] This has also been attested to by Pushpadanta in his *Mahāpurāṇa* where he says that the dead body was carried to burning ghat by four persons.[8] Those who attended the funeral were all regarded as unclean and they all washed themselves as well as their dresses.[9] It is reasonable to assume that no one went to take food in a family afflicted with death But, after the funeral, matters appear to have been again as usual.

Alberuni tells us that the heirs of the deceased had to make, above the door of the house, something like a shelf projecting from the wall in the open air, on which they placed every day a dish of something cooked and a vessel of water till the end of the ten-day period after the death.[10] On the tenth

1. *I A.*, I, p. 211.
2. *I.A.*, XII, pp. 222-24.
3. *Mahā.*, 28.1. etc.
4. Elliot and Dowson, *op. cit.*, I, p. 10; II, p. 45; Sachau, *op. cit.*, II, p. 169.
5. Sachau, *op. cit.*, II, p. 170.
6. *Ibid.*
7. *Ibid.*
8. *Mahā.*, 78.25 6-78.26.9.
9. Sachau, *op. cit.*, II, p. 170.
10. *Ibid.*, p. 165.

of the last-mentioned days, the heir spent, in the name of the deceased, much food and cold water. After the eleventh day, the heir sent every day sufficient food for a single person and a dirham to the house of the Brāhmaṇa, and continued doing this during all the days of the mourning year without any interruption until its end.[1] The duty of the heir towards the deceased in the first year consisted in his giving sixteen banquets, where every guest in addition to his food received alms also, *viz.*, on the fifteenth and sixteenth days after death; further, once a month during the whole year. The banquet in the sixth month was to be more rich and more liberal than the other. Further, the banquet on the last but one day of the year was devoted to the deceased and his ancestors and the final banquet was on the last day of the year.[2] If the heir was a son, he had to wear the mourning-dress throughout the whole year.[3] Nourishment was forbidden to the heirs for one single day in the first part of the mourning year.[4] These observations made by Alberuni do not hold good totally, but they are true to some extent even today. Hence it may safely be presumed that these customs were at least partly prevalent during the period of the Rāshṭrakūṭas.

The custom of *sallekhanā* or fasting unto death, according to Somadeva,[5] was to be followed when the body was about to perish, like a dry leaf or a lamp without oil. The hour of this last act of life, according to him, comes when every day the body loses strength and power of enjoyment, and is beyond remedy. Self-restraint, study, austerities, worship, and charity all become useless if the mind is not pure at the last hour of life. One had to renounce one's affection for friends, infatuation with riches and illwill towards enemies, and then to take proper steps (*i.e.*, resort to *sallekhanā*) after confessing all sins before the head of the congregation. Food was gradually given up and then beverages, both sweet and

1. *Ibid* , p. 166.
2. *Ibid.*, p. 165.
3. *Ibid.*
4. *Ibid.*
5. K.K. Handiqui, *op. cit.*, p. 287.

pungent; and thereafter one had to abstain from everything with one's mind on the five Parameshṭhins. There were five factors that destroyed the efficacy of *sallekhanā* : the desire to live longer, the desire to die to avoid sufferings, longing for friends, recollection of past happiness and the desire for happiness in the next life.[1] This practice was mostly common among the Jain communities. Rāshṭrakūṭa rulers, most of them, patronised Jainism. Thus this practice might have been common among the people of the Deccan.

Abu Zaid further informs us that when a person, either man or woman, became old, and the senses were enfeebled, he or she begged some one of the family to throw him into the fire, or to drown him in the water.[2] According to Alberuni, "no man of distinction did it except the Vaiśyas and the Śūdras, especially at those times which were prized as the most suitable for a man to acquire in them, for a future repetition of life, a better form of condition than that in which he happened to have been born and to live. Burning oneself was forbidden to Brāhmaṇas and Kshatriyas by a special law. Therefore, if they wanted to kill themselves, they did so at the time of an eclipse in some other manner, or they hired somebody to drown them in the Gaṅgā, keeping them under water till they were dead."[3] These acts were different from what is called *sallekhanā*, and may be termed as suicide.

Mahādāna had great importance in the society.[4] The Andura Plates[5] of Govinda IV mention some more important *mahādānas* such as *Hiraṇyagarbha*, *Ubhayamukhī*, *Gosahasra* and *Kalpavṛksha*.[6] *Tulāpurusha Mahādāna* was made by

1. जीवितमरणाशंसे सुहृदनुरागः सुखानुबन्धविधिः ।
   एतेसनिदानाः स्युः सल्लेखनतानये पञ्च ॥
   Quoted by Handiqui, *op cit.*, p. 287, fn. 8.
2. Elliot and Dowson, *op. cit* , I, pp. 9-10.
3. Sachau, *op cit.*, II, p 170.
4. *Mahā.*, 19.1-19.4 and 28.1. etc.
5. *E I.*, XXXVI, p. 259.
6. For *Mahādāna*, see Hemādri, *Chaturvargachintāmaṇi Dānakhaṇḍa*, Vol. I (Banaras ed.), pp. 226f. The *Ubhayamukhī* is the gitt of a cow just while giving birth to a calf.

Govinda IV without getting down from the pan of the *Tulā* (the balance). Another example of such donation we find in the time of Indra III, who after his coronation ceremony went to Kurundaka to perform *Paṭṭabandha* ceremony where he was weighed against gold for the *Tulāpurusha Mahādāna.*[1]

Superstitious Beliefs

There were a number of superstitious beliefs prevalent in the society. The *Yaśastilaka* informs us that at the time of the procession after the coronation of a king, women in periods, eunuchs, men with deformities and chāṇḍālas were considered to be inauspicious and so they were removed from the sight.[2]

Somadeva observes that, at the sight of poison in food, crows and cuckoos cry in an unwonted fashion, mungooses and peacocks are overjoyed, the Krauñcha bird sleeps, the cock crows in a harsh tone, the parrot vomits, and the monkey evacuates bowels; while the eyes of the chakora bird lose colour, and the goose limps.[3] These things seem to have no scientific base, but some of them are still current in the society today.

It was believed that if certain vows and conditions were observed, gods could be compelled to do the needful. From one of the Raṭṭa records from Saundatti we learn that Kesirāja of Banahatti had sworn to Unborn : If disease and trouble should ever manifest themselves among those whom I protect, I will never come to you.[4]

Catching a serpent alive was regarded as a signal proof of chastity; Sugatādevī, the wife of Maṇḍaleśvara Varma, had caught a serpent alive in her hand, and a temple was built in her honour as the chastest lady of the land. Spells and enchantments against serpent bites were current, but evidence

1. *E.I.*, XXXVI, pp. 223-38.
2. *Yaś* , p. 28.
3. *Ibid.*, p. 113.
4. *J.B.B.R.A.S.*, X, p. 281.

is available to show that their futility was often realised.[1]

Sometimes some loyal subjects used to take the vow that they would offer their own heads, if their king were to be blessed with a son.[2] There are others who used to vow to offer their own heads in case a son was born to them, cases are on record to show that such vows were actually kept.[3] There is the instance of King Amoghavarsha Nṛpatuṅga[4] who offered one of his fingers to goddess Mahālakshmī to ward off a terrible epidemic.

Ibn Khurdadba informs us that persons who had grown very old and weak, very often used to commit suicide in holy places, either by drowning or by burning themselves on some auspicious days.[5] The famous Chandella King Dhaṅga has been given as an example of having died by drowning at Prayāga when he was very old.[6] Women treating their husbands with herbs and medicines to keep them under their control was also in practice.[7]

Certain beliefs popular in our period recorded in the *Yaśastilaka* are : the moon of the fourth lunar day was believed to cause disputes;[8] a dove alighting inside a house was supposed to forebode its destruction;[9] the trumpeting of a female elephant at the commencement of a journey and the braying of a donkey from behind were evil omens;[10] a shower of crested tadpoles on a house was an evil portent indicating destruction of wealth and prosperity;[11] and elephants were supposed to be possessed by a spirit called Madapurusha, of

1. *I.A* , XII, p. 99.
2. *RATT*, p. 352.
3. *E.C.*, IV, Introduction, p. 9.
4. *E.I* , VIII, 248.
5. Elliot and Dowson, *op. cit* , I, p. 10.
6. *RATT*, p. 353.
7. *Ibid.*, p. 352.
8. K.K. Handiqui, *op. cit.*, p. 407.
9. 'अगारान्तरायतितः कपोत इव निर्वास्य', Book III.
10. K.K. Handiqui, p. 407.
11. 'गेहे शिखण्डिमण्डूकवृष्टिश्च श्रीच्छिदेद्विषः', (2.72).

terrible aspect, like lightning fire.[1] Alberuni informs us that people considered the crepitus ventris as a good omen and sneezing as a bad omen.[2] Pushpadanta also considers cow touch and *peepal* tree touch as productive of good results and sitting of crow overhead as a bad omen.[3]

According to an inscription[4] of Amoghavarsha I, dated A.D. 906, Mugina Kāḍamma, Erenāga, Kuppa and Māda were holding the rights of *Okkaltana* (cultivation rights) in the village Māvinuru. For the proper utilisation of this land it was believed that if they were to destroy this gift, they would incur the sin of destroying Vārāṇasī, the seven crores of ascetics, a tank, a garden and a cow.

Astronomy and Astrology

The sciences of astronomy and astrology were well developed in our period as revealed through the epigraphical evidences. Many of the grants were issued on some auspicious days such as full-moon day or on the day of Saṁkrānti. The copper plate of Dhruvarāja, 783 A.D. from Kāsārśiri, was issued when it was the day of solar eclipse in the month of Mārgaśīrsha.[5] The Anjanavati Plates[6], Devali Plates[7] and Lohārā grant[8] of Govinda III were all issued on the days of the solar eclipse. The Jethwai Plates of the Rāshṭrakūṭa queen Śīlamahādevī[9] were also issued in 786 A.D. on the day of the solar eclipse of the month of Āśvina. The Jharikā grant of Govinda III, dated 803 A.D., was made on the day of the lunar eclipse in Kārtika. The copper plates from

1. 'ज्वलज्ज्वालवज्रवैश्वानरकरालमूर्तिना मदपुरुषेणाधिष्ठिततया द्विगुणीभूतभीमसाहसनिकाय', Book III.
2. Sachau, *Alberuni's India*, I, p. 182.
3. Sudarshan Mishra, *op. cit.*, p. 4.
4. *E.I.*, XXVI, pp. 59-62.
5. *JASB*, XLIII-XLIV.
6. *E.I.*, XXIII, p. 10.
7. *E.I.* XXXV, p. 270.
8. *Ibid.*, XXIII, p. 213.
9. *Ibid.*, XXIII, p. 98.

Gaonai issued by Govinda IV bear a date equivalent to January seventeen, 930 A.D., which was a day of lunar eclipse.[1] If an attempt is made to search out dates in all the Rāshṭrakūṭa inscriptions in this light, we may find many such inscriptions issued on the day of lunar or solar eclipse. Similarly, the Saṁkrānti is also important in this context. For example, the Nesarikā grant[2] of Govinda III, dated 805 A.D. was issued on the occasion of the Saṁkrānti on the thirteenth day of the dark half of the month of Pausha. Like today, dāna on such dates had more importance and we find its evidences in our inscriptions. Such functions must have been held on as per preplanned dates. To find out a suitable date in the above mentioned fashion it required a good knowledge of astronomy.

Astrology, too, had great influence on the society. From the Kadba plates of Govinda III[3] we learn that even the Jains had taken to astrology; for, the record states how a grant was made in favour of a Jain Maṭha because its head had removed the evil influence of Saturn from which a feudatory Chālukya prince was suffering. Saturn was indeed tremendously dreaded in our period; the Śilāhāra prince Aparājitadeva[4] and Mahāmaṇḍaleśvara Govuṇarasa[5] are seen talking with pride about the title of 'Śanivāravijaya,' 'the one who is successful (even) on Saturdays.' Marco Polo also states that people gave importance to signs and omens. Thus it can be easily concluded that people were much influenced by their belief in the signs of astronomy and astrology.

Importance of Regnal Years

Sulaiman and Masudi[6] write that on the Tatariya coins of the Ballahara (the Rāshṭrakūṭas) the date of the accession

1. *E.I.*, XXXIV, p. 123.
2. *Ibid.*, XXXII, p. 160.
3. *Ibid.*, IV, p. 340.
4. *Ibid.*, III, p. 269.
5. *E.I.*, IV, p. 340.
6. S.S. Nadvi, *op. cit.*, p. 24.

of the king to the throne was impressed. Sulaiman says that while the era of the Arabs began with the year of Hijrat, that of the Rāshṭrakūṭas with the coronation of the king. This is, really speaking, the regnal year of the king.

Charitable/Meritorious Works

The Smṛti law of our period declares the gift of land as the most meritorious of all the gifts.[1] The *Matsya Purāṇa*[2] and the *Liṅga Purāṇa*[3] give at great length the description of sixteen *mahādānas* (great gifts) which involve the distribution of gold among the Brāhmaṇas. These laws follow the older tradition also such as digging of wells, ponds and tanks, construction of temples, distribution of food and laying out of gardens. The inscriptions and other historical records of this period give many instances of the observance of these rules. Apart from numerous examples of construction of temples and donation of lands to Brāhmaṇas and others, we have several instances of *tulāpurusha*[4] and *hiraṇyagarbha*[5] which are included in the list of sixteen *mahādānas*. Records also refer to the construction of monasteries and alms-houses, digging of wells and similar activities. We have several instances of gift of land for the encouragement of learning.

The fragmentary Rāshṭrakūṭa inscription from Kandhār[6] records some of the charitable works mentioned above. The first deed referred to in this record is the construction of a

1. *HCIP*, IV, p. 392.
2. *Matsya Purāṇa*, II, 274.89.
3. *Liṅga Purāṇa*, II, p. 28f.
4. It involves the weighing of the donor on a balance against gold which is thereafter distributed among the Brāhmaṇas. Cf. *E.I.*, IX, pp. 33f. and *E.I.* VII, p. 36. Here we find Rāshṭrakūṭa Kings Indra III and Govinda IV performing *tulāpurusha* respectively.
5. It involves the performance of sacraments on the donor seated in a golden vessel which is thereafter broken and distributed among the Brāhmaṇas. Cf. *E.I.*, XVIII, pp. 243f. Here we find Rāshṭrakūṭa King Dantidurga performing *hiraṇyagarbha*.
6. *E.I.*, XXXV pp. 107-09.

maṇḍapa (pavilion) named *Sarvalokāśraya* (a place for shelter of the general public) near the temple of the well-known local deity Śiva called Kshetrapāla. Then follows the description of the setting up of five centres for the distribution of water (*prapā*), for the amelioration of the suffering of the people during summer, at five places, *viz*., (i) the *makara toraṇa* (the gateway with *makara* motif) in the royal palace (*rāja-gṛha*), (ii) the *Yaksha-dvāra* (another gateway endowed with Yaksha-figures) adorned with Maṇḍalasiddhi Vināyaka, (iii) the front of the temple of Kāmadeva close to the area where the chief courtesans of the king lived (*pradhāna-rāja-vilāsinī-pāṭaka*), (iv) the courtyard of the temple of the god Kālapriya, and (v) the above-mentioned pavilion named *Sarvalokāśraya*. These were the centres for free distribution of water during summer.

Similarly, fire-places (*agnisthitikā*) were constructed at five places for saving the poor people from suffering from cold during winter. These five places were : (i) the pavilion called Sarvalokāśraya in the courtyard of Maṇḍalasiddhi, (ii-iii) two places near the temple of Kālapriya, (iv) the front of the temple of the god Sagaraveśvara situated on the embankment of the tank called Jagattuṅgasamudra, and (v) the vicinity of the temple of Baṅkeśvara situated towards the north of the Sagaraveśvara temple.

We get here some evidences of free feeding house (*sattra-śālā*) also. At Kandhār there was provision for offering meals to the (Brāhmaṇas) numbering thirty, who were engaged in reciting the Vedas.[1] On the occasion of the lunar eclipse Govinda II made grants of land etc. and also ordered the donation of a village called Payalīpattan situated on the western boundary of Mānyakheṭa. The object of the grant was to establish a *sattra* or charitable feeding house where 1000 Brāhmaṇas of different denominations were to be fed from the proceeds of the village every day. The number of each class of Brāhmaṇas to be fed is specified as follows :[2]

1. *E.I.*, XXXV, pp. 107-09, ll. 8f.
2. *E.I.*, XXIII, pp. 101-13 and also P.K. Gode, *Studies in Cultural History*, Vol. III, pt. II, Poona, 1969, p. 22.

Karnātaka Brāhmaṇas of Mānyakheṭa	360
Brāhmaṇas of Kaṇva-Śākhā	300
Brāhmaṇas from Karahāṭaka	240
Brāhmaṇas of the Chatuścharaṇa	72
Sahasrasāmānya or common to the thousand	28
Total	1000

To our surprise, we find the Muhammadan Governor of Samayan *Vishaya* under the Rāshṭrakūṭas who arranged free ferry near Sammayan, and a feeding house, where śāli rice, curries and ghee were catered free of cost.[1] It is a rare example of charitable work for establishing communal harmony.

Forced Labour

One of the socio-economic institutions that had some direct bearing on the taxation system was the practice of exacting *vishṭi* which has been variously rendered as forced labour, unpaid labour, impressed labour, free labour etc. The practice of exacting forced labour prevailed in the Deccan during our period.

In the inscriptions of the Rāshṭrakūṭas the forced labour is mentioned as *biṭṭi*, the currupt form of the Sanskrit term *vishṭi*. It is interesting to note that in Sanskrit and Kannada literary works there are frequent references to *biṭṭi* and its variant forms. For example, in the *Yaśastilaka* of Somadeva Sūri a spy reports to the king against the minister who engaged in exacting *vishṭi* when labourers were busy in sowing. In the *Vikramārjuna-Vijaya*[2] of Pampa, the greatest Kannada classical poet of the tenth century A.D., the term *mūviṭṭi*

1. *E.I.*, XXXII, p. 57. Also H.D. Sankalia, 'When the Ādivāsī was King,' *The Times of India*, a daily newspaper from Delhi. September 19, 1982 (Sunday Review), p. 2.
2. Ch. IX, v. 2.

which means three types of forced labour occurs twice. The term *mūviṭṭi* mentioned in the literary works and epigraphs of Karnataka of the tenth century A.D. signifies that the use of unpaid labour in the battlefield continued as late as the tenth century A.D.

From the inscriptions of Karnataka also we get glimpses of the nature of the employment of forced labour. From an inscription of about 958 A.D. we learn that the people were expected to cut fodder for the king's horses and elephants.[1] From the references occurring in the inscriptions like *biṭṭi-baṇḍi*[2] etc. we learn that the people were expected to supply the king with carts and other necessary implements without any rent or remuneration in return. Though details are not forthcoming, we can quite reasonably assume that the unpaid labour was employed for the construction and maintenance of roads, bridges, excavation and maintenance of tanks, for the construction of temples and works of public utility.

Since forced labour formed a very negligible source of State income, the rulers were not very particular about it. But the donees of villages, who received the rights to exact forced labour deemed it a special privilege to have forced labour at their disposal. Thus, with the gradually increasing number of village grants during Rāshṭrakūṭa times, the strong forts of feudalism were built and with them references to *biṭṭi* become quite a regular quite feature. Moreover, comparative lack of coined money during the Rāshṭrakūṭa times, must have made payment of government dues in the form of labour service compulsory.[3]

Forced labour was so popular with the feudal lords, but we cannot expect it to be equally popular with the peasants. An inscription from Chincholi (Dharwar district), dated 798 A.D., provides some clue to the unpopularity of the forced labour, for the inscription states, "His act is of religious merit who exempts (people) from tax on irrigation and forced labour."[4]

1. *E.C.*, XI, p. 6.
2. *E.C.*, V, Hn. 84 and 139.
3. *JKU*, XII, p. 151.
4. *SII.*, I, No. 15.

A record of the Rāshṭrakūṭa King Indra III, dated 915 A.D., grants a village called Tenna to a Brāhmaṇa with the accompanying right to forced labour as an occasion presents itself.[1] It is remarkable to note that Somadeva takes exception to forced labour only at the time of sowing. It seems that forced labour was the poor men's terror.[2] The Arab merchant Sulaiman also observed that the Indian kings had numerous troops, who were not given any pay, but maintained themselves without receiving anything from the king.[3] This, perhaps, refers to the armies of the Pratīhāras and the Rāshṭrakūṭas.

Above we have discussed about people without pay. But we have got some hint about remuneration for certain works from the Kandhār inscription of Kṛshṇa III[4] which is valuable for us for comparing the payments. The first reference is to the bards (*vandījana*) who used to praise the noble qualities of one and received (each) two hundred *drammas* together with a pair of clothes, probably per year. Next, provision of a hundred *drammas* and a pair of clothes is made for each of a group of persons whose duty was to recite sacred texts four times a day. The third provision of fifty *drammas* and a pair of clothes was made in favour (of each) of another group of reciters. These look like payments to be made to the palace servants.

Corruption

We get an appalling picture of the corruption and exploitation of the minister in the tenth-century work, the *Yaśastilakachampū* of Somadeva, which mainly reflects the conditions prevailing in the later Rāshṭrakūṭa period. A spy of the king is shown as reporting that the minister is responsible for three things: demanding unpaid labour at the time of sowing, collection of dues while the corn is still

1. *E.I.*, Vol. IX.
2. K.K. Handiqui, *op. cit.*, p. 117.
3. *HIED*, I, p. 7. Also Buddha Prakash, *Aspects of Indian History and Civilization*, Agra, 1965, p. 224.
4. *E.I.*, XXXV, p. 107.

unripe, and the unbridled movement of troops in the harvesting season.[1]

He further says that the minister misappropriates the funds even of religious and charitable endowments,[2] melts down the image of the gods and replaces them by those of lesser value, sells an image and with the proceeds institutes a religious festival[3] and robs the people like a *thug* and with the money, thus obtained, gives charities to the Brāhmaṇas. This typical minister professes bravery only in the presence of merchants and physicians and exhibits courage only before the weak and deformed, but huddles down silently, like an ape, in the company of warriors and desperadoes.[4]

The spy in his report describes that minister as a monster of financial corruption.[5] The spy sums up his character by stating that "he is darkness embodied, sin personified, evil incarnate and the Kali age in human form."[6]

Crime and Punishment

Certain details concerning crime and punishment are preserved in the *Yaśastilaka.* In a story, the priest Śrībhūti who is found guilty of breach of trust is given three types of choice by the king: he must either swallow three bowls of cow-dung, or receive thirty-three blows to be given by powerful wrestlers, or forfeit his entire property. The minister prefers the last choice and all his wealth is confiscated; and he is smeared with clay teeming with worms, and made to wear garlands of potsherds and abandoned platters, and expelled from the city seated on the back of a donkey. Similar treatment is meted out to another culprit by the enraged citizen. He is pelted with clods of earth and severely

1. Kedar Nath Sharma (ed.), *Yaśastilakachampū*, III, 172, Nirnaya Sagar Press edition, p. 427. Also see K.K. Handiqui, *Yaśastilaka and Indian Culture*, Sholapur, 1949, pp. 91, 117-18.
2. *Ibid.*, III, 236, p. 458.
3. *Ibid.*, III, 227, 235, pp. 453, 457.
4. *Ibid.*, III, 190, p. 439,
5. K.K. Handiqui, *op. cit.*, p. 119.
6. Kedar Nath Sharma (ed.), III, 223, p. 452.

whipped and turned out of the city on the back of a donkey, clothed in rags from the cremation ground, and wearing a garland of platters with the head shaven at random with the blade held in the reverse direction, and Bilva fruits suspended from the tuft of hair on the crest of the head. For adulterous adventure people were exiled by the king after indictment in the presence of all the people. Somadeva also refers to the torture of thieves. A thief accused of robbing and murdering a barber was condemned by the judges and put in such a condition so that he might lose his life in ten or twelve days.[1]

Some details about cruelty to animals are also recorded by Somadeva. A buffalo is tortured to death with revolting cruelty for killing the king's horse. We are told that the legs of the animal were tied together, and burning coals heaped upon the body, while salt water was poured over the wounds, and he was allowed to drink water mixed with boiled extracts of peppers. On the other hand, the epitaphs on the dog and the peacock who were accidentally killed, bear testimony to the love of animals.[2] The Ātakūr inscription on a memorial stone tells us about a gift of land in memory of a hound, who had attacked and killed a boar, but was himself killed in the fight.[3]

Sulaiman, an Arab traveller, informs that the punishment for adultery and thiefing was death sentence. For executing this punishment the culprit was forced to sit on a pointed and circular log of wood which penetrated from the lower portion of the body to the throat and ultimately killed the culprit.[4]

Place Names: An Observation

The study of Indian inscriptions reveals the fact that while many of the place-names have survived without any change or with only minor changes through the centuries,

1. K.K. Handiqui, *op. cit.*, pp. 122-123.
2. *Ibid.*, p. 113.
3. *Sources of Karnataka History*, Vol. I, p. 97.
4. Syed Sulaiman Nadvi, *Arab our Bharat Ke Sambandh*, Allahabad, 1930, p. 26.

scores of other place-names have undergone significant changes, in some cases the original place-names having been replaced by totally different ones.

We learn from the Māvali inscription[1] of Rāshṭrakūṭa Govinda III, of about the end of the eighth century A.D., that the village was known by the name Perguñji. Māvali is a modern village in the Soraba Taluk of Shimoga District in Karnataka. This is an excellent example of how a village came to lose its original Kannada name and gained a Sanskritised form. Perguñji is made up of two parts '*per*' and '*guñji*'. The first part means 'big' and the second part 'creeper.' In keeping with the fashion of those days, the Kannada place-name Perguñji was transformed into Sanskrit as Mahāvallī. Here *per*=*mahā* and guñji=vallī. This form came into popular use. In due course, the original name Perguñji went out of use and the Sanskritised form Mahāvalli also came to be used with slight change as Māvali.[2]

In our period, names of some places were changed and the places renamed after the V.I.Ps. The Sanskrit name Kṛshṇa appears in the Kannada records as Kannara, Kannāra, Kanhar, Kanhāra, Kandara, Kandāra, Kandhar and Kandhār.[3] The mention of Kṛshṇa III as the lord of Kandhārapura in the epigraphs of the Raṭṭas no doubt proved the existence of a city called Kandhārapura named after a Rāshṭrakūṭa ruler Kṛshṇa.[4]

Another such example is Baṅkāpura. A record[5] belonging to the reign of the Western Chālukyas records that the king was ruling from his capital Baṅkāpura. Baṅkāpura, which has retained its name to the present day, is a big village in the Shiggaon Taluk of the Dharwar District in Karnataka.

1. *E.C.*, X, Sb. 10.
2. K.V. Ramesh, 'Some Observations on Indian Place-Names' in Madhava N. Katti (ed.), *Studies in Indian Place Names*, I, Mysore, 1980, pp. 95-96.
3. Cf. *JIH*, XXXVII, p. 40, *Bomb. Gaz.*, I, Pt. I, p. 2444; Pt. II, pp. 334, 410 note, 1,468, 526 etc. The Prakrit name Kannara was also sometimes re-Sanskritised as Karṇa, *R.ITT*, p. 122.
4. *E.I.*, XXXV, p. 109.
5. *Ibid.*, XXXVI, p. 69.

This place was originally named after Baṅkeya of the Chellaketan family, who was the minister of the Rāshṭrakūṭa King Amoghavarsha I (814-78 A.D.) and was governing the Banavāsi province under that emperor.

A monastery was also named after the King Amoghavarsha. The grants[1] made by Indra III from Vajirkheda, dated 914 A.D., register a gift of two villages to a Jain monastery, Amogha by name, and the site of the monastery itself to the preceptor Vardhamāna. Amoghavarsha I was a true follower of Jainism and hence a Jain monastery named after him is quite logical. One of the *liṅgas* installed in a temple of Mānyakheṭa was probably named after the Rāshṭrakūṭa King Govinda IV as Govindeśvara.[2]

1. *Ibid.*, XXXVIII, p. 6.
2. *Ibid.*, XXXVI, p. 259.

4

Education and Literature

A. EDUCATION

Education is considered to be the fifth of the essential needs of the society next only to food, cloth, house and hospital. It was well developed and organised during the time of the Rāshṭrakūṭas. Buddhist monasteries were on decline under the influence of Rajput powers. Especially during the time of the Rāshṭrakūṭas the progress of education and literature was unique. Rāshṭrakūṭa emperors donated open-heartedly for educational purposes. Trading communities and rich persons also made donations for the establishment of educational institutions and their maintenance.

Our epigraphical materials do not throw any light on the arangements made in the ordinary village for the primary education. Any discussion on this part would be hypothetical only. We find many institutions of higher learning as well as numerous literary works of very high standard. On the basis of these we can easily conclude that the system of education was well organised right from the primary stage.

We have ample evidence to show that the arrangements for higher education in our period meant learning of Sanskrit and Veda, Vyākaraṇa (grammar), Jyotisha (astronomy and astrology), Sāhitya (literature), Mīmāṁsā, Dharmaśāstra, Purāṇas, Nyāya (logic), Tantra, Painting, Carpentry, Sculpture, Music, Drama and use of war weapons etc.[1] Training in good handwriting, mathematics, Kāvya, linguistics, stories, musical instruments etc. has been suggested especially for women in the *Mahāpurāṇa* of Pushpadanta.[2] The donee of the Dhulia plates of Rāshṭrakūṭa King Dhruva, dated 779 A.D., is described as well versed in Vedas, Vedāṅgas, history, Purāṇas, grammar, Mīmāṁsā, logic, Nirukta, and liturgy.[3]

Arrangement for higher education was made in three kinds of institutions or places, *viz.*, maṭhas associated with temples endowed by the state or private charity, *agrahāras* granted to Brāhmaṇa settlements, and special educational institutions conducted by private individuals or village people.

There existed a maṭha at Hebbal in Dharwar district of Karnataka where an inscription, dated 975 A.D., records the grant of fifty *mattars* of land for the maṭha. Here students were fed and taught.[4] The donation given to the Buddhist monastery Kanheri by Bhadravishṇu in the reign of Amoghavarsha I, was meant for purchasing books.[5]

The word *agrahāra*, found in the epigraphs, signifies a particular form of land-grant mentioned in the Dharmaśāstras. It was a technical term applied to the endowment of such villages as were in exclusive and undisturbed enjoyment of a Brāhmaṇa beneficiary or a group of such beneficiaries. Endowments were made on account of a desire to acquire religious merit and a zeal to found higher educational institutions. The grantees of an *agrahāra* village were the new leaders of the old rustics. Their advent brought about significant

1. *Mahāpurāṇa*, 5.6.5-5.7.3.
2. *Ibid.*, 5.18.4-8.
3. *E.I.*, VIII, p. 182.
4. *E.I.*, IV, p. 358.
5. *I A.*, VII, p. 67.

changes in the social and cultural life of the village.[1]

The system of forming the *agrahāra* began during the period of the Kadambas who were contemporaries of the Guptas of North India. The *agrahāras* were not too many at that time. The later rulers, *viz.*, the Chālukyas of Bādāmi, the Rāshṭrakūṭas etc., gave great encouragement for the spread of education and hence innumerable *agrahāras* came into existence during their regimes from the sixth century onwards.

There are instances where more than one village were granted as an *agrahāra* and in such cases, two or more villages were clubbed together to form one *agrahāra*. The reason for such clubbing seems to be that a single village was not sufficient to meet the requirements of an educational institution, which was intended to be installed. This might have necessitated the inclusion of one or more villages to form an *agrahāra*. To illustrate an example of this type, we may cite a Rāshṭrakūṭra record of Nityavarsha, dated 968 A.D., from Kyāsāpura in Chitradurga district, which refers to the formation of an *agrahāra* after clubbing the two villages, *viz.*, Bidiravalli and Bīravūr, by an officer named Pandayya.[2]

Śālotgi is a large village, ten kilometres south-east of Iṇḍī, which happens to be the chief town of the Iṇḍī taluk of the Bijapur district. It was then situated in a small district of Karṇapurī *Vishaya*, a part of the bigger division of Tardavādi-100, which covered the major portion of the present Bijapur district. A stone pillar which was set up, here originally, bears three epigraphs engraved on all the four sides, described by the editors as A, B and C respectively and is now preserved in the Bijapur Museum.[3] This record, dated 945 A.D., tells us that Nārāyaṇa (surnamed Gajāñkuśa), the minister of peace and war under the Rāshṭrakūṭa Kṛshṇa III, got a *śālā* built

1 R.N. Nandi, 'Social Life in the Agrahāras of the Deccan', *Proceedings of the Indian History Congress*, 28th Session, Mysore, 1966, p. 97. For detailed discussion see S. Leela Shantakumari, *History of the Agraharas, Kanataka, 400-1300*, Madras, 1986.

2. *E.C.*, XII, Cd. 50.

3. *E.I.*, IV, pp. 60ff; also Cf. *S.I.I.*, XVIII, No. 26.

in the above village. He also helped this *śālā* with a huge amount collected from levy imposed on marriage and such other ceremonies and revenue collected from land. It was an *agrahāra* of considerable antiquity.

This *śālā* received a magnificent gift of land from Govindabhaṭṭa's son, Chakrāyudha, the chief of the village of Pāviṭṭage. As an *agrahāra*, the place was evidently a centre of education and the institution (*śālā*) therein must have been a renowned centre of learning, as it could attract students hailing from different regions.[1] Twenty-seven dwelling places were provided for those students. The inhabitants of the village significantly enough, voluntarily came forward to contribute the stipulated amount of the institution.[2] The *śālā* of this place must have flourished for a fairly long time as a renowned centre of learning and education; for, it has transformed the very name of the village as: Śālā + Pāviṭṭage= Śālotgi. The meaning of the latter term, Pāviṭṭage, is not quite clear. The Kannada term *iṭṭage* or *iṭṭige* (Sanskrit *ishṭakā*) means brick. The term *Pāviṭṭage* means a step, or a stair, in Kannada. How and why this village came to be called *Pāviṭṭage*, we have no means to explain.[3] A later inscription from the same place informs us that when the college hall built in 945 A.D. crumbled down, it was erected again by a local feudatory.[4]

Another example of an *agrahāra* is available to us from the Kalas inscription from Dharwar district.[5] This inscription is dated in the reign of Govinda IV (930-935A.D.). but it may be presumed that this institution was flourishing throughout the tenth century. Here, there was a Sanskrit College. All its two hundred Brāhmaṇa house-holders are described in v. 30 of the record as well-versed in grammar,

1. *Atra vidyārthinaḥ saṁti nānā-janapadodbhavāḥ.*
2. *Śālā vidyarthi-saṅghāya.*
3. S. Gururajachar, *Studies in Indian Place Names*, Vol. I, Mysore, 1980, pp 88-91.
4. *E I.*, IV, p. 64.
5. *E.I.*, XIII, p. 317.

polity, the science of literary composition etc.[1] The main purpose of the grant was to meet the requirement of payment of teachers' salaries there.

In the Rāshṭrakūṭa inscription at Kandhār[2] it is mentioned that there was provision of two *prasthas*[3] of oil and one *prastha* of salt daily in order to meet the requirement of the college (*Vidyāsthāna*), situated on the bank of the Nāndī in the Godāvarī valley[4] and belonging to Brāhmaṇas engaged in studies. For this purpose, arrangements had to be made for the storing of nine *khaṇḍikās*[5] of oil and four and a half *khaṇḍikās* of salt by purchasing the articles from the *grāma-kaṭaka*, *i.e.* the villages and valleys around the town where the inscription was set up. For the bulk purchase of the articles, arrangements were made for the daily payment, in a lump sum, of the price of oil and salt required per day.

Thus we see that these institutions were financed partly by the State aid and partly by private donations. The endowment village soon developed into a centre of higher learning. Teachers and specialists, who formed an important section of the *agrahāra* village, were maintained on separate plots of productive land. Students, who flocked to the endowment village, soon became important members of the educational establishment. Promising students were often maintained on state-subsidies. The Bahur plates of Nṛpatuṅgavarman record a grant of three villages for the maintenance of a college made by the king at the request of his minister.[6] The Kanhere cave inscription of the time of King Amoghavarsha I informs us about the provision made for clothes and books for the students.[7]

1. A.S. Altekar, *Rāshṭrakūṭas and their times*, Poona, 1967, pp. 402-03.
2. *E.I.*, XXXV, Pt. III, p. 109.
3. A *prastha* is variously regarded as 6 lb or 32 *palas* being equal to 4 tolas.
4. *Godāvarī-taṭ ādhyāsini Nāndī taṭe*.
5. *Khaṇḍikā* is the same as modern candy often regarded as equal to 560 pounds—D.C. Sircar.
6. *E.I.*, IV, p. 180.
7. *I A.*, XII, p 215; XIII, p. 133; XX, p. 421.

Life in an *agrahāra* village was not wholly given to the monotony of colourless religious service and dry academic pursuits. The village shrine was the nucleus of rural culture. Festive occasions were not a rarity. Regular provision was made for dance and music, both vocal and instrumental, in order to entertain the deity.

These *agrahāras*, sometimes, were called *ghaṭikāas* also. The meaning of *ghaṭikā* as a time measure of twenty-four minutes is well known throughout India. But the fact that it also denoted an educational institution in ancient and medieval Karnataka is very little known.

The word *ghaṭikā* is derived from the Sanskrit original root *ghaṭ* which means "to take place" or "form" and several scholars have given other meanings too. But we have positive evidence, in a few inscriptions, of the *ghaṭikā* being a centre of advanced learning in Karnataka.

The earliest example of a *ghaṭikā* in Karnataka is to be found in Dharwar district at Kalas then known as Kāḍiyūru.[1] The inscription of this place, dated 929-30 A.D., describes the land of Kāḍiyūr, and learned men studying in its *agrahāra* and *ghaṭikā*. The transformation of *ghaṭikā* into Kannada *ghalige* had taken place by the tenth century A.D. In the *ghalige* of Kalas, the Brāhmaṇas studied grammar, polity, literature, history, the great logic of Ekāksharamuni and commentaries on them.[2]

Karhāḍa, which is the same as Karād in Satara district (Maharashtra) was undoubtedly a famous centre of education in the Rāshṭrakūṭa period, for we find many of the donees of Rāshṭrakūṭa grants hailing from that town. This, for instance, is the case with the donees of the Samangad plates of Dantiturga[3], the Bhore State Museum Plates of Dhruva[4] and the Sanjan charter of Amoghavarsha.[5] The donee of the Bhore State Museum Plates is Vāsudevabhaṭṭa who was the son of

1. *E.I*, VII, p. 329.
2. *Ibid.*, p. 337, v. 10.
3. *I.A.*, XI, pp. 111ff.
4. *E.I.*, XXII, p. 181.
5. *E.I.*, XVIII, pp. 235ff.

Durgābhaṭṭa, and was famous for his proficiency in the interpretation of the Vedas and the Vedāṅgas. This Charter would easily show that Karâd was a centre of scholarship where Vedic exegesis was also given attention to.

B. LITERATURE

(a) Sanskrit : General Works

The glorious regime of the Rāshṭrakūṭas saw at once the flowering of literary activity both in Sanskrit and Kannada. The curriculum of advanced studies in this period was so wide as to include Veda, Vyākaraṇa, Jyotisha, Sāhitya, Mīmāṁsā, Dharmaśāstra, Purāṇas, Nyāya and Smṛtis.[1]

Grammar and logic (Tarka) seem to have been considered very important subjects. If Nayasena was a distinguished grammarian turned poet, Somadeva, the author of *Yaśastilaka*, was a seasoned logician turned poet. In one of the opening verses of *Yaśastilaka*, we are told that just as the cow yields milk by eating grass, similarly his intellect produced the beautiful utterances of poetical composition, by feeding on the dry logical studies, to which he had devoted himself since his childhood.[2]

It is remarkable that, unlike the grants of the early Chālukya princes, those of the Rāshṭrakūṭas contain accounts in verse of the ancestors of the granter, and most of the verses are of the nature of those we find in the ordinary Sanskrit literature, possessing the same merits and faults. The Rāshṭrakūṭas, therefore, must have been patrons of learning, and probably had poets in their service.[3]

One of the epigraphs of this period mentions *Kaumara* or the Kātantra system of grammar in which specialists were

1. A.S. Altekar, *op. cit.*, p. 400.
2. K.K. Handiqui, *op. cit.*, p. 10.
3. R.G. Bhandarkar, *The Early History of the Deccan*, Poona, 1983, p. 105.

available.[1] The famous commentary (*vṛtti*) on the *Kātantra-sūtras* was written by Durgāsiṁha belonging to this period. It not only explains but amplifies the text.[2] Durgāsiṁha has also written a gloss on his own *vṛtti.*

Like the *Jainendra* system, Karnataka founded another system of Sanskrit grammar renowned as the *Śākaṭāyana* school. While compressing *Pāṇini* and *Jainendra* in a convenient form, this Jaina Śākaṭāyana, a protege of the Rāshṭrakūṭa King Amoghavarsha I, anticipates in his arrangement the example later followed by *Kaumudī* texts. The *sūtras* are arranged topic-wise and make for easy comprehension. Besides being the author of the *sūtras* known as *Śabdānuśāsana*, Śākaṭāyana himself has also added his own commentary on them known as *Amoghavṛtti*, in honour of his patron.[3]

The history of the Rāshṭrakūṭas was almost a forgotten chapter in the history of India till the end of last century. The discovery in the present century of numerous inscriptions and copper plates, mostly in Sanskrit, has come in handy to write a dependable history of this great ruling dynasty. Each one of the Sanskrit records is, indeed, a poem by itself. Each of these Sanskrit plates is replete with the graces and beauties of language met with in classical writers like Bāṇa and Bhāravi. One of them, the Begumra Plate of Indra III, dated 915 A.D.,[4] deserves to be noticed here in particular. Its author is Trivikrama, the same as the author of the first and the only datable *champū-kāvya* in Sanskrit literature, *viz*, *Nala-Champū*.[5] This establishes the fact that Karnataka had its own signal contributions to make in the field of pure literary forms also.

The origin of the word *champū* itself is obscure; but Prof. R.S. Mugali in his *History of Kannada Literature* thinks

1. *E.I.*, V, p. 22.
2. S K. Belvalkar, *System of Sanskrit Grammar*, p. 86.
3. *Ibid.*, p. 70.
4. *E.I.*, IX, p. 28.
5. P.B. Desai (ed.), *A History of Karnataka*, Second Edition, Dharwar, 1981, p. 307.

that the word is of Kannada origin. Anyway, *Champū* is the most elaborate and artificial form in Sanskrit literature, calculated to afford to the poet the amplest opportunities to display not only his erudition but also his command over prose as well as verse in one and the same composition. Up to the tenth century, compositions were either in prose or in verse almost exclusively; and even when they were in prose and verse intermingled, the latter was used occasionally and for some definite purposes. But the yearning of poets to display their mastery over both simultaneously seems to be responsible for the rise of this altogether new form in Sanskrit literature.[1]

Trivikramabhaṭṭa's composition, the *Nalachampū*, also called *Damayantīkathā*, in prose and verse, both highly literary and embellished, runs to seven long chapters. He pays compliments to Bāṇa and Subandhu in the beginning. He does not slavishly follow the original *Mahābhārata* in his treatment of Nala's story. He has made highly romantic and ingenious innovations of his own. Nala's minister, Śrutaśīla, is assigned an important role here in bringing about the union of Nala and Damayantī. There are conventional descriptions of nature, and the story ends with Damayantī's rejection of the love-suit of the gods.

Trivikrama was the son of Nemāditya and grandson of Śrīdhara of Śāṇḍilya gotra. He was a poet at the court of Indra III for whom he composed Navasari inscription in A.D. 915. He was a staunch adherent of the Śaiva faith.[2] Another ornate work from the pen of this author is *Madālasāchampū*.

Amoghavarsha I or Nṛpatuṅga (814-878 A.D.) was not only interested in literature, but was himself a scholar and composer of a very high order. A short and sweet philosophical lyric in Sanskrit *Praśnottararatnamālikā*, 'the Jewel-Garland of Questions and Answers', is his composition; though it is sometimes wrongly attributed to Vimala or

1. *H.C.I.P.*, Vol. IV, p. 188.
2. K.K. Handiqui, *Yaśastilaka and Indian Culture*, Sholapur, 1949, p. 37.

Śaṅkarāchārya. The verses, in *Āryā* metre, are all in the form of questions and answers, a figurative device known as 'praśnottara'.

The morality taught in these questions and answers of the *Praśnottara-ratnamālikā* is general human morality and not specifically Jainistic, and it is as simple as the language in which it is couched. We find verses like the following :

V. 8. "What does one fear ? Death. Who is in even worse plight than the blind man ? The passionate man. Who is not disconcerted by the arrows of the glances of a beautiful woman ?..."

V. 10. "What is unfathomable ? The conduct of women. Who is intelligent ? He who is not deceived by this. What is poverty ? Discontent. What is dignity ? Entreating.

V. What is hell ? Dependence upon another. What is good fortune ? The renunciation of all desires. What is truth ? The welfare of the beings. What do the beings like ? Life."

VV. 26-27. "What shall I tell you, that is as difficult to find on the earth as a wishing-jewel ? Certainly it is fourfold good. And what is the special name given to it by those who have driven away the darkness of ignorance ? Gifts, accompanied by friendly speech, knowledge without arrogance; heroism coupled with forbearance, and wealth hand in hand with self-sacrifice. This fourfold good is indeed difficult to find."

The *Smṛti*-writers, Kātyāyana, Āngirasa, Yama and Vishṇu are all usually assigned to this period; one is not certain whether any of these hailed from the Rāshṭrakūṭa domain.

Indranandin wrote *Jvālāmālinikalpa* in Sanskrit. It deals with a mystic fire-cult associated with the goddess Jvālāmālinī. This work was composed in A.D. 939 at Mānyakheṭa when King Kṛshṇarāja was on the throne.[1]

Halāyudha is the author of the *Abhidhānaratnamālā*, a famous lexicon known after his name. He has followed in

1. K.K. Handiqui, *op. cit.*, p. 6

the footsteps of Amaradatta, Vararuchi, Bhāguri and Vopālita in writing this great work. He has also written the *Kavirahasya* and the *Mṛtasañjīvanī*. The former is really a *dhātu-pāṭha* or list of verbs with meanings, written in verse. It explains the conjugational peculiarities of roots having the same form, and its preface mentions expressly the patronage given to him by Kṛshṇa III (A.D. 939-67). The latter is a commentary on the basic text of prosody, Piṅgala's *Chhandaḥ-Sūtra*. The work is a treatise on metrics.

The *Mṛtasañjīvanī* was composed in honour of King Vākpati Muñja of Dhārā, while the *Kavirahasya* eulogizes the deeds of Kṛshṇa III of the Rāshṭrakūṭa dynasty. Thus it seems that Halāyudha was originally an inhabitant of Mānyakheṭa, but later on he migrated to Ujjain and was admitted into the patronage of Vākpati Muñja[1] of the Paramāro dynasty.

This was the golden age which saw the rise of the great Advaita philosopher Śaṅkarāchārya (A.D. 788-820). He was given encouragement to establish his *maṭha* at Śṛṅgerī in the Chickmanglur district (Karnataka state).

The numerous *bhāshyas*, or learned commentaries, written by him on the major Upanishads, Brahmasūtras and the Bhagavad-Gītā, taken together with his moving devotional hymns (*stotras*) and manuals of philosophy, started a new age in philosophical thinking and living. Some of his greatest disciples, like Padmapāda, the author of *Pañchapadika*, Sureśvara, the author of *Bṛhadāraṇyaka-ślokavārttika*, *Taittirīya-ślokavārttika* and *Naishkarmyasiddhi*, were also settled in Karnataka. The great tradition of Advaita was thus born and nourished in this land.

It is a moot question among scholars whether Maṇḍana Miśra was himself Sureśvara and whether Viśvarūpa was not his other name. The fact is further complicated by the suggested identities of Sureśvara, Umveka and Bhavabhūti in addition.

1. Ganga Prasad Yadava, *Dhanapāla and His Times*, New Delhi, 1982, p. 82. Also, K.A. Nilakanta Sastri, *A History of South India* (Hindi, Second edition), Patna, 1978, p. 301.

The celebrated commentary called *Bālakriḍā* on the *Yājñavalkya-smṛti* is by Viśvarūpa, who is generally identified with Sureśvara. In the words of Mm. P.V. Kane : "The style of Viśvarūpa is simple and forcible and resembles that of the great Śaṁkara. He quotes profusely from Vedic works, mentions the Charakas and Vājasaneyins, the Kāṭhakas, and very often supports his position by quotations from the *Ṛg-Veda*, the *Brāhmaṇas* and the *Upanishads*. Though saturated with the lore of the *Pūrva-mīmāṁsā*, his philosophical views are identical with Śaṁkara's."[1]

Sarvajñātman, the great systematiser of Śaṁkara's thought in his *Saṁkshepaśāriraka*, was a pupil of Sureśvara and is, therefore, to be assigned to our period.

Another very great writer who flourished under the Chālukyas of Lemulavāḍa (or Vemulavāḍa), feudatories of the Rāshṭrakūṭas, was the Jaina Somadevasūri, who made substantial contributions to Jaina religious literature. "He is one of the most versatile talents in the history of Indian literature. He is a master of prose and verse, a profound scholar, an authority on Jaina dogma, a close student of the art of government, a political thinker, and a keen observer of men and manners."[2] He was a contemporary of Kṛshṇa III (A.D. 939-68). He belonged to an order of Jaina monks known as Devasaṁgha and was the disciple of Nemideva who in turn was the disciple of Yaśodeva, and had the following honorific titles[3] : Syādvādachalasiṁha ('A lion on the mountain of Syādvāda'), Tārkika-Chakravartin ('The Lord of the logicians'), Vādībha-pañchānana ('A lion to elephants, to wit, the disputants'), Vākkallolapayonidhi ('An ocean of the waves of eloquence'), and Kavikularāja ('The king of the poets'). He continued the *champū* tradition started by Trivikrama and took it to sublime heights.

1. P.V. Kane, *History of Dharmaśāstra*, Vol. I, pp. 252f.
2. K.K.Handiqui, *op. cit.*, p. 3.
3. *Ibid.*, p. 1.

Somadevasūri wrote his *Yaśodhara-Mahārāja-Charita* (*Yaśastilaka*) in 959 A.D., while his patron was camping with his overlord Kṛshṇa III at Melpāṭi in the Chittoor District, having vanquished the Pāṇḍya-Chola, Chera, Ceylonese and other kings.[1] Somadeva's statement is remarkable for its historical accuracy, as it is corroborated by the Karhād plates[2] of the great Rāshṭrakūṭa emperor Kṛshṇa III, issued on the 9th March 959 A.D., at Melpāṭi, a few weeks earlier than the composition of Somadeva's *Yaśastilaka*. Although Somadeva was contemporary of Kṛshṇa III, his work was not composed at Mānyakheṭa, but at an obscure place called Gaṅgadhārā[3], which seems to have been the capital of a prince named Vādarāja, the eldest son of a Chālukya chief named Arikesarin, a tributary of Kṛshṇa III. It is, however, certain that he was intimately acquainted with court life, and may have passed sometime in the Rāshṭrakūṭa capital. The court life, so minutely described by him in Book III of his *Yaśastilaka*, does not apply to a petty feudatory chief like that of Gaṅgadhārā, and can be true only of the sovereign of an imperial status, who receives embassies from foreign courts, declares war against refractory kings, and has at his disposal requirements drawn from different parts of India.[4]

The *Yaśastilaka* represents a lively picture of India at a time when the Buddhist, Jaina and Brahmanical religions were still engaged in a contest that drew towards it the attention, and wellnigh absorbed the intellectual energies of all thinking men.[5] The story in prose and verse is of the hero Yaśodhara's different births and sufferings, popular among Jainas, but in the treatment of the same, Somadeva has shown such an encyclopaedic genius that a scholar today could reconstruct

1. 'शकनृपकालातीत संवत्सरशतेष्वष्ट स्वेकाशीत्यधिकेषु (अंकतः 881) सिद्धार्थ संवत्सरान्तर्गत चैत्रमासमदन त्रयोदश्यां......मेल्वाटीप्रवर्धमान-राज्यप्रभावे श्रीकृष्णराजदेवे सति।'
2. *E.I.*, IV, 278.
3. Gaṅgadhārā has been identified with Gaṅgawati in the Raichur district quite near the modern Dharwar in Karnataka.
4. K.K. Handiqui *op. cit.*, p. 6.
5. Peterson's Report, I, p. 33.

all shades of Vedic, Agamic, Tantrika and popular thought and wisdom current in the time by dint of patient research on this work. There is nothing secular and religious, social or political, that escapes the far-flung net of the great author. It can be regarded as a unique work in Sanskrit literature. This work contains eight Books called Āśovāsas.

The contents of this work are briefly as follows[1]: King Mādridatta has ascended the throne at an early age and is entirely given to sensual pleasures. At the advice of his family priest he prepares to offer a great sacrifice to his family goddess Chaṇḍamāridevatā, consisting of a pair of every living creature, including human beings. Mādridatta himself is to perform the sacrifice. Then the servants drag in a youth and a maiden, a pair of ascetics whom they have selected for the human sacrifice. At the sight of them a change comes over the king. It occurs to him that these might be the twin children of his own sister, who were said to have renounced the world and joined the Jain community. He asks these two to tell him their history, and it is revealed that they are indeed their relatives. The major part of the story deals with their experiences in various rebirths, but many explanations regarding the doctrines of the Jaina religion are interwoven. Many famous poets, such as Bhāravi, Bhavadhūti, Bhartṛhari, Gunāḍhya, Vyāsa, Bhāsa, Kālidāsa, Bāṇa and others are mentioned, all of whom are supposed to have done honour to the Jaina religion. The last three sections also form an independent book, entitled Upāsakādhyayana ("Readings for Laymen"), which serves as a work of edification for Jaina laymen. The work ends with the conversion of Mādridatta and his family goddess to the Jaina religion.

Somadevasūri was a prolific writer, and another work which deserves some consideration here is his treatise on politics, the *Nītivākyāmṛta*.[2] Here he pays homage to the

1. M. Winternitz, *A History of Indian Literature*, Vol. II (Second edition), New Delhi, 1977, p. 534.
2. It has been printed recently by the Orient Research Institute, Mysore.

state, the root of *dharma*, *artha* and *kāma*.[1] It is modelled on Kauṭilya's *Arthaśāstra* and has been recently translated into Italian. Such is its unique significance as one of the very few dealing exclusively with politics and statecraft. It has thirty-two chapters dealing, among other things, with the values of life, the sciences, the minister, preceptor, general, envoy, spy, the *saptāṅgas* (the seven limbs) of a State, judiciary and diplomacy. He gives a picture of the imperial court besides throwing light on the problems of government affecting war and peace.[2]

The other works of this author, not extant today are : *Shaṇṇavatiprakaraṇa*, *Mahendramātali-saṁkalpa* and *Yukti-Chintāmaṇisūtra*[3] as we know from the colophon of his *Nīti-vākyāmṛta*.

A copper-plate inscription in Sanskrit found at Parbhani[4] (in Maharashtra State) not only gives us a glimpse of Somadeva seven years after the composition of *Yaśastilaka*, but also furnishes a genealogy of the feudatory Chālukya chiefs in whose territory he lived and worked. The inscription records the grant of a village, Vanikaṭupulu[5] by name, to Somadeva by Vadya's son Arikesarin IV in 966 A.D. for the repairs and upkeep of a Jaina temple called Śubhadhāmajinālaya, built by Vadyaga in the capital. It is clear from this record that in 966 A.D. Somadeva was incharge of Śubhadhāma temple and seems to have carried on his literary activities undisturbed as a hitherto unknown work *Syādvādopanishad* is here attributed to him. He was held in the highest esteem by his contemporaries, and kings and feudatory chiefs are described as reverently bowing to his feet.[6]

1. 'अथ धर्मार्थ कामफलाय राज्याय नमः' ।
2. Ganga Prasad Yadava, *Dhanapāla and His Times*, New Delhi, 1982, p. 236.
3. K K. Handiqui, *op. cit.*, p. 1.
4. Nathu Ram Premi, *Jain Sāhitya aur Itihāsa*, pp. 90ff.
5. K.K. Handiqui, *op. cit.*, p. 5.
6. 'अखिलमहासाम (न्तसी) मन्तप्रान्तपर्यस्तोत्तं सस्त्रक्सुरभिचरणः सकल-विद्वज्ज कर्णावतं सीभवद्यशः पुण्डरीकः सूर्य इव सकलावनिभृतांशिरः श्रेणिषु शिखण्डमण्डनायमानपादयद्मोऽभूत्' ।

Muñjārya Vādighaṅghala Bhaṭṭa was one of the contemporaries of Somadeva. He is known to us from the Kudlur plates of the Gaṅga King Mārasiṁha, dated 963 A.D.[1] Mārasiṁha was a tributary of Kṛshṇa III, and the grant of a village to Vādighaṅghala Bhaṭṭa by the former forms the subject of the inscription, which eloquently describes the great Jaina teacher's attainments and influence. Vādighaṅghala Bhaṭṭa was a distinguished grammarian and seems to have propounded a system of grammar on a sure and sound basis.[2] He was expert in Lokāyaṭa, Sāṁkhya and Buddhist philosophy as well as Vedic interpretation[3], a great master of Jaina doctrine and an eminent poet. He was intimately connected with the Gaṅga King Būṭuga II and Kṛshṇa III and the Rāshṭrakūṭa capital. We are told that his faultless eloquent elucidation of literature made Gaṅga Gāṅgeya (Būṭuga II), 'cuckoo in the pleasure garden of learning', his pupil. He was honoured by the learned men of Vallabharāja's capital, who were enlightened by his exposition of all branches of political science;[4] and Vallabharāja seems to be no other than Kṛshṇa III who is called Vallabhanarendradeva in the Karhād grant[5], and Vallabhanarendra and Vallabharāya in Pushpadanta's work.[6] Kṛshṇa III is, moreover, explicitly mentioned in inscriptions, which declare that Kṛshṇarāja, who with his tributaries honoured the master, conquered the regions by acting upon his counsel, which was 'sound in relation to the present as well as the future'.[7] It would thus appear that while Somadeva was preoccupied with the theoretical principles of statecraft, Vādighaṅghala Bhaṭṭa played the role of a practical statesman and acted as a political adviser to the Rāshṭrakūṭa emperor.

1. Text and Translation in *Annual Report of the Mysore Archaeological Department*, 1921.
2. 'निःसंशयनिर्विवादव्युत्पादित व्याकरणप्रकारः', ll. 159-60.
3. 'वेदार्थविचारचारुधिषणः', l. 162.
4. *Yaś.*, ll. 165-69.
5. *E.I.*, IV, 278.
6. *Jasaharachariu*, 1.1.3 and *Nāyakumārachariu*, 1.3.2.
7. *Yaś.*, ll. 169-71.

The glory and achievements of the empire seem to have opened new vistas before the thingking men of the age. The disruption of the Rāshṭrakuṭa empire after Kṛshṇa III must have been a rude shock to cultural possibilities in the Deccan.

In the theological field too, the Jainas of this period produced monumental works. Some of the most exhaustive and authoritative commentaries on the Jaina Canon known as *Shalkhaṇḍāgama* were completed under Rāshṭrakūṭa patronage. Vīrasena and Jainasena were teacher and disciple who jointly completed the gigantic commentaries known as *Dhavala* and *Jayaahavala*, together running to some one lac *ślokas*.[1]

Jinasena, the friend of king Amoghavarsha I (A.D.814-878), was also a master-poet who wrote the magnificent *Ādipurāṇa* dealing with the epic story of Bharata and Bāhubalī. It is a *Kāvya* and *Parāṇa* in one. The work, though very voluminous, remained incomplete till it was completed by Jinasena's gifted pupil Guṇabhadra whose supplementary work is known as *Uttarapurāṇa* The importance of these works would be realised only if we see how Jinasena's work set the tradition of Kannada *Champū* poetry for a period of four centuries, starting from Pampa.

We have fairly accurate information regarding the time when the *Mahāpurāṇa* was written. It is stated at the end of the work that it was consecrated on a date equivalent to June 23, 897 A.D., during the reign of the Rāshṭrakūṭa king Kṛshṇa II Akālavarsha by Guṇabhadra's pupil Lokasena. Jinasena was a pupil of Vīrasena. He is not identical with Jinasena, the author of the *Harivaṁśa-Purāṇa*.[2]

The *Ādipurāṇa* and the *Uttarapurāṇa* are remarkable specimens of the Jaina literature in Karnataka during the early medieval age. A.N. Upadhye[3] rightly observes that it is not only a systematic exposition of the Jaina traditional lore and principles, but also an exquisite specimen of Sanskrit literature, rich in exuberant descriptions and full of poetic embellishments, both of sense and sound. The *Ādipurāṇa* has forty-seven chapters and deals mainly with the life of the first Jina,

1. H.L. Jain, *Introduction to Shalkhaṇḍāgama*, p. II.
2. M. Winternitz, *op. cit.*, p. 499.
3. A.N. Upadhye (ed.), *Ātmānuśāsana*, Introduction, p. 9.

Ṛshabhadeva and his son, Bharata. Forty-two chapters are composed by Jinasena and the remainder is added to it by his disciple Guṇabhadra. The *Uttarapurāṇa* contains the biographies of all the remaining great figures of the Jaina tradition. The *Mahāpurāṇa* contains the stories of all the sixty-three excellent men of the Jaina tradition.[1]

Another literary work of Jinasena, equally significant, is *Pārśvābhyudaya*, which gives the life story of Pārśvanātha, and at the same time, by a very ingenious device of *samasyā purāṇa* incorporated the entire text of Kālidāsa's *Meghadūta*. For every single line of Kālidāsa, Jinasena adds three more of his own and achieves the intended meaning relating to Pārśvanātha. This work has proved most useful in deciding Kālidāsa's text and readings.[2] Asaga's *Vardhamāna-Purāṇa* in Sanskrit is also a work written in this period. He was equally great as a poet in Kannada literature too.

Finally, this survey would be incomplete if the progress achieved by Jaina logic is not indicated. Recent researches in Jainology have shown that Akalaṅka (720-780 A.D.), an astute philosopher and dialectician, lived under the Rāshṭrakūṭa king Śubhatuṅga or Kṛshṇa I. His scintillating intellect and incisive insight are revealed in a number of works of Jaina logic, epistemology and metaphysics.[3] It is interesting to note here that the invocatory verse found at the beginning of numerous epigraphs of the Rāshṭrakūṭas happens to be the composition of this brilliant writer Akalaṅka, and it occurs as the invocatory verse of his *Pramāṇa-saṅgrah* also.

The Kolagall inscription[4] of Khoṭṭiga, dated Śaka 889 expired, *i.e.*, A.D. 967, in its verse twenty-two gives the ancestry of the poet Madhusūdana who composed this *praśasti*. We do not know anything more about this poet.

1. R.B.P. Singh, *Jainism in Early Medieval Kurnataka*, New Delhi, 1975, p. 10.
2. K. Krishnamoorthy, in his paper read in a Seminar at the Mythic Society, Bangalore, 1983.
3. For a fuller account of these, see Mahendra Kumar Jain, *Introduction to Siddiviniśchaya*, Kashi, 1959, pp. 62-70.
4. *E.I.*, XXI, pp. 260-67.

Rājaśekhara, the author of *Viddhaśālabhañjikā* (Sanskrit) and *Karpūramañjarī* (Prakrit play),[1] also flourished at the court of the Pratīhāras of Kanauj and that of the Kalachuris of Tripurī respectively. Due to Rāshṭrakūṭa king Indra's raid at Kanauj he was forced to migrate to Tripurī. His contributions in Sanskrit language made during the period of our study are remarkable.

(*b*) *Sanskrit : Scientific Works*

A noteworthy work on Indian mathematics written under the patronage of Amoghavarsha I is Mahāvīrāchārya's *Gaṇitasārasaṅgraha.*[2] It is simpler than the work of Brahmagupta and deals with geometrical progression.[3]

Kalyāṇakāraka[4] is a celebrated name in the annals of Jaina medical literature. It is a Sanskrit work by Ugrāditya who appears to have been a contemporary of the Rāshṭrakūṭa king Nṛpatuṅga (814-78 A.D.). The copy that has been procured gives at the end a long discourse in Sanskrit prose on the uselessness of a flesh diet. He is said to have delivered a lecture at the court of Nṛpatuṅga, where many learned men and doctors had assembled.[5] The work begins with the statement that the science of medicine is divided into two parts, namely, prevention and cure.

A copper plate[6] dated 797 A. D. from Maṇne, in Nalamangala taluk, informs us that the Gaṅga King Śivamāra was skilled in poetry, grammar, drama in all its branches, and the management of elephants as taught by the sage Pālakāpya, that he wrote a treatise on the treatment of elephants and that

1. *V.V. Mirashi Felicitation Vol.*, pp. 409-10.
2. *HCIP*, Vol. IV, p. 200.
3. 2, 4, 8, 16 . . . or 3, 9, 27, 81 . . . etc.
4. V.P. Shashtri (ed.), *Ugrādityāchāryakṛta Kalyāṇakāraka*, Sholapur, 1940.
5. *Archaeological Survey of Mysore*, Vol. II, p. 40. Also K.K. Handiqui, *op. cit.*, p. 91.
6. *Ibid.*, p. 10; also *E.C.*, IX, No. 60.

he was anointed to the kingdom by the crowned king Govindarāja.

(*c*) *Apabhraṁśa*

Perhaps the greatest Apabhraṁśa poet that has come to light so far is Pushpadanta who wrote his *Mahāpurāna,*[1] *Nāyakumāra-chariu* (story of Nāyakumār)[2] and *Jasahara-chariu* (Yaśodharacharita)[3] under the patronage of the ministers of the Rāshṭrakūṭa king Kṛshṇa III and his successor. Pushpadanta carries to perfection the possibilities of Apabhraṁśa as a vehicle of poetry. His charming style. striking figures of speech and occasional double *eutendres* recall the best traditions of classical Sanskrit poetry. In his *Mahāpurāṇa* he has beautifully delineated the lives of the sixty-three great men(*śalākā-purushas* of the Jaina faith),[4] while in the other two works he has narrated the lives of two other religious heroes.

The poet himself tells us that his parents were originally Brāhmaṇas of Kāśyapa gotra and belonged to the Śaiva faith, but later on they got converted to Jainism.[5] His father's name was Keśavabhaṭṭa and that of his mother was Mugdhā Devī. Pushpadanta, who remained a life-long bachelor and averse to sensuous pleasures, had an extremely dark complexion and

1. This book has been edited by P.L. Vaidya in three parts and published by Manikchandra Digambara Jain Granthamala in 1937, 1940 and 1941 respectively.
2. This book was edited by Hira Lal Jain and published by Balatkarana Jain Publication Society, Karanja, Berar in 1933. Now its second edition with Hindi translation edited by Dr. Jain has been published by Bharatiya Jnanapitha, New Delhi in 1972.
3. Critically edited with an Introduction, Glossary and Notes by P.L. Vaidya and published by the Ambādās Chawre Digambara Jain Granthamala in 1931. Now it has been edited with Hindi translation by H.L. Jain and published by Bharatiya Jnanapitha in 1972.
4. P.L. Vaidya, *Introduction to Jasaharachariu*, Poona, 1931. p. 20.
5. Nathu Ram Premi, *Jain Sāhitya aur Itihāsa*, Bombay, 1956, p. 225.

was ugly in appearance with a very lean and thin physique.[1] The poet lived at the court of some prince;[2] but some calamity befell him there which compelled him to undertake the long journey to Mānyakheṭa where his poetic genius was rekindled by Bharata, the minister of king Kṛshṇa III.[3]

In one of the verses prefixed to various *sandhis* of his *Mahāpurāṇa*, the poet makes mention of the ravages of Mānyakheṭa by the king of Dhārā.[4] Obviously, this event is no other than the invasion by Sīyaka II of Dhārā during the reign of the Rāshṭrakūṭa king Khoṭṭigadeva, the successor of Kṛshṇa III. This event, according to the author of *Paiyalachchhi-nāma-mālā*, took place in V.S. 1029 (= A.D. 972), and the mention of it by Pushpadanta proves that his literary activity continued for at least seven years after the completion of his *Mahāpurāṇa* in S. 887 (= A.D. 965), the writing of which had commenced in 959 A.D. This book consists of two parts, an *Ādipurāṇa* in thirty-seven and an *Uttarapurāṇa* in sixty-five chapters. Pushpadanta's reference to the destruction of Mānyakheṭa (which event occurred in A.D. 972) in a work completed in A.D. 965 seems to be an interpolation, because this reference is not found in *all* copies of the manuscript, and at various places in the different copies of the text. The period of *Nāyakumāracharìu* is supposed to be 966-68 A.D. and that of *Jasaharacharìu* between 968-72 A.D.

Pushpadanta has shown his great poetic feat by narrating in different ways the same dreams of mothers of twenty-four

1. R. Upadhyaya, *Sanskrit and Prakrit Mahākāvyas*, Varanasi, V.S. 1992, p. 44. Also *Mahāpurāṇa*, 1.3.6; 1.9.12; 4.31.2 and 38.4.2.
2. Dr. Premi is of the opinion that the poet might have belonged to Berar. *Ibid.*, p. 229.
3. *H.C.I.P.*, Vol. IV, p. 218.
4. दीनानाथधनं सदाबहुजनं प्रोत्फुल्लवल्लीवनं
   मान्याखेटपुरं पुरंदरपुरीलीलाहरं सुन्दरम् ।
   धारानाथनरेन्द्र कोपशिखिना दग्धविदग्धप्रियं
   केदानीं वर्सात करिष्यतिपुनः श्रीपुष्पदन्तः कविः ॥

   —म. पु., संधि 50 की प्रशस्ति ।

Jinendras.[1] Some of the epithets of this great poet as known from his works are as follows :

Kavikula-Tilaka,[2]
Mahākavi,[3]
Kavivara,[4]
Kāvyakāra,[5]
Kāvya-Ratna-Ratnākara,[6]
Kāvya-Piśācha,[7]
Vara-Vāṇi-Vilāsa,[8]
Vimala-Sarasvatī-Janita-Vilāsa,[9]
Sarasvati-Nilaya,[10]
Vāgīśvari-Devī-Niketa.[11]

1. *Mahāpurāna*, 3.5.5-32; 38.12.1-21; 40.4.1-4; 41.4.15-28; 42.4.4-10; 43.5.1-19; 44.4.1-9; 46.3.1-22; 47.7.1-6; 48.6.4-14; 49.6.3-10; 53.5.1-10; 55.5.1-8; 58.5.1-13; 59.3.12-59.4.5; 63.2.7-11; 64.4.1-7; 65.3.6.9; 67.4.12.67.5.8; 68.4.1-14; 80.6.4-11; 87.12.3-11; 94.14.1-14; and 96.8.3-12.
2. 'कइकुलतिलएं सरसइणिलएं'
—*Mahā.*, 38.4.3.
3. 'णिग्गि वण्णउ थिउ जाम महाकई'
—*Mahā.*, 38.2.2.
4. 'इय णिसुणेवि विउद्धउ कइवरु'
—*Mahā.*, 38.2.4.
5. 'हउ कव्वपिसल्लउ कव्वकारि'
—*Mahā.*, 81.2.4.
6. 'भो-भो केसवतणुरुह णवसरुहमुह कव्वरयणरयणार'
—*Mahā.*, 1.4.10.
7. 'ता जंथिउ कव्वपिसल्लएण'
—*Mahā.*, 1.8.8.
8. 'ता जंपइ वरवायाविलासु'
—*Mahā.*, 38.4.3.
9. 'विमलसरासय जणियविलासें'
—*Mahā.*, 1.4.1.
10. 'कइकुलतिलएं सरसइणिलएं'
—*Mahā*, 102.14.4.
11. 'तहुं वाइंसरिदेवीणिकेउ'
—*Nāyakumāracharıu*, 1.2.6.
The order in which the epithets have been indicated above is ours.

This poet declares himself a self-respecting man.[1] He wrote perhaps one more book before coming to Mānyakheṭa, *Kathāmakaranda*, which is now not available.[2]

The *Karakaṇḍa Chariu* of Kanakāmara, admittedly inspired by the poetry of Pushpadanta, is noteworthy for its subject-matter and historical references.[3]

Earlier Apabhraṁśa poets were Svayambhū and Chaturmukha. Svayambhū may be assigned to eighth or ninth century A.D. whose works are *Paumachariu* and *Riṭṭhaṇemichariu.*[4]

(*d*) *Kannada*

The Kannada script, language and literature received impetus and manifested spectacular growth in the period under review. The Kannada alphabet assumed round and beautiful shapes and forms. Epigraphical records engraved in the Kannada script and language were produced in large numbers. Emperors and potentates patronised Kannada learning, language and literature side by side with Sanskrit.[5] Kannada attained productivity and classical dignity. Several poets and authors of note came forth with their monumental literary creations. The Rāshṭrakūṭa rule witnessed a golden age of the Kannada literature.

After Tamil, Kannada possesses the oldest literature in South India.[6] Among the Kannada works of the period may

1. णण्ण हो मंदिरि णिवसंतु संतु अहिमाण मेरु [=अभिमान मे] कइ पुप्फयंतु—*Jasaharachariu*, 1.1.4;
   पुप्फयंतकइणा चुयपंके जइ अहिमाणमेरुणमंके [अभिमान म'रु नामांकित]
   —*Mahā.*, 102.14.11 and
   कं यास्यस्यभिमानरत्न निलयं श्रीपुष्पदंत विना
   —*Mahā.*, Praśasti of ch. 80.
2. 'पइ' णण्णिउ बण्णिउ वीरराउ'
   —*Mahā*, 1.6.11.
3. *HCIP*, Vol. IV, p. 218.
4. K.K. Handiqui, *op. cit.*, p. 7.
5. P.B. Desai (ed.), *A History of Karnataka*, Dharwar, Second edition, 1981, p. 151.
6. T.V. Mahalingam, Sectional Presidential Address, *Proceedings of the Indian History Congress*, Jaipur Session, 1951, p. 108.

be mentioned the *Kavirājamārga* of the Rāshṭrakūṭa king Amoghavarsha I. It is the first literary treatise on Kannada poetics. The early period of Kannada literature extending from the fifth to the ninth centuries, is well reflected in the *Kavirājamārga*. The author mentions several of these writers.

The *Kavirājamārga* contains sentiments as beautiful as they are original. It lays down that a poem, if it is to stand the test of greatness, must deal with nature, and describe the sea and the mountains, the sunrise and the moonrise, the waxing and waning of the seasons. Other themes of poetry are heroic life, romance, adventure, games and festivities; and of course, it is the poetic fire that in the final analysis turns the mere themes into imperishable poetry. Amoghavarsha I throughout illustrates his principles by frequent citations, and it is plausible to assume that he was generally guided in his work by Daṇḍin's Sanskrit classic, *Kāvyādarśa*.

As an author and a patron of letters, Amoghavarsha's name lives as long as Kannada language and literature lives. However, the authorship of this work is disputed between Nṛpatuṅga or Amoghavarsha I, the well-known Rāshṭrakūṭa king of the ninth century A.D. and a poet in his court who had the title of Kavīśvara but whose real name is unknown. The prevalent opinion is that Kavīśvara was the real author; but he was so much benefited by Amoghavarsha in writing this poem that he wanted posterity to think that it was written by his patron only. This practice of a court poet fathering his work on his patron is not quite unknown in the history of Indian literature.[1]

The poet was a member of the court and he was fully conversant with matters relating to administration. Some of the verses are addressed to a king, who is referred to as 'you'. There are also verses which contain praises of a king's liberality and prowess, and some others contain the praise of a king who had the titles of Nṛpatuṅga, Atiśaya-Dhavale,

1. G.S. Dikshit, 'Some Aspects of Administration in the ninth and tenth centuries as illustrated by contemporary Kannada works', *Proceedings of the Indian History Congress*, Nagpur Session, 1950, pp. 121-23.

and Vīra-Nārāyaṇa, and who is no other than Amoghavarsha himself. From all these, it is evident that the poet has introduced as illustrations in his work, verses which he wrote in praise of his patron or in reference to him.

The *Kavirājamārga* is a singular literary composition in Kannada. The very character of this literacy art and the enumeration therein of a good many Kannada writers that flourished earlier, stand testimony to the state of development and maturity which this southern speech attained by this time. It also defines the extent of the Kannada-speaking area from the Godāvarī in the north to the Kāverī in the south. The truth of this statement is vouchsafed by the presence of Kannada inscriptions ranging from the early centuries to as late a period as the fourteenth century throughout this extensive area, and particularly in the northern tracts extending as far as the former river. This is also supported by cultural vestiges. It further speaks highly of the literacy and cultural attainments of the Kannada people of those days :

> Twixt sacred rivers twain it lies
> From famed Godāvarī
> To where the pilgrim rests
> His eyes on holy Kāverī.
> The people of this land are skilled
> To speak in rhythmic tone
> And quick to grasp a poet's thought
> So kindred to their own.
> Not students only, but the folk
> Untutored in the schools
> By instinct use and understand
> The strict poetic rules.[1]

The inscription of Jurā, known as Jurā *praśasti*,[2] of Rāshṭrakūṭa Kṛshṇa III, is an epigraphical landmark of

1. P.B. Desai, *op. cit.*, p. 152. Also *H.C.I.P.*, Vol. IV, p. 221.
2. *E.I.*, XIX, p. 287.

classical Kannada literary composition, with charming poetic diction in polished *Kanda* metre. Its theme is the trimphs of this great monarch in the fields of politics and moral discipline. Here we cite the specimen :

> This lusty Elephant Rider
> uprooted the roots of that proud Chola
> who had extirpated the family of Pāṇḍya,
> whose ancestor of epic fame, a compeer of
> Lord Indra to share his seat on elephant's back,
> had participated in the Bhārata war.
> This Son of Another's wife
> never casts a glance of passion
> on another's wife.
> Adoring her more than his mother
> who nourished him with her milk,
> his mind never lost restraint.[1]

This epoch ushered in the golden age of Kannada literary renaissance heralded by master architects like Nṛpatuṅga, Ādi-Pampa, Nāgavarma, Ponna and Ranna. The last two of these had the privilege of being fittingly honoured by emperors with the illustrious title, 'emperor among poets'.

A prose work, *Vodda-ārādhana*, recently discovered,[2] is probably the earliest of all extant Kannada works. Its author, Śivakoṭyāchārya, was a Jain, and its prose style has been much praised. Like many Jain works, *Vodda-ārādhana*, too has a professedly didactic aim. It seems, however, not to be clearly established that *Vodda-ārādhana* belongs to a period earlier than A.D. 850, the probable date of *Kavirājamārga*. In any case, these two early Kannada works must have clearly been preceded by some centuries of literary activity.

The Jains, Vīraśaivas, and Vaishṇavas have all enriched Kannada literature, and hence it is often divided into three periods, called the Jain, Vīraśaiva, and Vaishṇava periods

1. P.B. Desai, *op. cit.*, p. 152.
2. *H C.I.P.*, Vol IV, p. 222.

respectively. But this is misleading, for the so-called periods overlap considerably and hence this classification is chronologically not of much value. If we take the *Kavirājamārga* of Amoghavarsha I as our starting point, for about three centuries (A.D. 850 to A.D. 1150) Jain predominance seems to be clear enough.

The tenth century brings us to one of the great periods of Kannada literature. It was in this century that the three "gems"—Pampa, Ponna, and Ranna—flourished, and it was in this century that Nāgavarma I wrote the first Kannada treatise on Prosody entitled *Chhandombudhi* or the "Ocean of Prosody", which is even now reckoned as one of the classics on the subject.

Pampa I, or Ādi Pampa (b. 902 A.D.), is usually regarded as the greatest Kannada poet. His father, a Brāhmaṇa, was converted to the Jain faith; and the son remained a staunch Jain. Pampa appears to have been the court poet of a minor prince Arikesari. In A.D. 941, when Pampa was only thirty-nine years old, he composed the two great poems, *Ādipurāṇa* and *Vikramārjuna-Vijaya* (also called, more popularly, *Pampa-Bhārata*). The former of these is a history of the first Tīrthaṅkara,[1] in other words, the first of the brave heroic souls who have crossed the disturbed and muddy sea of human frailty and misery, and reached the shores of unending indefinable peace. The first Tīrthaṅkara, Ṛshabha, for instance, is described as the father of Bharata, the king who gave his name to Bhārata-Varsha, i.e., India. Pampa's *Ādi Purāṇa* tells in a beautiful language the story of Ṛshabha, the first (*ādi*) Tīrthaṅkara.

In his *Pampa-Bhārata* he narrates a number of episodes pertaining to his patron Arikesari and other rulers of the Chālukya dynasty.[2] The majority of Kannada poets appear to have been as familiar with the art of writing as with the art of warfare, and some of them handled the sword and quill with equal facility. Pampa declares that he was not only

1. Written in both ways, *i.e.*, as Tīrthaṅkara and Tīrthakara.

2. P.B. Desai, *op. cit.*, p. 16.

a *Kavi* (poet), but also a Kali (hero)—*em-kaliyo-sat-kaviyo*.[1] Critics unanimously concede him to be the best Kannada poet of his time.

At the root of chivalry, compassion and charity, stood courage and conviction. Chivalry itself was classified into three distinct forms—*yuddha-vīra* (the hero in war), *dayā-vīra* (the hero in compassion) and *dāna-vira* (the hero in munificence). The compassionate and the munificent were required to sacrifice as much as the hero on the battlefield. In Pampa's words :

> He, who cannot uproot enemy kings,
> nor protect those who cling to his feet,
> nor leave an imprint of clarity by parting with
> his gold, yet longs to live—oh Marāntaka,
> should he be called a human or a
> mean worm in the country-fig.[2]

Other famous poets who flourished at this time were Raṇṇa (b. 949 A.D.), the celebrated author of the *Gadāyuddha* (982 A.D.) and the *Ajitapurāṇa* (993 A.D.), Asaṅga and Jinachandra. But Raṇṇa was patronised by Chālukya King Taila II and his successor and so we will not go here with a detailed picture of his writings. They enriched the Kanarese language. Chāmuṇḍāchārya, who was a general of the Gaṅga Kings Mārasiṁha and Rāchamalla IV, composed the *Chāmuṇḍarāya-purāṇa* (978 A.D.), which contains a complete history of the twenty-four Jinas. It is the oldest extant specimen of a book, written in continuous prose.[3]

(*e*) *Telugu*

Many of the Rāshṭrakūṭa kings who encouraged Kannada poets also likewise encouraged Telugu poets. In fact, the

1. S. Settar and Gunther D. Sontheimer (eds.), *Memorial Stones*, Dharwar, 1982, p. 18.
2. Pampa, *Vikramārjuna-Vijaya*. K.V. Puttapa (ed.), Mysore, 1973, V, v. 75.
3. E P. Rice, *A History of Kanarese Literature*, p. 32.

relation between these two literatures has been so intimate that some writers have distinguished themselves equally in both.

Ponna, one of the celebrated Kannada poets, hailed originally from Punganūr in Kammanādu in coastal Andhra. He was a good scholar and an eminent poet in both the Telugu and Kannada languages. He wrote the *Ādipurāṇa* in Telugu, under the name Sarvadeva. The Rāshṭrakūṭa king Kṛshṇa III conferred upon him the title of 'Ubhayakavi-chakravartin' or supreme among the poets of both (Sanskrit and Telugu) languages.[1] Ponna was a Jain. He wrote *Śāntipurāṇa*[2] in Sanskrit, which gives history on the basis of the stories of the sixteenth Tīrthaṅkara. His book *Bhuvanaikarāmābhyudaya* is now not available.

(f) Marathi

About the ninth century the Marathi language which was already the spoken language of the people, was first made the vehicle of written literature. This fact can be corroborated by one of the Shravan-Belagola inscriptions dated Śaka 905.[3] The progress of the Marathi language was further enhanced by the propounders of the Mahānubhāva sect. By the middle of the thirteenth century when the poets Mukundarāja, Jñāneśvara and Nāmadeva wrote their important verses, it

1. M Rama Rao, *Karnataka-Andhra Relations*, Dharwar, 1974, p. 78. Also see N. Venkata Rao, *Andhra-Karnataka Sārasavatamulu-Parasparā Prabhāvamu*, pp. 69-74. But Dr. Moraes in his sectional presidential address a the time of the 15th Indian History Congress at Gwalior, 1952 (*Proceeding Vol*, pp. 116-17) says that this title was conferred upon Ponna for his knowledge in Sanskrit and Kannada. In our opinion Sanskrit seems to be a common language for educated people of that time. Thus M. Rama Rao's version is correct, because the writings of Ponna in Telugu must have been considered an extra merit for him. Moreover, he belonged to the Telugu region too However, A.S. Altekar (p. 412) and K.K. Handiqui (p. 6) are in favour of Sanskrit and Kannada.
2. *Proceedings of the Indian History Congress*, 15th Session, Gwalior, 1952, pp. 116-17.
3. S.G. Tulpule, *Prāchīna Marāṭhī Koriv Lekha* (Marathi), No. 4, Pune, 1964-67, pp. 18ff.

came of age. It was at this time that Marathi attained the exalted status of the court language of the Yadava kings of Devagiri.[1]

(g) Trilingual or Bilingual Inscriptions

There is a tenth-century poetic inscription from Kurkiyal in Karimnagar district of Andhra Pradesh. This unique inscription written in three languages, Sanskrit, Kannada and Telugu, contains an eulogistic account of the great Kannada poet Pampa. It was got written by the poet's brother Jinavallabha who was also a noted scholar of the period.[2]

One bilingual inscription has been found at Oratte in Chingalput district of Tamilnadu.[3] This inscribed hero stone is lying in front of a dilapidated Śiva temple, presently known as Parameśvara temple in the centre of the village. It was engraved in Kannada and Tamil characters and issued in the twenty-sixth regnal year of the Rāshṭrakūṭa king Kṛshṇa III. It records the offering of his head by Kanchaya to the deity Mahādeva (to ward off the calamity to the village during its raid by the soldiers of Kannaradeva).

There is another Tamil inscription available to us at Kuranganilmuttam of North Arcot district in Tamilnadu. Its language is Tamil and it was engraved during the time of king Kannara.[4]

The main Rāshṭrakūṭa empire was spread fully over modern Maharashtra and Karnataka states and partly over Tamilnadu and Andhra Pradesh. If we closely conduct a language survey of the Rāshṭrakūṭa inscriptions found in these states it would be very easy to conclude that people in general and the Rāshṭrakūṭa kings in particular always considered the importance of the local language at the time of engraving any inscription. There is no need of citing the example of an inscription engraved in the Sanskrit or Kannada language.

1. *A Panorama of Maharashtra*, p. 9.
2. P.B. Desai (ed.), *A History of Karnataka*, Dharwar, 2nd revised edition, 1981, p. 12.
3. *Indian Archaeological Review*, 1976-77, p. 62.
4. *Ibid.*, 1974-75, p. 50.

All the inscriptions found in the Maharashtra region are written in Sanskrit while in Karnataka they are written either in Kannada or in Sanskrit. This is quite obvious. We do not find any inscription of Marathi language because during the time of the Rāshṭrakūṭa rule this language had just started cropping up. We have seen above examples of bilingual or trilingual inscriptions found in the transitional zones. We have also seen two Tamil inscriptions[1] engraved on the pillars of the rock-cut Trimūrti cave temple in the village Kuranganilmuttam in the district of North Arcot of Tamilnadu. One of these inscriptions dated in the twenty-fourth regnal year (A.D. 963-64) of the Rāshṭrakūṭa king Kannara, the conqueror of Kachchi and Tanjai, records a taxfree gift of land by the administrative boarder *Ur* of Pallavapuram in Erikilnadu, a sub-division in Kaliyur-Kottam for food offerings to the deity (Tiruvadigal) in the temple called Kalmandagam. The other inscription dated in the twenty-fifth regnal year of the same monarch records a gift of ninety sheep by somebody (details lost) for maintaining lamps in the said temple. To sum up, we can say that most of the inscriptions of the Rāshṭrakūṭa empire were engraved in the local language only, and bilingual or trilingual inscriptions were put in the transitional zones.

Thus we find different languages flourishing in different parts of the Rāshṭrakūṭa empire. In the South the dialects were alien in structure and vocabulary to Sanskrit, therefore, from the beginning, was the language of the learned only influencing the development of the dialects.[2]

1. *Indian Archaeological Review*, 1974-75, p. 56.
2. R.C. Majumdar (ed.), *The Age of Imperial Kanauj*, Bombay, 2nd ed., 1964, p. III.

5

Agriculture and Industry

SECTION I

Agriculture

India's socio-economic base has been oriented towards agriculture. Consequently the majority of the people have always found employment on land. The foremost factor which helped the growth of economic prosperity of the region during the Rāshṭrakūṭa period was the physical background of the Deccan. It also helps us in tracing the chief agricultural commodities grown and the forest wealth that contributed to the growth of economy of that period.

The discovery of the techniques of producing food from land was a major breakthrough in the history of human civilization. Since then agriculture has been a major industry in all countries and at all stages of civilization.

Types of land

The physical condition of land under the Rāshṭrakūṭa empire was almost the same as today. Mainly there were there types of land :

(a) Wet land,
(b) Dry land, and
(c) Hilly or forest land.

The Daṇḍāpur inscription of the Rāshṭrakūṭa king Prabhūtavarsha, dated A.D. 918, records the grant of seventeen *mattars* of land exempted from taxes, and further states that two *mattars* of wet land granted by Kesabbe should meet this tax.[1] From this statement itself we can easily understand that wet land was superior to dry land or ordinary land, because tax of only two *mattars* of wet land equals the tax for seventeen *mattars* of ordinary land. Wet land did not mean inundated land. Here wet land means the land where water for irrigating the crops was easily available, either by natural or by man-made means, and dry land means the land where no facility of water for crops was available. In that case, the cultivation depended only on rain water. Hilly or forest land was wasteland and was under the direct control of the State.

Ownership and Transfer Right of Land

From early times, lands were owned by the royalty as well as by private citizens. The right of cultivating royal lands was held by officials serving under the king as is evidenced by Vaḍḍarśe inscription.[2] Gifting of royal lands to temples and Brāhmaṇs, to private citizens of the agricultural class as also to deceased warriors, was in vogue under the Rāshṭrakūṭas.

The object of Bandora Plates[3] (in Goa territory) is to record the king's grant of one *hala* of *khajjana* lands as well as a piece of land including a house site, a garden and a tank belonging to an unnamed Rāshṭrakūṭa. In addition to this, some land to be reclaimed by clearing the forest (*araṇya-karshaṇa*) by employing four batches of workers (*preshya-kula*)

1. *K.I.*, II, pp. 11-14.
2. K.V. Ramesh, *A History of South Kanara*, Dharwar, 1970, pp. 271-72.
3. *E.I.*, XXXIII, pp. 293-95.

was also granted. The gift was exempted from all taxes (*paṅga*).[1] This inscription further records that the donee Hastyārya would enjoy the produce of the land by putting up a bund to prevent the salt water from entering the field on the sea-shore. This is how the owners of lands along the sea-coast cultivated their lands.

The above mentioned gift was made for securing the welfare and final beatitude of the king as well as of Nāgapadda, Malladatta and Achal. It appears that these three persons were the real donors of the gift and the land etc. belonging to the Rāshṭrakūṭas, appears to have been purchased by them for the purpose of the gift. The expression *khajjana* occurs in some other records of this region. This word is the same as the modern Marāṭhī as well as Konkanī *Khājan* meaning 'a rice field created out of the nullah on a sea-shore by putting embankments after the ebb-tide'. It is interesting to note that this meaning is supported by our inscription in question which states that the donee would cultivate the land by putting up an embankment to prevent the sea water.

The Kāsārśirsi Copper Plate of Dhruvarāja, dated Śaka 705,[2] gives an expression *kṛshataḥ karshayataḥ*. In this expression it can be seen, with an amount of certainty, the roots of the mode of cultivation of the owned agricultural lands some twelve centuries ago. The owned agricultural land could be cultivated personally by the holder (*kṛshataḥ*) or it could be got cultivated with the help of other labour, in some form or other (*karshayataḥ*). There is another alternative for the enjoyment of the fruits of the agricultural lands in addition to *bhuñjataḥ* and *bhojayataḥ*, that is enjoying himself or caused to be enjoyed. It is expressed by the term *pratidiśataḥ* which means otherwise. This leads to the suggestion that this mode of enjoyment of the lands refers to the use of the land by keeping it fallow and appropriating only the grass, fruits

1. This word is found invariably in the inscriptions of the fifth to the fourteenth centuries which indicates a levy in general.
2. *JASB*, XLIII-XLIV (New Series), 1968-69, pp. 94-105.

and foliage of plants and trees, and trees themselves. Such a connotation, the only plausible explanation of the expression is supported by the expression "*tṛṇakāshṭhodakopetasavṛksha-mātānidhinikshepasahita*"[1] meaning that the grant included grass, woods, water, tree-grove and underground stones.

A copper plate charter[2] of the Rāshṭrakūṭa King Kṛshṇa I, dated 23 March, 768 A.D., donates the village of Koregaon (Kumārigrāma) to a group of Brāhmaṇas from Karhad. The river and all neighbouring villages have been recognizably named in the grant, when the locality was under permanent agricultural settlement before the eighth century.[3]

Let us now consider the question whether the land was freely transferable or not. There is sufficient evidence to show that the transfer of land was not an affair with which only the seller and the purchaser were concerned. A record from Saundatti,[4] which is unfortunately fragmentary, records a gift of land to a Jain temple, which was made with the consent of fifty agriculturists. It seems very probable that these agriculturists were the Mahājanas of the locality; if so, it is clear that the sales of the land required the consent of the village community. An inscription from Belgaum district records that when the Raṭṭa ruler Kārtavīrya gave 800 *kammas* of land to a temple at Nesarge, the six headmen of the place received a gift of money 'like that which was customary to give at the time of buying'.[5] It would thus seem that even when the owners of the land were alienating landed property, they had to pay a certain duty to the village headman. This customary gift to the village headmen seems to have been due to the necessity of getting the consent to the village community. The consent of the neighbours also was merely to avoid any quarrel about the boundaries.[6]

There is evidence to show that if a village or land was owned by several cosharers, no new owner could be introduced

1. *E.I.*, XXIII, p. 281.
2. *Ibid.*, XIII, pp. 275-92.
3. D.D. Kosambi, *Myth and Reality*, Bombay, 1962, p. 146.
4. *J.B.B.R.A.S.*, X, p. 208.
5. *Ibid.*, p. 257.
6. *RATT*, p. 363.

except, with the consent of the whole body. The Śivapur inscription of Mahāśivagupta, belonging to *c.* 800 A.D., assigns one-fourth of five villages to fifteen Brāhmaṇas. The grant was hereditary, but on the condition that the grantees and their descendants continued to be men of learning and high moral character. The record expressly adds that if a sharer died heirless, or was ignorant, or immoral, his share was to be assigned to some other relative by the remaining cosharers, and not by the king.[1]

Unit of Land Measurement

Our records speak about grants of land. Sizes of granted lands are expressed in different terms : *kamma*, *mattar*, *nivartana* and *veli*. Though our list may not be exhaustive but uses of *mattar* and *nivartana* have occurred more frequently.

In an inscription from Mulgund, we find a king named Kanna granting six *mattars* in Pareyaloku to the west of the boundary of Sugandhvatī or modern Saundatti[2] A record from Soratur,[3] dated 951 A.D., records the gift of twelve *matters* of land made by the officer of the division for the *maṭha* there. In the Bhujjabeśvara temple at Hebbal in Dharwar district there were five dancing girls in the middle of the tenth century, each one being assigned four *mattars* of land for her maintenance.[4]

The Konnur inscription of Amoghavarsha I[5] states that at the request of his favourite general, Bankeya, he gave to a Jain temple twelve *Nivartanas* of land. The above mentioned Mulgund inscription also mentions a grant of twelve *Nivartanas* of land situated in the *Śivaṭa* of that village. Mahāsāmanta Pṛthvīrāma, a contemporary of Kṛshṇa II, is said to have erected a Jain temple in *c.* 875 A.D. His grandson was also a

1. *E.I.*, XI, p. 192.
2. *JBBRAS*, X, p. 199.
3. *I.A.*, XII, p. 253.
4. *RATT*, p. 295.
5. *E.I.*, VI, p. 29.

Jain, but the latter's grandson was a follower of Hinduism and is known to have made a grant of twelve *Nivartanas* of land to his preceptor who was well versed in the three Vedas. The educational institution at Śālotgi had an endowment of twelve *Nivartanas* of land, necessary for meeting the lighting charges of the institution; and the pay of the principal of the college was the income from the fifty *Nivartanas* of land. Dr. A.S. Altekar estimates one *Nivartana* equal to five acres of land. The Lohārā grant of Govinda III also gives the measurement of land in *Nivartanas*.[1]

A Belgaum district inscription records that the Raṭṭa ruler Kārtavīrya gave 800 *Kammas* of land to a temple at Nesarge.[2] In the list of several South Indian Inscriptions we find the land measurement given in terms of *veli*.[3] This term was more common in the Tanjore region. The Rāshṭrakūṭas had sway up to Ceylon also, though temporarily; hence we have included this unit of measurement current in Tamil Nadu at the time. However, more common terms were *mattars* and *Nivartanas* as indicated above.

Dr. (Mrs.) Shobhana Gokhale[4] gives some information about the unit of land measurement. They are *dhur*, *khandika*, *prastha*, *adhak and pal*, which were also common in the Rāshṭrakūṭa period. *Dhur* (= 1/20th of a *bigha*) has occurred in the Chinchini plate[5] of Indra III. But it may be noted that the Kandhār inscription records the purchase of a *khandika* of oil and 4½ *khandikas*[6] of salt from the neighbouring grāma-katakas to meet the requirements of the college situated on the bank of river Nandi. Hence the use of *khandika* as a unit of land measurement is doubtful.

1. *E.I.*, XXIII, p. 213.
2. *JBBRAS*, X, p. 257-
3. *S.I.I.*, Nos. 1, 3, 4 & 5 etc.
4. In a seminar under the auspices of the Mythic Society of India, Bangalore, January 1977.
5. *E.I.*, XXXII, pp. 61-75.
6. *E.I.*, XXXV, p. 111.

Main Crops

The climatic conditions of the Deccan during the period of the Rāshṭrakūṭas were hardly different from now. On this assumption we are in a position to say that cotton was produced in a large quantity. Cotton-yarn and cloth are mentioned among the articles of export from Bharoach by the *Periplus*[1] in the first century A.D., by Marco Polo in the thirteenth century[2] and by Tavernier in the seventeenth century.[3] It is obvious that in our period too this region must have been producing cotton, as it does even today.

Indigo is known to have been extensively exported from Gujarat and Thana in the thirteenth[4] and seventeenth[5] centuries A.D. and the crop was probably raised in our period too.

The *Abhidhanaratnamālā* refers to an amazing variety of foodgrains and cereals including rice, barley, wheat, sugarcane, etc. This fact is also testified to by the Arab travellers and writers who were very much struck by the fertility of the soil and the rich variety of products grown in India. Their testimony with regard to the conditions is particularly relevant to western India with which they were familiar.[6]

The chief crops in the Deccan must have been *jawari*, *bajri*, oilseeds, coconuts, betelnuts, rice,[7] sandal, teak, ebony wood etc.[8]

Arab traveller, Ibn-Hauqal (956 A.D.)=350 H informs us that here honey is also produced in large quantity.[9] Sugarcane too was one of the main crops of the region.

1. Schoff, *The Periplus of the Erythrean Sea*, London, 1912, p. 39.
2. Cordier, *Yule's Travels of Marco Polo*, London, 1926, p. 393.
3. Tavernier, *Travels in India*, Calcutta, 1905, p. 52.
4. Cordier, *op. cit.*, pp. 393 and 398.
5. Moreland, *From Akbar to Aurangzeb*, London, 1923, p. 160.
6. T.V. Pathy, *op. cit.*, p. 39.
7. S.S. Nadvi, *op. cit.*, p. 64.
8. *RATT*, p. 354.
9. S.S. Nadvi, *op. cit.*, p. 64.

Fruits and Spices

Sulaiman Saudagar (851 A.D.=237 H) expresses surprise and says that in India there are all varieties of fruits but there is no tree of *chhuhārā*. He further says that here is one fruit which is not found in his country. It is mango. Ibn Hauqal also praises mango. He says that mango-lovers of India should know how much respect is there for mango in the eyes of the Arabs.[1]

Masudi writes—"Orange and lemon are particular products of India. From India they took them to Arabia, but the tastes differ."[2]

Coconut and betel-nuts also find mention in the Arab accounts. In these accounts we invariably find the mention of cardamom, clove, nutmeg, bay leaf, etc. These things were harvested in surplus quantities so that they were easy to export.[3]

Garden and Forest

The Rāshṭrakūṭa empire had vast stretches of waste lands, forests etc. Several inscriptions belonging to the period under review explicitly mention grants of flower and fruit gardens to the temples. For instance, the Konnur inscription of Amoghavarsha I refers to the grants such as flower garden situated in Taleyar village and twelve *Nivartanas* of land from each of the thirty villages in one sub-division made over to a Jain temple.[4]

Forests yield an immense wealth by way of timber, fruits, spices and a variety of herbs. Indian traders carried a brisk trade in sandalwood, teakwood, shishum and ebony with countries like Egypt, Mesopotamia, etc. It is interesting to note that Indian teak is found in Ur and in the palace of Nebuchadanezzar (sixth century B.C.).[5] The Arab traders had

1. *Ibid.*, pp 27 & 63.
2. *Ibid* , p. 63.
3. *Ibid.*, pp. 54-56; 62-64.
4. *RATT*, p. 237.
5. H.G. Rawlinson, *Intercourse between India and Western World*, Cambridge, 1916, p. 3.

settlements in the Rāshṭrakūṭa territories. It may be, therefore, concluded that the Rāshṭrakūṭa kingdom which included vast areas of forest such as the Western Ghats, the sandalwood forests of Mysore and the teakwood areas of the Chanda and Balharshah, produced an immense wealth.[1]

Prices of agricultural lands and their produce have been discussed in detail by Dr. Altekar.[2] The discussion on this aspect of agriculture would be merely a case of repetition, and so we would not take up this aspect here.

Irrigation Works

The Rāshṭrakūṭa empire included river systems such as the Narmadā, Tāpti, Godāvarī, Kṛshṇā and Tuṅgabhadrā. It is interesting to note that from the earliest times, all civilizations and empires flourished on river banks, as water is the main source of nourishment. Therefore it may easily be concluded that the river water must have helped the irrigation system also. Further, the inscriptions from Tondaimandalam[3] during the period of its occupation by Kṛshṇa III, suggest the construction of irrigation tanks and canals on a large scale.

A survey in the Karnataka State[4] reveals that there were four tanks constructed, one renovated and thirty-three referred to in the Rāshṭrakūṭa inscriptions. There have been found references to ten ponds too. In this survey references to four channels and one well have also been traced. Here Dr. G.R. Kuppuswamy's study is based on the *Epigraphia Carnatica* series and limited to south Karnataka only. He has given tables for districtwise performances of each dynasty. He tries to prove that the regions which were closer to the capital were more benefited than the other regions. He also lays stress on the point that the less work done in a region does

1. T.V. Pathy, *op. cit.*, p. 40. Also S.S. Nadvi, *op. cit.*, p. 27.
2. *RATT*, pp. 378-94.
3. T.V. Pathy, *op. cit.*, p. 39.
4. G.R. Kuppuswamy, 'Irrigation System in Karnataka Dynastic Analysis', *JKU*, XVI-XVII, pp. 75-86.

not always mean that the emperor did not show interest in that region; maybe, he did not get adequate cooperation from the local people. Secondly, environmental factors there must have also contributed towards such result.

So far as the local public support is concerned, we have instances to show that the people did not lack in supporting works of their own interest. An inscription of A.D. 918 from Daṇḍapur[1] records that the people of that place resolved upon collecting levies in order to maintain in good repair a big irrigation tank in that area. The levies were : three *drammas* on each Brāhmaṇa marriage, two on each *upanayana*, one on each Śūdra marriage, and one *paṇa* on every occasion of a *prāyaśchitta.* Numerous instances of such voluntary levies by particular sections, guilds or merchants, caste organisations, and so on, for serving more or less limited purposes may be gathered from the inscriptions.[2]

Agricultural Taxes

The ownership of culturable lands was vested in private individuals and families. The state could confiscate them only if the revenue demand had not been complied with. The taxation structure under the Rāshṭrakūṭas was more or less similar to that in northern India. Land tax, variously called as Udraṅga or Bhogakara, was the sheet anchor of the government finance. Its incidence was about 25% and it used to be generally collected in kind in two or three instalments. Lands given as grants to Brāhmaṇas and temples were taxed at a lower rate. Petty taxes in kind were collected on fruits, vegetables etc.; they were called Bhogakara and were usually assigned to local officials as part of their pay. Octroi and excise duties were levied on a number of articles; these were collected sometimes in cash.[3]

1. *I.A.*, XII, p 223.
2. R.C. Majumdar and K.K. Dasgupta (eds), *A Comprehensive History of India*, Vol. III, Pt. I, p. 741.
3. A.S. Altekar, *State and Government in Ancient India*, Delhi, 1958, pp. 363-64.

Examples of assessment on the whole village are not lacking. The Bevinahalle inscription of the time of Rāshṭrakūṭa Khoṭṭiga tells us that the revenue of the two villages, *viz.*, Madhur and Malagavādi, was fifty gadyāṇas.[1] But the assessment of land revenue was generally on individual holdings. Local assignees in their turn had made their arrangements to assess the individual holdings, within their jurisdiction. This is evident from the following example. In A.D. 941 "The thousand (mahājanas) of Kumbhise (Susmi in Shimoga district of Karnataka) made the following settlement for each *mattar* of low lands on the old channel, the paddy of the two channels. For the paddy fields from which the water is cut off cultivation to cease."[2]

Dr. A.S. Altekar states that land tax was usually collected in kind and rarely in cash.[3] The learned scholar has rightly pointed out that "...the taxes in kind were those realised from lands and those in cash from other sources."[4] Thus, for example, we have the instance of the actual taxation of a village in Gangawadi which used to pay tax of 20 Kalañjus and 2000 measures of paddy.[5] In this case, 2000 measures of paddy was the land revenue and the 20 Kalañjus might refer to the income from miscellaneous taxes. Similarly, in the case of Beli-ūr in Gangawadi province, the revenue assessed was 80 gold coins and 800 measures of paddy in A.D. 887.[6] Of this, 800 measures of paddy alone might refer to the land revenue and tax in gold might refer to the commercial taxes etc. But, with regard to the Cambay Plates of Govinda IV,[7] which mention the average land revenue of each one of the 1400 villages to be 500 *suvarṇas*, Dr. Altekar argues that "the Dharmaśāstras laud to the skies gifts of gold and land, but not of corn; that may have been another reason for

1. *E.C.*, XI, Chitradoorga, No. 74.
2. *E.C.*, VIII, Sb. No. 83.
3. *RATT*, p. 226.
4. *Ibid.*
5. *I.A.*, VI, p. 94.
6. *Ibid.*, p. 103.
7. *E.I.*, VII, p. 26.

starting the revenues of these villages in gold rather than in corn."[1] But this does not explain as to why the other records of the same time mention land revenue in corn and not at all in gold. There is another difficulty in accepting Altekar's argument that the land revenue was "usually collected in kind and rarely in cash" during the time of the Rāshṭrakūṭas. In the epigraphs of this period *siddhāya* is invariably calculated in gold coins and rarely in measures of corn. For example, an inscription from Daṇḍapur, dated 918 A.D., mentions that the chief *dvijas* gave joyfully as an income to *perggere* of the place from out of the village revenue in gold.[2] For this another explanation may be offered. In all the above cited examples the revenue assessed was on the entire village lands and not on individual holdings. With regard to the collection from individual holders, it appears that in the same village some cultivators might have paid in cash and others in kind. And it is true that the revenue of 1400 villages mentioned in the Cambay Plates, stood for the collection of land revenue in both cash and kind. It may be suggested here that in the local records entries of the receipt of the tax was made both in terms of cash and units of corn. And while making the same entries of tax, collections in the central register were calculated in terms of gold coins. Thus, it may be concluded that, as in earlier times, during the Rāshṭrakūṭa times also land revenue was collected both in cash and kind, and there was no rarity collection in cash as suggested by Altekar.

According to Appadorai, the formidable list of taxes in the epigraphical sources has led the scholars to conclude that the burden of taxes on the people was very heavy and they were expected to pay a large number of taxes. But a careful and critical examination of records would reveal that the burden of all taxes did not fall on one and the same individual, but was properly distributed among the various sections of the society. In case of taxes being imposed arbitrarity or heavily, they were opposed too. The Roṇa inscription of the time of Rāshṭrakūṭa King Kṛshṇa III,

1. *RATT*, pp. 226-27.
2. *K.I.*, II, pp. 11-13.

dated A.D. 942,[1] records an interesting historical fact that certain Būtayya, an officer, laid siege to Roṇa for collecting certain taxes such as *bhattaya* and *perohi* (?) and for establishing the right of using the village threshing floor (*kaṇa*). The record further states that at the instance of the Mahājanas of the place, he was opposed by one Pampayya of *Vāji-kula* who in the tumult lost his life.

Time of Agricultural Tax Collection

The land revenue was usually collected at the time of the harvest only. Thus the harvest time may be regarded as the commencement of the revenue year. From a passage in the *Vaśastilaka-champū* it appears that the ministers and officials in-charge of land revenue collection were instructed to approach the cultivators for the same at the time of harvest only.[2]

Exemption from Taxation

Exemption from taxation has been claimed as a privilege of the learned Brāhmaṇas in most of the Smṛtis. But in our records we find exemption from taxation for general agriculturist people during the time of natural calamities like famines.[3] There are some direct instances to show that the assessment of land revenue was revised on certain occasions. The Banvāsi inscription of A.D. 941[4] refers to a fresh settlement necessitated by the drying up of an old irrigation canal. Thus it appears that during the time of drought and drying up of canals and tanks, the Rāshṭrakūṭa rulers were obliged either to revise or remit the land revenue.

Sometimes taxes were exempted on certain happy occasions like the coronation, birth of a child, etc. For

1. *Yaśastilaka*, XI (i), p. 22.
2. *Yaśastilaka*, Book III, p. 172; also K.K. Handiqui, *op. cit.*, p. 30.
3. A.S. Altekar, *State and Government in Ancient India*, Delhi, 1958, pp 363-64.
4. *E.C.*, VIII, Sb. No. 83.

instance, an epigraph of the Rāshṭrakūṭa King Kṛshṇa III and the Cambay plates of Govinda IV record the grant of 1800 villages free from all imposts on the occasion of their respective coronations.[1]

Love for Cattle

Cattle-taming is a part of agricultural life in India. Most of the pet animals serve people in their own way. Cow, ox, buffalo, horse, dog etc. are usually tamed for milk, manure, drawing cart or ploughing land and guarding property. Here we are not going to find out the names of animals tamed by the people of our period, but we wish to see how they showed love and sacrifice to these useful animals.

At the places of large gatherings or maket places food and water for the cattle were arranged by the State. In the fragmentary inscription at Kandhār[2] we find that arrangements were made for the provision of two tankfuls of water (*jala-droṇyau*) and troughtfuls of fodder for the cattle (*go-grāsaḥ*) at five places, *viz.*, (i) the market of Gurjars (*Gūrjar-āpaṇa*), (ii-iv) the temples of the deities Vīranārāyaṇa, Śrīkṛshṇeśvara and Kshetrapāla, and (v) the much frequented market place (*kshuṇṇahaṭṭikā*). To meet the expenses of the above, the amount of fifty *drammas* was allotted per day.

Honouring the noble souls who laid their lives for a noble cause and erecting memorials to perpetuate their memory is an old-age practice common to all times. In our period, memorial stones were set up in the memory of the heroes who died even in fights involving cattle-lifting or *go-grahaṇa*. Examples of such memorials (*vīragals*) are many. Of the two hero-stones of the ruler of Palasige-12000 country, one at Tambūr (932-33 A.D.) mentions the Rāshṭrakūṭa monarch, Govinda IV, and his feudatory, Kanniha mahārāja, and records the death of Anniga of Tambūr in battle; the other of the same family, found at Kiravatti (984 A.D.), mentions that when the *mahārāja* (name lost) was ruling the country

1. *E.I.*, VII, p. 36.
2. *E.I.*, XXXV, p. 108.

of the Palasige-12000, and Sariyabbarasī was administering Kiravatti, a certain hero died in a scuffle arising out of a cattle-raid.[1]

Mention must be made here of a stone set up to commemorate the heroism, not of a human being but of a devoted animal, the dog. This inscribed slab is found at Ātkūr[2] in Karnataka state. It describes the famous battle of Takkolam between Rāshṭrakūṭa Kṛshṇa III and the Chola prince Rājāditya. In this battle which Kṛshṇa III won, Gaṅga Būtuga II, a subordinate of the king, pleased with the valour of his servant Manalara, presents him a dog named Kālī. Once this dog attacked a wild boar obviously to protect his master, and in the fight lost his life. The affectionate master commemorated the heroism of the dog by setting up the stone on the top of which is depicted the fight between the two animals.

These two examples are enough to show how people during the Rāshṭrakūṭa rule sacrificed their lives in protecting cattle just out of sheer love for them, and perpetuated the memory of their pet animals.

SECTION II

Industries

There were several factors which helped the growth of economic prosperity of the Deccan during the Rāshṭrakūṭa period. The economic life of the people was largely conditioned by the physical background of the country. The mineral wealth also determined the structure of economic activity. Megasthenes of the late fourth century B.C. pointed out the working system of mines such as gold, silver, copper, iron, red lead, mercury, manganese, mica and also an amazing variety of precious and semi-precious stones.[3] This is

1. S. Settar (ed.), *Memorial Stones*, Dharwar, 1982, p. 222.
2. *E.C.*, III, Md. 116 & 22; VII, Sk. 159; VIII, Sb. 232; IX, Bn. 32; X, Sp. 82; XV, Hn. 128-29 and *S.I.I.*, IX, 37.
3. J.W. McCrindle, *India as described by Megasthenes and Arrian*, London, 1877, pp. 36-38.

corroborated by his contemporary Kauṭilya's *Arthaśāstra* wherein it is stated that superintendents were appointed to supervise the mines and to manufacture copper, tin, lead, mercury, brass etc. Yet another superintendent was entrusted with the exploitation of the ocean mines such as shells, diamonds, precious stones, pearls and corals.

Mineral Resources and Industries connected with them

The mineral resources coupled by the agricultural produce boosted industry, and the surplus goods were traded both within and also outside. Agriculture, industry, and trade and commerce were interdependent and complementary to one another and they greatly increased the prosperity of the people.[1] As discussed earlier, agriculture was the main industry of the people.

In mineral wealth, the Rāshṭrakūṭa empire was perhaps richer than any region in India. It is interesting to note that right from the Indus Valley period, gold was supplied from the Kolar gold mines (Karnataka) and Ramāgiri gold mines (Anantapur District, Andhra Pradesh).[2] Again, the diamonds of Kohinoor and Vajrakarur in Andhra Pradesh are famous even today and the geological conditions could hardly differ over a time lapse of a thousand years. Copper and iron have been found in the districts of Cuddapah, Kurnool, Bellary, Chanda, Ahmadnagar, Bijapur and Dharwar.[3] Some of the areas in the Deccan, it is reported, contain huge deposits of gold, diamonds and iron even in modern times. It may be pointed out that copper was highly valued in those days and was perhaps costlier than now. Its large-scale use is vouchsafed by the discovery of several copper objects from the historic levels of the deposits excavated at Nasik, Jorwe, Nevasa, Bhokardan and Ter.[4] Extensive use of copper for

1. T.V. Pathy, *Elūra: Art and Culture*, New Delhi, 1980, p. 39.
2. R.C. Majumdar (ed.), *The Vedic Age*, p. 184
3. A. Ball, *A Manual of Geology of India*, Pt. III, Ch. V.
4. H.D. Sankalia and others, *Report on the Excavations at Nasik and Jorwe*, Poona, 1955, pp. 188-9; *From History to Pre-History at Nevasa*, Poona, pp. 409-22 and S.B. Deo, *Excavations at Bhokardan*, Nagpur, 1974, pp. 180-84.

household purposes is clearly shown by the rich variety of vessels, spoons, etc., uncovered in the excavations referred to.

More prolific than copper deposits, there are rich aggregations of precious and semi-precious stones in the Deccan. Prior to the commencement of the Rāshṭrakūṭa rule, the traders of this region traded in a variety of beads prepared out of precious and semi-precious stones such as amethyst, garnet, topaz, sapphire, jasper, agate, chalcedony, carnelian, crystal, etc. Some of the excavated sites in the Deccan have not only yielded thousands of such beads but also revealed the existence of factories where such beads were wrought. Furthermore, there are several stone moulds and sharpeners used for the manufacture of beads. Beads of different shapes reported from excavations have also got parallels in the paintings of Ajantā[1] and the sculptures of Elūra.[2] The necklaces, ear-reels and pulleys, armlets, waist ornaments and head jewellery depicted in the Ajantā paintings and Elūra sculptures are bedecked with such precious stones. Therefore, it is very clear that the mineral wealth of this region was thoroughly exploited by the artisans and that there was a brisk trade in surplus goods. The mineral deposits extensively found in the hilly tracks of Ajantā, Elūra, the Western Ghats, Cuddapah. Kurnool and Golconda continuously yielded good quality of minerals for metal industries.

The above description gives a fairly good idea about the existence of mineral resources in plenty in the Rāshṭrakūṭa territories. Naturally, it accelerated the setting up of industries. Industries in ancient times were run by guilds of workers, skilled persons and artisans who inherited family skills. The organisation of trade and workers' guilds helped the growth of production, trade and commerce, which has been discussed in the next chapter. The contemporary evidence is insufficient to study the growth of industry. Yet one may

1. M.K. Dhavalikar, *Ajantā: A Cultural Study*, Poona, 1970, pp. 68-70 and Plate XXXV.
2. T.V. Pathy, *op. cit.*, Plate XXII.

conclude on the basis of literary and epigraphical evidences that industry was well developed.

Agate and carnelian stones, worked into a variety of bowls, knife-handles, paper-weights, beads and bangles were exported from Bharoach. Such raw materials were available in plenty in Cambay and Ratnapur. This industry was known from the days of Pliny.[1] It is interesting to note that ivory carving was well-known in certain parts of the Deccan. The three ivory figurines reported so far from Ter,[2] in Osmanabad and Bhokardan[3] in Aurangabad and third from Pompeii in Italy, suggest common source and identical workmanship. It may also be assumed that the establishment of industries, particularly in the absence of quick transportation, depended mainly on the availability of raw materials.

The industries based on mineral products were mainly for the production of vessels and utensils, ornaments, war weapons, agricultural tools, tools for village industries, etc. Other industries also contributed to the growth of production and thereby augmented the economy of the region. Science and technology were, without doubt, very well advanced, right from the Gupta period. The Pālas of Bengal and the Cholas of Tanjore, the two important contemporaries of the Rāshṭrakūṭa rulers, were great patrons of art and learning, during whose period bronze images were cast on a large-scale uprecedented in the art history of India.

Mānyakheṭa, the Rāshṭrakūṭa capital, which was much nearer the diamond fields, must have been the main industrial centre for producing precious stones in beautiful shape and size.

Mysore was very rich in elephants and so we may well presume that it may have been a centre of ivory industry.[4]

Textile Industry

As stated earlier, the Rāshṭrakūṭa kingdom comprised

1. George C.M. Birdwood, *Industrial Art of India*, London, 1915, p. 219.
2. Douglas Barret, *Ter*, Bombay, 1960, p. 8.
3. S.B. Deo, *Excavations at Bhokardan*, Nagpur, 1974.
4. *RATT*, pp. 356-57.

predominantly black cotton soil conducive to the growth of textile industry. *The Periplus of the Erythrean Sea* refers to Bharoach and Damarike *i.e.* Dravid country as the main exporting centres of cloth. The manufacturing centres in this region were Gujarat, Ujjain, Paithan, Bhokardan[1] and Tagara (Ter). Literary references are made to different varieties of textiles, such as fine and rough varieties of cotton fabrics, woollen and hempen yarns.[2] Medhātithi states that widows and destitutes were gainfully engaged in weaving and lace-making.[3] Paithan, the capital city of the Sātavāhanas, continued to be an important centre for textile. Paithan, known as Pratishṭhānabhukti[4] in the grants of Govinda, was famous for Paithani sarees, woven out of pure silk and jari, fine texture and durability. Similarly. Tagara was known for producing muslins and mallow cloth. Tagarapura figures prominently in the Śilāhāra epigraphs.[5] It is fairly interesting to note that the recent excavations carried out to Bhokardan,[6] Paithan and Ter show that several hundreds of bone and ivory points were used for weaving purposes. Marco Polo and Tavernier have noted that Gujarat, Thana, Warangal and Burhanpur were the prolific centres of textiles and produced fine varieties of calicos. The Indian muslins are proverbial for their diaphonous texture.

Leather Industry

Like the textile industry, tannage must have been in a flourishing condition in Maharashtra. According to Marco Polo Thana and Bharoach exported leather in large quantities to Arabia and to the Persian Gulf.

By virtue of his visit to Kanbaya (Cambay) in A.D. 915, Masudi is able to give us a fairly good description of the

1. S.B. Deo, *op. cit.*, p. 8.
2. R.C. Majumdar (ed.), *op. cit.*, p. 595.
3. *On Manu-Smṛti*, IX.75.
4. *E.I.*, I, pp. 52-58.
5. *I.A.*, VI, p. 73; *E.I.*, III, pp. 269, 273.
6. S.B. Deo, *op. cit.*, p. 605.

conditions prevailing then. He names the local ruler, Bania, who is said to have governed Kanbaya on behalf of the Ballahara (Skt. Vallabharāja, *i.e.*, the Rāshṭrakūṭa king). He describes the ebb and flow near Kanbaya, also the famous shoe-industry which flourished here and adjoining places of Sandan and Bubara.[1] Shoe-makers were treated as semi-untouchables.[2]

Sugarcane Industry

The area of the Rāshṭrakūṭa empire today is very rich in sugarcane growing. The Kolhapur-Ratnagiri region is today well known for its *gur* and sugarcane industry, and the Kolhapur *gur* is famous throughout India. It will be interesting to see how old this industry is in this area. It is difficult to answer this question in so far as the upper limit is concerned in the absence of any evidence on the point. However, we have definite evidence to show that this industry was in a highly developed state in this region at least from the eleventh century A.D., the evidence consists of certain place names occurring in a few inscriptions of the Śilāhāras, the Rāshṭrakūṭas and the later Chālukyas of Kalyāṇa. We are here interested only in the evidence from Rāshṭrakūṭa inscription.[3]

The Nesāri plates of the Rāshṭrakūṭa king Govinda III, dated A.D. 805, state that the emperor donated the village of Nesarikā in the Chandagaḍa *vishaya* to a Brāhmaṇa hailing from Ikshugrāma.[4] The donated village is probably identical with the modern Vasgaon in the Dapoli Taluk of the Ratnagiri

1. K.A. Fariq, *Ancient India in Arabic Literature* (Urdu), New Delhi, 1973, p. 182. Also S.S. Nadvi, *op. cit.*, p. 55.
2. R.C. Majumdar & K.K. Dasgupta (eds.), *A Comprehensive History of India*, Vol. III, Pt. II, New Delhi, 1982, p. 985.
3. Ajoy Mitra Shastri, 'Fresh light on the Antiquity of the Jaggery and Sugar Industries in Southern Maharashtra', in Madhava N. Katti (ed.), *Studies in Indian Place Names*, I, Mysore, 1980, pp. 43-46.
4. *Sources of the Medieval History of the Deccan*, Vol. I, p. 21, text line 47.

district of Maharashtra. As indicated by the first Sanskrit constituent of the name, the village was perhaps famous for its sugarcane crop. It is interesting to note that the first part of the present name of the village also has the same connotation in Marathi. The evidence derived from the place-name goes well with the fact that the Ratnagiri region is even now reputed for *gur* and sugar industry.

Coir Industry

While Sulaiman does not mention cocount, Masudi, Istakhri and Hauqal state that it was grown in Malabar, Dibjat islands, Sarandib and in places near Thana. A very important industry was connected with cocount fibre, and India supplied coir threads to West Asia for use in ships. Coir industry was probably in existence in India during the tenth century A.D.[1]

Boat Industry

We cannot deny the fact that in the Rāshṭrakūṭa period there were considerable shipping activities. Thus there must have been some industry for boat-making.

Abu Zaid, the Arab traveller of the ninth century, indicates that cocount area is famous for ship or boat-making. There carpenters get heavy work. They cut coconut tree and then they allow it to dry up. After it is dried up fully and seasoned, they make planks out of it. They make ropes with the help of coconut bark. With these two things they make boat and its mast. Coconut leaves are woven for the purpose of oar.[2] Thus coconut tree served the complete purpose of boat-making.

1. A.K. Nizami, *India in the early Arabic Travelogues* (unpublished thesis of Bombay University), 1978, p. 224.
2. S.S. Nadvi, *op. cit.*, p. 62.

Oil Mill Industry

The oil mill industry was also a major industry, which catered to the needs of the common man, temples and royalty, as it is referred to so frequently. In one of the records of our period we find mention of one *ulakku* (*okkalu*) of oil to be supplied per day as long as the moon and the sun endure instead of thirty kalañjus of gold.[1] We also find sesame oil as one of the items of export in Arab accounts.[2]

Bangle Making

The making of bangles was an important industry though references are found only to bangle sellers.[3] H. D. Sankalia states that glass bangles came during the Bahmani period.[4] He refers to Ajantā paintings and says that in no case it is possible to single out any specimen as made of glass. Thus according to him, the existence of glass bangles prior to the fourteenth century cannot be proved archaeologically, from literature, sculpture and paintings.[5] But Sanskrit and Kannada literary sources prove the existence of glass bangles, much earlier. In *Yeśastilaka* we find mention of glass bangles (*sphaṭikavalaya*).[6]

Other Industries

Though we do not find evidences of their existence as an industry in our records, but many other things are found in Arab accounts, such as mats, bamboo, sal wood, perfumes, betel nuts etc. among the articles of export.[7] Until and unless

1. *E.* ., XXVI, pp. 230-35.
2. *RATT*, p. 354.
3. *E.C.*, VIII, p. 235.
4. *BDCRI*, VIII, pp. 252ff.
5. *Ibid.*, p. 254.
6. K.K. Handiqui, *op. cit.*, p. 120.
7. S.S. Nadvi, *op. cit.*, pp. 55 and 57-58.

they nre produced in surplus quantities, it is practically not possible to export them. On this assumption we can very easily think of industries connected with the manufacture of these items. Hence those industrial units may be for betel-processing, rope making, mat making and basket making etc., perfumery manufacture and so on. These industries are quite possible in the Rāshṭrakūṭa region, because raw materials for these industries are readily available there. Rāshṭrakūṭa temples built of stone slabs remind us of industries connected with stone cutting.

6

Trade and Commerce

D.C. Sircar, while addressing the Indian History Congress as its General President remarked[1]: "Of the few theories popularised during (recent times),[2] mention may be made of the belief that the feudal system began to develop in India and reached its climax during the period 300-1200 A.D. as is supposed to be indicated by the paucity of coins and the consequent shrinkage of trade. As a matter of fact, however, many of the most powerful monarchs and prosperous kingdoms flourished in our country during this period. Contemporary Arab merchants refer to the Rāshṭrakūṭa king of the ninth century as one of the greatest rulers of the earth, comparable to the Chinese emperor and the Khalifa of the Muslim world and his Gurjar and Pāla neighbours as maintaining even larger forces, the Pāla army having included fifty-thousand elephants and ten to fifteen thousand washermen. They also speak of silver coins prevalent in the Rāshṭrakūṭa kingdom and Gurjar riches as well as of muslin

1. 'Some Problems of the Study of Early Indian History', *Proceedings of the Indian History Congress*, Vol. 41, Bombay Session, 1980, p. 7.
2. Here he used 'this period' by which he meant the latter part of the current century.

and other articles of trade". This statement is a clear hint on the status of trade during our period under discussion.

A. Appadorai[1] has made exhaustive use of the Arab sources for a study of trade. Arab sources have been recently re-assessed by many scholars like G.F. Hourani,[2] W.H. Siddiqui,[3] S.S. Nadvi[4] etc. Further new information about the internal trade in India and trade between India and the Eastern Archipelago through Rāshṭrakūṭa centres is to be found in a recently edited Prākṛt text *Kuvalayamālā* of Uddyotanasūri[5] who wrote it in 779 A.D. Somadevasūri's *Yaśastilaka*[6] also contains some information about trade which has not been made use of by earlier scholars. All this new information added to the fresh study of the old material gives a much fuller picture of the trade of the Rāshṭrakūṭa times than the one we had earlier.

Arab-Rāshṭrakūṭa Trade Relations

The Rāshṭrakūṭas and the Abbasid Khalifas were two great contemporary powers in the eighth, ninth and tenth centuries. Though we do not have any Rāshṭrakūṭa accounts of the Arabs, we have Arab accounts of the Rāshṭrakūṭa rulers, dominions and the people in those dominions and also what these people thought of the Arabs. From these accounts, it is clear that each had great respect for the other. Sulaiman (9th century) says, "The inhabitants of the

1. A. Appadorai, *Economic Condition in South India* (1000-1500 A.D.), Vol. II, Madras, 1936, pp. 485-513.
2. G.F. Hourani, *Arab Seafaring in the Indian Ocean in Ancient and Medieval Times*, Princeton N.J., 1951.
3. W.H. Siddiqui, 'India's Contribution to the Arab Civilization', *India's Contribution to World Thought and Culture*, Vivekanand Rock Memorial Committee.
4. Syed Sulaiman Nadvi, *Arab aur Bharat ke Sambandh* (Hindi translation by Ram Chandra Verma), Prayag, 1930; also 'Arab Navigation', *Islamic Culture*, XV, 1941, pp. 435-38; XVI, 1942, pp. 72-86, 192-98 and 402-22.
5. A.N. Upadhye (ed.), *Kuvalayamālā*, Bombay, 1970.
6. K.K. Handiqui, *Yaśastilaka and Indian Culture*, Sholapur, 1949.

Balhara's country say that if their kings reign for a long time, it is wholly in consequence of the favour shown to the Arabs. In fact among all the kings there is no one to be found who is so partial to the Arabs as Balhara and his subjects follow his example."[1] Khurdadba (early tenth century) says, "The greatest king of India is the Balhara". He also seems to account for his greatness in the following way : "On his ring is inscribed the following sentence 'what is begun with resolution ends with success'."[2] Al-Idrisi, a Moroccan traveller of the eleventh-twelfth centuries, who based his work on earlier writings, says in an oft-quoted passage, "The Indians are naturally inclined to justice and never depart from it in their actions. Their good faith, honesty and fidelity to their engagements are well-known and they are so famous for these qualities that people flock to their country from every side; hence the country is flourishing and their condition prosperous."[3]

The Arab name was as much respected in India as the Indian name was respected in the Arab countries. The Arabs were allowed to erect their mosques and celebrate their prayers publicly. They not only participated in our export and import trade, but also took part in the internal trade within South India.

Ports and Indian Coast

When the Caliphs established a world-wide empire, their capital Baghdad became a great commercial centre. To bring goods from India by way of the Persian Gulf to this capital, a few sea-ports and river-ports became prominent. Basra at the head of the Persian Gulf came to be known as the Gateway of India. An equally big port which subsequently overshadowed Basra was the port of Siraf also on the Persian Gulf. The

1. H.M. Elliot and J. Dowson, *History of India*, Second edition, Calcutta, 1956, pp. 4-5.
2. *Ibid.*, p. 17.
3. *Ibid.*

city of Ubla at the confluence of the Tigris and the Euphrates became an attractive emporium of Indian commodities. There were many other markets and godowns of Indian woods like teak.[1] On the Indian side, confining ourselves to the Rāshṭrakūṭa dominions, the Arabs mention Subara (Sopara), Siolan (Sanjan), Saimur (Ghaul) and Sindabur (Goa).[2]

Kalyāṇa which was a natural port of export for the northern Deccan was the next port of importance. It was one of the five important ports trading in cloth, brass and black wood logs. Naosari, Dabhol, Jayagad, Devagad and Malvan were other ports of minor importance, engaged chiefly in coastal trade.[3]

Coast of Komkom : Most of the Arab writers mention Komkom or Konkan. According to Sulaiman the Balhara kingdom begins on the sea coast, called the country of Komkom.[4] The coast of Komkom is said to belong to the Balharas.

A perusal of the Arabic passages shows that the coast of Komkom was well-known to the Arabs by virtue of their long maritime association with it. Komkom is to be identified as Konkan, the coastal land between Thana and Goa.

It appears in the Sanskrit texts and ancient edicts as Konkana, whence is derived the Arabic Komkom. Konkan played a prominent role in the development of the Rāshṭrakūṭas' commerce.

Coast of Thana and adjoining places : A lot of references are made in the Arabic writings to the coast of Thana, which was dotted with a number of cities and ports. The most famous cities on the coast of Thana and the adjoining region were Thana, Subara, Sandan, Saimur, Sandbur, Kanbaya and Barus, which were regularly visited by the Arabs

1. W.H. Siddiqui, *op. cit.*, p. 581.
2. Maulana Syed Sulaiman Nadvi, *Arab aur Bharat ke Sambandha* (Hindi translation by Babu Ramchandra Verma), Prayag, 1930, pp. 46-47.
3. A.S. Altekar, *op. cit.*, p. 358.
4. *Silsilat*, I, p. 28 as quoted in A.K. Nizami, *India in the early Arabic Trevelogues* (Unpublished thesis), Bombay, 1978, pp. 40-42.

in connection with trade. Every Arab writer has thrown light on the conditions of these cities. During the ninth and tenth centuries A.D. they were wealthy and prosperous cities.

Among the travellers with whom we are concerned, Masudi traversed widely on the coast of Thana. Around 303 A.H., *i.e.*, 916 A.D., he was in Kanbaya (Cambay) and Thana region. Sulaiman, Istakhri and Hauqal too possibly visited this region. They mention this coast and its ports and cities.

The accounts of Thana and adjoining places given by other writers aɪe equally elaborate and interesting. Most of the narratives and Buzurg's *Ajaibal Hind* carry useful details regarding the coast of Thana. The Sicilian geographer, besides others, presented a detailed picture of the coast of Thana and other places. His accounts are quite informative.[1]

Thana was intimately known to the Arabs during the ninth and tenth centuries A.D. By this time a large number of Muslims had already settled in this region and their colonies came up. Buzurg cites many persons who were deeply knowledgeable. Such people were handy to get information.[2]

Trade Routes

The *Kuvalayamālākahā* of Uddyotanasūri was completed on 21 March, 779 A.D.[3] It was composed at Jāwālipur which is identified with Jalor, 120 km from Jodhpur on the left bank of the Sukarī river. It is very remarkable that the trade centres and the trading activities of the Rāshṭrakūṭa empire are frequently mentioned in this book. The importance of Sopara and Paithan was so well-known that they have occurred at several places in Uddyotanasūri's description.

In his narrations of voyages fourteen searoutes have

1. *Ibid.*, p. 42.
2. *Ibid.*
3. Prem Suman Jain, *Kuvalayamālākahā kā Sāṁskṛtika Adhyayana* (Hindi), Vaishali, 1975, p. 6.

been traced,[1] out of which five routes originate from Sopara:

1. Sopāraka to Babbarakula (65.33),
2. Sopāraka to Svarṇadvīpa (66.1),
3. Sopāraka to Chīna and Mahā-Chīna (66.2),
4. Sopāraka to Mahilārājya (Tibet) (66.3),
5. Sopāraka to Ratnadvīpa (66.4).

In the period of our discussion these voyages were very difficult and risky. Persons who took these voyages were only those who wanted to earn money through overseas trade. They took with them goods of their own places and sold them at higher prices in the foreign countries and used to bring back foreign goods at very cheap rates to sell them in their own country at very higher rates; and thus their earnings were manyfold.

Trade inside India was carried on mostly through land or river routes. On a keen analysis of the materials contained in the *Kuvalayamālākahā* as many as twenty-eight routes have been noticed.[2] Many of them passed through the Rāshṭrakūṭa empire or at least touched the periphery of the empire, which may be enumerated below:

1. Ayodhyā to Vijayapurī (mod. Vijayadurga in Ratnagiri district)[3] passing through Kośāmbī, Vindhyāṭavī, Narmadā river, Sahyādri, Chintāmaṇi-pallī and Kāñchī.
2. Ujjayinī to the Narmadā river.
3. Vārāṇasī to Pratishṭhāna and from Pratishṭhāna to the bank of the Narmadā.
4. Takshaśilā to Sopāraka passing through Dakshiṇā-patha.

1. *Ibid.*, p. 211.
2. *Ibid.*, pp. 216-17.
3. *Ibid.*, p. 72.

5. Sopāraka to Kosala, Uttrāpatha, East Country, Vārāvatī and Babbarakula.
6. Vindhyāvāsa to Bharukachchha.
7. Vindhyāṭavī to the Narmadā river in the south direction.
8. From Deva Aṭavī on the south bank of the Narmadā to Bharukachchha.

These routes were very popular in those days and utilized by the trading community too.

Sixteen itineraries[1] are olso given by Al-Biruni of the early eleventh century A.D. The information seems to have been communicated to him by the Sultan Mahmud, who had marched on some of these roads with huge armies. In addition, the information was also probably derived from merchants, sailors, pilgrims and travellers both Hindu and Muslim.

Out of these sixteen trade routes the following route numbers were concerned with the Rāshṭrakūṭa empire:

Route No. 4 : From Kanauj southward, as far as Benvasi on the south coast, this route touched at Gwalior and Kalanjar and passed through the realms of Kajurah (Khajuraho) and Mannakara (Balhara), *i.e.*, Mānyakheṭa.

Route No. 8 : From Dhar towards the Godāvarī, the road went to Bhumihara, Kand, Namuvur (on the banks of the river Neribudda) Alispur (Ellichpur) and reached Manlagir on the banks of the Gadavar (Godāvarī).

Route No. 9 : Dhar to Tana (Thana) on the Indian Ocean. The route lay across the Mahratta-Desh (Maharashtra) and the province of Kunkan to reach Thana, its capital.

Route No. 10 : From Bazana to Somnath on the South Coast of Kathiawar. On the way lay Anhilwara (Pattan).

Route No. 11 : From Pattan to Thana, on the west coast. This route passed through Bhiroj (Broach).

1. Nafis Ahmad, *Muslim Contributions to Geography*, Lahore, 1947, pp. 143-45.

Though the period of Al-Biruni is slightly later than the period of the Rāshṭrakūṭas, these routes were not new. They must have been common routes for the people of the Rāshṭrakūṭa period also. Here, in the above-mentioned routes we have included the route passing through Gujarat also, because a minor Rāshṭrakūṭa dynasty ruled in that region.

Indian Commodities and their Popularity[1]

Sulaiman says that extremely fine Indian cotton cloth which could pass through a small fine ring was imported by the Arabs and distributed throughout the then known world. Pratishṭhāna (Paithan) and Tagara (Ter) continued to be the centres of trade. These cities were the principal centres of the cloth trade. Besides these, the principal centres in the Deccan were Minnagar, Gujarat and Ujjain. Paithan and Warangal were and still are, particularly famous for their muslins.[2]

Of the kinds of wood sent from India, teak came first. According to Ibn Rosteh, teak was exported from the Rāshṭrakūṭa kingdom of western India where it was extensively grown.[3] This tree at that time furnished the inhabitants of Siraf with the wood of which they built their houses. It was also used in ship-building by the Arabs.

Al-Istakri (A.D. 951) refers to Indian drugs, perfumes and condiments. The Arabs imported a sort of poison which was called Besh. This word appears to be a corruption of *visha* or poison. It must have been used in the making of drugs. The Arabs also imported black salt in large quantities. Masud and Bushari say that fine shoes of Cambay were very much liked by the Arabs. Indian swords of different varieties were variously termed as *Saif, Muhamud, al-hind, Hinai, Hinduani*, and *Handuvani.*

1. W.H. Siddiqui, *op. cit.*, pp. 581-82.
2. A.S. Altekar, *op. cit.*, p. 356.
3. *H.C.I.P.*, Vol. IV, p. 403.

Indian commodities became very popular in Arabian countries. We may learn this from their equivalents in the Arabic language. Indian *mushk*, *henna* and *ood* were popularly known as *Hindi*. *Kapur* became *kafur*, *pippal*, *filfil* and *sagawan*, *saj*. "The love of Arabs for Indian commodities and everything connected with India was so much that they used to name their favourite fair daughter as *Hinda* and *Saifi-Hindi* after their dreamland India".

The most important article of import into India from the Arab countries was the horse. The *Kuvalayamālākahā*, a Prākṛt work written in A.D. 779 enumerates eighteen kinds of Indian horses. The Arabs supplied three kinds of horses which they called *Voltaha*, *Kayaha* and *Seraha*. The Arab traders supplied good horses. Gradually the names of Indian horses as given by Bāṇa and Daṇḍin were taken away from the market and were replaced by Arabic names, until at last the *Mānasollāsa* and Hemachandra in *Abhidhānachintāmaṇi* completely left out Indian names and replaced them by Arabic names.[1]

According to Dr. Gode,[2] the first reference to the Arab horse occurs in Jayadatta's *Aśvavaidyaka* (*c*. Śaka 972= A.D. 1050) where the Tājika has been mentioned along with Pārasīka. Tājī is an Arabic word meaning Arab country and also Arab horse. It is to be noted that the original Arabic phoneme Tājī has been adopted in the Sanskrit works in the form of Tājika, belonging to Tājī, Arabia.[3]

The Arabs who came to India were not motivated either by political ambitions or missionary zeal; and their main business was trade handed down to them by their forefathers from pre-Islamic times. In the Deccan the Muslims found conditions congenial to them. Friendly intercourse existed

1. A.N. Upadhaye, *op. cit.*, p. 116.
2. P.K. Gode, 'Some references to Persian Horses in Indian literature from A D. 500-1800', *Poona Orientalist*, XI, Nos. I & II; also G.H. Khare, *Sources of the Medieval History of the Deccan*, Poona, 1930.
3. Devising Chauhan, 'Arab Horses in India', *A.B.O.R.I.* XLVIII-XLIX, pp. 391-94.

between the Deccan and the Muslims of South-West Asia. Hindu kings who wanted Arab horses gave encouragement to Muslim traders. The Rāshṭrakūṭa king Amoghavarsha I ordered that the Muslims within his kingdom should not be molested. They were allowed to construct mosques in the country.[1]

Among the articles of export were included mats, hides, indigo, incense, perfumes, betel-nuts, coconuts, sandalwood, sesame oil,[2] ivory, clove, nutmeg, pearl, pepper, bamboo, rattan, mace, cardamom etc., diamond, elephant, rhinoceros, peacock etc.[3] and among the articles of import were dates, gold, Italian wine and small quantity of copper, tin, lead, topaz, storax, sweet cloves, flint glass, antimony, gold and silver coins, singing boys and girls etc.[4]

Slave Trade

Slave trade is quite different from the trade items mentioned above, and so we intend to give it a separate treatment. This trade continued before and after the Rāshṭrakūṭa period; we are, however, restricting ourselves to our own period itself.

There are some literary works, which throw light on slave trade. Mention may be made of the following : the *Niśīthachūrṇi* (*c*. seventh century A.D.), the *Samaraichchakahā* (*c*. first half of the eighth century A.D.), the *Kuvalayamālākahā* (779 A.D.), the *Gaṇitasārasaṅgraha* (850 A.D.), the *Upamitibhava prapañchakathā* (905 A.D.), the *Kathākośa* (*c*. tenth century A.D.), and several other works of the later period. The Muslim and the Arab accounts, such as the *Futuhu-l Buldan* (892-93 A.D.), and many other writings of the following centuries also supply information about the problem in

1. T.V. Mahalingam, Sectional Presidential Address, *Proceedings of the Indian History Congress*, Jaipur Session, 1951, p. 104.
2. A.S. Altekar, *op. cit.*, p. 358.
3. Saiyad Sulaiman Nadvi, *op. cit.*, pp. 55; 57-58.
4. A.S. Altekar, *op. cit.*, p. 355 and also S. S. Nadvi, *op. cit.*, pp. 67-8.

question. Though not many, some Indian inscriptions of the early medieval period available in the *Epigraphia Carnatica*[1] contain materials relating to slave trade. A few other inscriptions also throw light on the internal slave trade of this period.[2]

With the contacts of the Arabs and the Turks the slave trade, along with trade in general, witnessed a vigorous increase. In spite of the prescription of the *śāstras* to the contrary, trade and traffic in slaves were gradually increasing as a lucrative profession during the tenth-twelfth centuries. These slaves were mainly used for domestic and luxury purposes.[3]

Out of the above-mentioned literary works, the author of *Gaṇitasārasaṅgraha*, Mahāvīrāchārya was patronised by the Rāshṭrakūṭa king Amoghavarsha I. Mention of trade in female slaves and high prices for the girls of younger age here indicates the probability of slave girls brought for luxury purposes.[4] The evidence of slave trade in the literary works of our own period clearly proves that this practice was in vogue during the Rāshṭrakūṭa times as well.

Internal Trade

From the *Kuvalayamālākahā*, we get a pen picture of trade within India in Rāshṭrakūṭa times and in Rāshṭrakūṭa centres. It contains the account of a *Sārthavāha* (merchant) in Takshaśilā by name Dhanadeva, nicknamed as Lobhadeva because of his greed. He told his father that he wanted to increase his family wealth by trading in Dakshiṇāpatha. He took his caravan from Takshaśilā to Śūrpāraka which was the biggest port then on the west coast. Lobhadeva camped with an old *Śreshṭhin* there. In due course, he sold horses which

1. Vols. III, V and VIII, etc.
2. O.P. Srivastava, 'Slave Trade in Ancient and Early Medieval India', *P.I.H.C.*, 39th Session, Hyderabad, 1978, pp. 124-36, especially p. 125.
3. *Ibid.*, p. 132.
4. P. 89.

he had brought and earned enormous wealth. In Śūrpāraka, there was a guild of local merchants (*Deśi Vaniya Meli.* Whenever a merchant from outside came, a reception was held in his honour. The reception also served the purpose of acquainting the local merchants with the condition of trade in different parts of the country and even outside. Lobhadeva went to the club with his host to narrate his experiences and receive the formal presents, *gandha*, *mālya*, and *tāmbūla*. Local traders started talking about their respective adventures[1];

> "I went to Kosala with a troop of horses, and brought back an elephant in exchange", the first merchant said.
>
> "I went to Uttarāpatha with betel-nuts, and brought back horses in exchange", said the second.
>
> "I went to the eastern country (probably Assam) with pearls, and brought fly-whisks", said the third.
>
> "I went to Dvārāvatī, and brought conch-shells from there", said the fourth.
>
> "I went to the coast of Barbaricum (Sindh) taking fabrics with me, and brought pearls (probably of Persian Gulf) and ivory (of Africa)", said the fifth.
>
> "I went to Suvarṇadvīpa (Sumatra) taking flowers to the Palāsa tree, and brought gold from there", said the sixth.
>
> "I went to Chīna (Indo-China) and Mahāchīna (Mainland China) taking buffaloes and a kind of deer, and brought back silk," said the seventh.
>
> "I went to Ratnadvīpa with leaves of the *Nimba* tree, and brought gems from there," said the eighth merchant.

The above is a graphic picture of the commercial life of India during the eighth century, when Indian traders carried on a brisk commerce from Takshaśilā to Sumatra and

1. A.N. Upadhaye, *op. cit.*, pp. 31-32, 11c-19; also see Prem Suman Jain, *op. cit.*, pp. 190-192.

from China to Barbaricum or Sindh through the Rāshṭrakūṭa port of Śūrpāraka which was to India then what Bombay is at the present moment. Dr. Buddha Prakash in his paper 'An eighth century Indian document on international trade' has studied this trade conference in detail.[1]

The *Yaśastilaka* informs that the silk and cotton garments from Kosala were famous in Mānyakheṭa.[2]

We also find an account of a mart or an emporium described in Somadeva Sūri's *Yaśastilaka*, written in A.D. 959 at Gangadhara when Kṛshṇa III was celebrating his vistory over the Cholas at Melapāti. "The mart *Peṇṭhāsthāna* was furnished with tents, containing many compartments and large stores of merchandise, with stalls for cattle nearby. Water, fodder and fire-wood were easily available, and the establishment covered an area of four miles. It was closely guarded by troops, and protected by moats, gates, walls and ramparts and had avenues with arrangements for water-supply, eating houses, assembly halls and ware-houses for different classes of commodities. Gamblers, whoremongers, jesters and dancing masters were excluded from the precincts of the mart. Here merchants from many countries were allowed to carry on their business, rates of toll and rent being extremely moderate."

This mart was maintained by one Śrībhūti, a private individual. Somadeva's *Nītivākyāmṛta* (19.21) says that there were also state marts and observes that a mart 'maintained with justice' is a source of endless profits to the king. The toll at this mart was not at excessive rate, and whatever was stolen by thieves from the mart was to be restored by the king from his own treasury.[3] Thus these emporia gave proper facilities and protection to merchants. It is probable that this institution was responsible for the growth of trade and the high reputation for justice which the Indians then had acquired.

1. *Bulletin of the Institute of Traditional Culture*, Madras, 1970.
2. K.K. Handiqui, *op. cit.*, p. 92.
3. K.K. Handiqui, *op. cit.*, pp. 119-20.

One of the water-tanks and free fodder centres for cattle is stated to have been made near the shop of the Gurjars who may have been the people of that name settled in different parts of western India. Their presence at Kandhār may be compared to that of the merchants of Bhillamāla (mod. Bhinmal) in the Jodhpur district (Rajasthan), at Sanjan in the Thana district of Maharashtra as indicated by the Chinchini plates of the time of Kṛshṇa III himself.[1] This record also helps us in understanding the inland trade of that time.

Position of Traders

The *Mahāpurāṇa* of Pushpadanta throws welcome light on the relation between the king and the traders of his country. The traders had full freedom to enter the royal court.[2] Not only this, the king even encouraged them to have nuptial relation with his daughter.[3] It is a clear indication of the king's cordial relation with the traders.[4] In support of this fact we would like to place here the following argument too. In the famous Kailāsa temple of Ellūra the first idol which we meet in this temple is of goddess Lakshmī, though the main shrine is of Lord Śiva. By putting goddess Lakshmī, the chief deity of traders, at an important place, the Rāshṭrakūṭas have shown their importance.

Trade guilds played an important role in the economic growth of the country, and they acted as the trustees of

1. *E.I.*, XXXV, p. 111.
2. मगहाहिउ अत्थाणि बइट्ठउ, केण वि वणिणा पण विवि दिट्ठउ ।

—*Mahā* , 8 2.2.5.

3. तहु णिय सुय दिण्ण पिहिवीसुंदरि वामें ।

परिणिय पसयच्छि णं मिलंति रइ कामें ॥

....।

अवरु वि तहु दिण्णउ उद्धरज्जु ॥

—*Mahā.*, 101.14.21-101.15.3

4. udarshan Mishra. *Mahākavi Pushpadanta aur unkā Mahāpurāṇa*, Vaishali, 1987, p. 185.

endowments. Not only did they supervise such grants but also alienated large sums and lands to the temples. The trade guilds had a chain of continuity till the medieval period. Some of the inscriptions belonging to the Rāshṭrakūṭa period refer to the trade guilds. Lakmeśvar inscription records the grant made by the headman of a weaver guild for the maintenance of the local temple.[1] The term *seṇi* is undoubtedly a corrupt form of Sanskrit *śreṇī*.[2]

In this connection, it is worth quoting the opinion of a contemporary foreign authority, Al-Utbi. He says that "the kings of Hind, the chiefs of that country and rich devotees used to amass their treasures and precious jewels and send them time after time to be presented to idols, that they might receive a reward for their good deeds and draw near to their gods."[3] This piece of information is well corroborated by the inscription of Kṛshṇarāja, the excavator of the famed Kailása temple at Ellūra.[4] Here in this description, in our opinion, the rich devotees are none but the members of big trading houses.

Somadevasūri,[5] strangely enough, advises against the appointment of Brāhmaṇa and Kshatriya *amātyas*. He seems to be suspicious of the caste privilege of the Brāhmaṇas and the military character of the Kshatriyas. This injunction against these two higher castes may be attributed to the Jain prejudice against Brahmanic privileges and to the progress of trade and commerce in the Rāshṭrakūṭa empire.[6] But it is very doubtful whether the advice of Somadeva was actually enforced anywhere in that kingdom.

Paṭṭaṇkuḍi Plates of Śilāhāra Avasara II, dated Ś 910,[7] gives the names of three merchants, *viz.*, Nāgai-śreshṭhin, Lokai-śreshṭhin and Ādityavarman, who paid 40 *dīnāras* as a

1. *E.I.*, VI, p. 166.
2. *JKU*, VI, p. 196.
3. A.S. Altekar, *op. cit.*, p. 289.
4. *I.A.*, XII, p. 159.
5. *Nītivākyāmṛta*, 18.22-24.
6. B.B. Mishra, *Polity in the Agni-Purāṇa*, Calcutta, 1965, p. 100.
7. *E I.*, XXXVII, pt. II, pp. 56-60.

present (pūda—pūjā) to king Avasara II for obtaining the confirmation of their hereditary rights over villages Kimjala and Pulīsa[1] described as their source of maintenance (*jīva-loka*). It is here stipulated that in return these merchants should annually remit two lakhs of betel-nuts towards the expenses of the royal bag of betel-nuts (haḍap). It is also specified that the share received by Nāgai-śreshṭhin would be free from the taxes (*namasya*). This transaction was arranged with the knowledge of several officers who included *haḍap* and some committees like hañjamāna.[2]

Paṭṭaṇakuḍi is a place in Chikodi Taluk of Belgaum district, where the above-mentioned inscription was found. The date of the inscription was fifteen years after the extinction of the Rāshṭrakūṭa empire, but it gives the genealogy of the imperial Rāshṭrakūṭas from Kṛshṇa II to Karkka II. Moreover, this region was under the Rāshṭrakūṭas during their hey-day. Thus it may be presumed easily that the Silaharas (Avasara II) were one of the feudatories of the Rāshṭrakūṭas who later became independent. Thus the condition described in this charter was very true to the Rāshṭrakūṭa empire and period.

Dr. R.S. Gupte has convincingly analysed about 266 inscriptions found in the Western Indian Caves, and has convincingly shown that donors belonged to diverse professions and hailed mostly from the trading communities.[3] This analysis also proves the sound economic condition of the traders and their relative position in the society.

Coins and Currency System

Coins and currency system are the instrumental keys for the enforcement of any trade activity. Unfortunately, we do not have any coin available with us claimed to be of the

1. Whether these two terms denote names of villages or refer to any kind of land is not certain.
2. For details *E.I.*, XXXV, p. 291.
3. R.S. Gupte, *The Iconography of the Buddhist Sculptures (Caves) at Ellora*, Aurangabad, 1964, pp. 117-19.

Rāshṭrakūṭa period. It does not, however, mean that the trade and commerce was based on the barter system. We do have references to coins in our epigraphs and literary works of the time.

In our epigraphical sources, references are found to the terms *gadyāṇa* and *gadyaṇaka* as early as 733 A.D.[1] and 754 A.D.[2] respectively, and the same terms continued to be referred to in the inscriptions of the Rāshṭrakūṭas.[3] But by far, the most common term found in the records of this period is *dramma* which occurs profusely in the records of the Rāshṭrakūṭas and in those of other dynasties also.

We come across references in various areas to the sale of land in terms of *gadyāṇa*,[4] endowments made[5] or excise collected in *drammas*[6] and fines imposed in *kāṇam*.[7] But there is as yet complete absence of any specimen which may correspond to any of these coins. The term *gadyāṇa* has often been taken to represent a gold coin of 48 *ratis* on the evidence of Bhāskarāchārya's *Lilāvati*.[8] But, no coin-type available at present strictly corresponds to the standard of the *Lilāvati*.

Before going into a detailed discussion of the coin names, let us tabulate the coins available for our period in an alphabetical order. Obviously, the list[9] is not exhaustive,

1. *E.C.*, XVI, No. 75.
2. *E C.*, III, p. 7.
3. *E.I.*. XIII, p. 338.
4. *E.I.*, III, pp. 5 and 7.
5. *I.A.*, XIII, pp. 135-37.
6. *E.I.*, II, pp. 13-14.
7. *E.I.*, XX, pp. 46ff.
8. Brajadulal Chattopadhyaya, *Coins and Currency System in South India c. A.D. 225-1300*, New Delhi, 1977, p 119.
9. This list for the Rāshṭrakūṭa dominions and the Rāshṭrakūṭa period (roughly) has baen prepared by ourselves on the basis of, and out of the materials provided in, B.D. Chattopadhyaya's *Coins and Currency System in South India c. A.D. 225-1300*, Appendix I, 'A list of coin-names compiled from South Indian epigraphs', pp. 163-186. Categorisation and arrangement of coin-names in an alphabetical order and entries under a particular coin-name in a chronological order are entirely ours. Numbering too is consequently independent.

	Coin Name	Place	Date	Reference
	1	2	3	4
(I)	DHARAṆA			
	Roṇada-poṁdharaṇa	Dharwar	971-72	*I.A.*, XII, p. 256.
(II)	DRAMMA			
	Damma	Dharwar	970	*E.I.*, XVI, p. 258.
	Dramma	Mandya	907	*E.C.*, III, Mandya 14.
		Dharwar	914	*K.I.*, II, pp. 13-14.
			970	*E.I.*, XVI, p. 258.
		Nanded	936-37	*E.I.*, XXXV, pp. 107-108.
		Thana	997	*E.I.*, III, pp. 270, 276.
	Hera-dramma	Shimoga	991	*E.C.*, VIII, Sorab 479.
	Kariya-dramma	Dharwar	956-57	*I.A.*, XII, pp. 257-58.
	Vyavahārika-śreshṭhi	Thana	*c.* 950	*E.I.*, XXXII, p. 60, 1.38.
	Gambhuvaka-dramma			
(III)	GADYĀṆA			
	Gadyāṇa-ponnu	Coorg	887	*I.A.*, VI, p. 103.
	Paramesti gadyāṇa-ponnu	Cuddapah	9th-10th Century	*E.I.*, XXXVI, p. 67.

	Poṁ-gadyāṇa	Bijapur	8th Century	*S.I.I.*, XV, No. 453.
		Dharwar	945	*E.I.*, XIV, p. 366.
	Roṇada-aru-gadyāṇa	Dharwar	971-72	*I.A.*, XII, pp. 255ff.
(IV)	KĀṆAM	Trichinopoly	First half of 9th Century	*E.I.*, XX, pp. 46-52.
		Tinnevelly	*c.* 874	*E.I.*, XXI, p. 105.
		North Arcot	First half of 10th Century	*E.I.*, XXV, pp. 234-35.
(V)	KĀRSHĀ-PIṆḌA	North Kanara	Middle of 8th Cent.	*E.I.*, XXI, p. 179.
(VI)	KĀŚU			
	Īlak-Kāśu	Tanjore	936-37	*S.I.I.*, XVII, No. 466; *A.R.S.I.E.*, 1924, p. 231; *S.I.I.*, V, No. 720.
	Kāśu	South Arcot	988	*E I.*, XXI. p. 170.
	Palan-Kāśu	Trichinopoly	9th Cent.	*E,I.*, XX, pp. 46-52; Cf. *A.R.S.I.E.*, 1928, p. 66.

(*Contd.*)

1	2	3	4
(VII) MĀSHA	Chingleput	959	*E.I.*, XXVII, p. 303.
(VIII) MĀSAKA	Tanjore	10th Cent.	*S.I.I.*, III, pp. 257-58.
(IX) NISHKA	Chingleput	959	*E.I.*, XXVII, p. 303.
(X) PAṆA	Mysore	*c*. 750	*E.C.*, VI, Heggadadevan-Cote, No. 4.
	Mandya	*c*. 907	*E.C.*, III, Mandya, No. 14.
(XI) PON, PONNU			
Urkkarchemmai-pon	Chingleput	2nd half of 9th Century	*A.R.S.I.E.*, 1911, B. 262 (p. 79); *Ibid.*, 1913, p. 8, Nos. 158-59.
Ṭulaip-pon	Ṭanjore	Close of 10th Cent,	*A.R.S.I.E.*, 1912 (245 of 1911).

	Aneya-ponnu	Bellary	987	*S.I.I.*, IX (I), No. 75.
	Dharaṇa-ponnu	Bellary	987	*Ibid.*
	Gadyāṇa-ponnu	Coorg	887	*I.A.*, VI, p. 103.
	Paramesti gadyāṇa-ponnu	Cuddapah	9th-10th Century	*E.I.*, XXXVI, p. 67.
(XII)	RŪPAKA			
	Rūpaka	Nasik	709-10	*E.I.*, XXV, p. 235.
	Kṛshṇarāja-rūpaka	Nasik	709-10	*E.I.*, XXV, pp. 232 & 235.

because it would be an impossible task for an individual to do that. Nevertheless, an attempt is being made to study here with dates and distribution areas. The sources where the coin names compiled here occur, have also been listed in the last column. Unfortunately, the meaning of the majority of the terms is unknown.

A.S. Altekar has tried to analyze the weight of these coins and their approximate cost also.[1]

In the present list we have also included specimens slightly from outside the dominions and the time of the Rāshṭrakūṭas, but they would naturally help us in a distinct and clearer manner to understand the coinage prevalent during our period.

In addition to *dramma* and *gadyāṇa*, we also get references to *suvarṇa*,[2] but it is strange that so far not a single coin of this type belonging to the Rāshṭrakūṭa period has been discovered. The Cambay plates of Govinda IV state that on the occasion of his *paṭṭabandha* ceremony he bestowed on the Brāhmaṇas of different *agrahāras* three lakhs of *suvarṇa* coins and on temple eight hundred villages, four lakhs of *suvarṇas* and thirty-two lakhs of *drammas*.[3] The mention of golden bars (*suvarṇasalākha*) given as *Dakshinā* by Vibhurāja is very important. Nothing is known as to whether the bent bars bore any mark similar to the bent bars which were noticed at Taxila. G.S. Dikshit[4] has observed that no similar currency was known to have been current in this area. The Chinchini plates[5] specify the payment in coins minted by a trader named Śreshṭhi Gambhurak. It appears that this trader of Samyan enjoyed a licence for minting coins on behalf of the ruling authority.

Sulaiman, Masudi, Istakhri and Hauqal, the Arab writers, describe Tatariya coins. The first two of these writers tell us that they were current in the kingdom of Jurz and Ballahara (Rāshṭrakūṭa). Others write that they were in use

1. A.S. Altekar, *op. cit.*, p. 363.
2. *E.I.*, XXXVI, p. 266.
3. *E.I.*, VII, p. 26.
4. *E.I.*, XXIX, p. 174.
5. *E.I.*, XXXII, p. 57.

in Mansura, Khandahar and other places.[1] Anyway, this coin was also current in the Rāshṭrakūṭa empire definitely. Sulaiman while praising the Rāshṭrakūṭas writes : "They have coins also. On it there is a mention of king's year which begins with the date of his coronation."[2]

Maximum reference to a coin name which occurs in our records of the Rāshṭrakūṭa period is the reference to the *dramma*. It is a Sanskrit form of the Greek word *drachma* which denoted the weight of a coin. It was the unit of a coinage in Greece. Its weight was 67.5 grains. Some of the silver coins issued by Indo-Bactrian kings were *drachma* weighing about 65 grains. The Indo-Greeks also issued hemi *drachmas*, which were later limited to silver coins by the Śaka Kshatrapas, the Guptas. Traikūṭakas and the early Kalachuri king Kṛshṇarāja. The term *dramma* is not, however, noticed in early Sanskrit literature or inscriptions. The hemi-drachmas of Kalachuri Kṛshṇarāja were known as Kṛshṇarāja rūpakas.[3]

The earliest mention of the coin *dramma* is in the Kanheri Cave inscription of Pullaśakti,[4] dated Śaka 765, which belongs to the reign of Amoghavarsha I. According to Kielhorn's reading, this inscription records first some gifts to the Buddhist Saṅgha of Kanhagiri (mod. Kanheri) in *drammas* and in the last line, one more of 120 Kāñchana *drammas*. From this A.S Altekar infers that the gifts mentioned first were those of ordinary or silver *drammas* and that mentioned in the last line was of gold.[5]

Now the question arises whether *drammas* were ever known as gold coins. The only evidence so far known about the currency of gold *drammas* is the afore-mentioned Kanheri inscription. However, V.V. Mirashi on the basis of his fresh reading of this inscription has disposed of the wrong notion

1. A.K. Nizami, *India in the early Arabic Travelogues* (Unpublished Thesis), Bombay University, 1978, p. 226.
2. Maulana S.S. Nadvi, *op. cit.*, p. 24.
3. *C.I.I.*, IV, p. 151.
4. *I.A.*, XIII, p. 136.
5. A.S. Altekar, *op. cit.*, pp. 364ff.

held by scholars for a long time that *drammas* were coined also in gold.[1] He asserts that gold coins current in the medieval period were called *suvarṇas*, *nishkas*, *taṅkas* or *gadyāṇas*, but not *drammas*. On the other hand, *drammas* as silver coins were mentioned in the records of the whole of India.

Thus we can say that no Rāshṭrakūṭa inscribed coins have been found, either in gold, silver, or in copper. The silver coins with the name of Kṛshṇarāja and Gādhiyā type coins discovered in the Poona district have wrongly been attributed to the Rāshṭrakūṭas.[2] M.H. Krishna described eight coins which have the figures of four lions hunched around a tank on the obverse, and elaborate floral design on the reverse. He first attributed these coins to the Kadambas and then suggested that they might have been issued by the Rāshṭrakūṭas.[3] There is hardly any reason to support this attribution.

Gādhiyā coins were current in Rajasthan and Central India from *c*. A.D. 700-1200. Who their exact issuers were is not known, as they are uninscribed. It is not unlikely that the Guhilots, the Paramāras and the Chālukyas issued some of them. A hoard of these coins was found in Poona district in 1944; it has, therefore, been suggested that the Gādhiyā coins may have been issued in Maharashtra as well as by the Rāshṭrakuṭas.[4] This view, however, requires further evidence in its support.

Weights and Measures

A.S. Altekar[5] has enumerated measurement of weights

1. V.V. Mirashi, *Indological Studies*, Vol. IV, Varanasi, 1966, pp. 231-15
2. R.C. Majumdar and K.K. Dasgupta (eds.), *Comprehensive History of India*, Vol. III, pt. II, New Delhi, 1982, p. 1411.
3. *Mysore Archaeological Report*, 1939, p. 87; 1940, p. 75.
4. *Journal of the Numismatic Society of India*, Varanasi, Vol. XXVIII, p. 172.
5. *Op. cit.*, pp. 376-78.

as Śevudu, Arakku, Urakku, Uri, Nāri, Kuruṇi, Padakku, Tuni, Kalam and Kalañju etc. We do not find any one of them except Kalañju in the Rāshṭrakūṭa records. Altekar has taken them from a record of Tanjore in *c.* 1000 A.D. Though we do not have direct sufficient evidence to discuss here, but in such an advanced state of trade of a kingdom there must have been a well organised system of weights and measures. In one of the records of our period[1] we find mention of *Kalañju* measurement for gold and *ulakku* for oil. For 30 *Kalañjus* of gold one *ulakku* of oil is to be supplied as long as the moon and the sun endure.

Sometime towards the end of Amoghavarsha's reign or during the early years of Kṛshṇa II's reign, the early Ālupas, the rulers of South Kanara, were subjected to Rāshṭrakūṭa rule.[2] Of the weights and measures which were in vogue during the early Ālupa period, one of the Udiyāvara inscriptions of Māramma mentions the following[3] :

Saṅkura : It has been suggested that this may be the same as *saṅkara* in which case the word may stand for 'a double sack for manure and grain to be carried on the back of a bullock'.

puṭṭige : same as *puṭṭi* meaning 'a basket'.

malave : It has been suggested that this may be another form of *mana*, 'a maund'.

pala : a particular weight.

peru : a (head-) load.

Of these, though saṅkura, puṭṭige and peru, as understood above, are general terms denoting containers in the first two, and an unspecified quantity in the last cases, since they are noted in the record in the context of taxation, they may be taken to have denoted, in those days, a standard quantity fixed by convention or decree.

1. *E.I.*, XXVI, pp. 230-35.
2. K.V. Ramesh, *A History of South Kanara*, Dharwar, 1970, p. 91.
3. *E.I.*, IX, p. 22.

Thus we can say even without ample records of our period that there were systematized weights and measures in use.

Banking System

Trade and commerce thrives not only with the help of currency system, weights and measures, but also with the help of banking system. These organisations have been since early times in our country.[1] In the whole of the Deccan a network of guilds[2] was spread, which used to regulate trade and banking business, not only for their members but for the general public as well. The examples of guilds are available in inscriptions[3] as well as in literary works like *yājñavalkya-smṛti*[4] and *Nītivākyāmṛta*.[5]

Commercial Taxes

Octroi and excise duties were levied on a number of articles during the Rāshṭrakūṭa period. The term *Bhūtopātta-pratyāya* occurs in an early Rāshṭrakūṭa record from Konnūr.[6] The term ending with *āya* clearly indicates that it was a type of tax.

During the time of the Rāshṭrakūṭas the tax on classified butter was a prominent one. Tax on the sale of classified butter received its sanction from Manu who prescribes a 16% duty on the sale of ghee.[7] The Soraṭur inscription of the time of Rāshṭrakūṭa Amoghavarsha I, dated A.D. 867-68, registers a remission of taxes on ghee (tuppa), *i.e.* classified butter.[8] The same record also registers a grant of income

1. *RATT*, pp. 367-71.
2. *I.A.*, 1919, p. 82.
3. *E I.*, VI, p. 166.
4. II, p. 189.
5. XXIX, p. 9.
6. *E.I.*, VI, p. 29.
7. *Manu.*, VII, p. 131.
8. *S.I.I.*, XI (i), No. 12, p. 8.

from ghee. Similarly, another record from Śisuvinhalli of the time of Amoghavarsha I, dated A.D. 872 records that Devayya, the governor of Belavola-300 exempted the *mahājanas* of the place from taxes on classified ghee.

It is rather strange that during the time of the Rāshṭrakūṭas the tax on classified butter gained so much prominence in the records. It might be due to the fact that the tax on the articles being very heavy and consequently the price having shot up there must have been representations made by the people, particularly the *mahājanas* to receive exemption from this tax.

An inscription[1] from Shiggaon of the time of the Rāshṭrakūṭa Amoghavarsha I, dated A.D. 866, mentions *Kallavalla*, which was most probably a tax on the extraction of liquor. For the term *Kalla* undoubtedly means liquor.[2]

Tolls were levied on articles on water (*jala-suṅka*).[3] By this it may be understood that fishing and also the marine and riparian trades were subjected to taxation.

These are some of the examples available with us in our records to illustrate the existence of commercial or sales taxes and excise duties. Discussion on the structure of tax, on its mode of collection and officials involved in this task is beyond the scope of the present work.

The development of trade can also be estimated on the basis of the economic condition of the empire. The economic condition was so good that the magnificent Kailāsa temple was excavated during this period. Evidences of quite a good number of towns in addition to port cities already mentioned, *viz.*, Mānyakheṭa, Lattur, Elūra, Ajantā, Poona[4], Bankāpur[5],

1. *K.I.*, I, p. 15.
2. S.G. Ghatapanedi, *Taxation in Ancient and Medieval Karnataka* (Unpublished thesis), Karnataka University, Dharwar, 1977, p. 151.
3. *E.I.*, IX, p. 21.
4. *J.B.B.R.A.S.*, VI, pp. 231-38.
5. *Progress of Kannada Research in Bombay State, 1953-57*, Dharwar, 1958, p. 10.

Annigeri[1], Kandhār[2], Siggāma[3], Śurguduru[4], Mayurkhindi[5], Panhala[6], Kolhapur[7], Manalore[8], Melapāti[9], Paṭṭadakal[10], Śrimāla[11] and Achalpur, Alandi, Bhokardan, Jogeśwari, Panpur, Rohankheta, Tagara[12] etc. also show the flourishing economy in the region.

The account of Indian religious sects in *Fihrist*[13] is prefaced with a short note by Ibn Nadim which while describing Mānyakheṭa reads :

> "...in that city there are for the ordinary people one million elephants which carry the merchandise....In this temple there are about twenty thousand idols made of a variety of precious metals like gold, silver, iron, brass, copper and ivory and various carved stones mounted with shaped and artistically worked precious jewels....In that house is an idol whose height is twelve cubits and

1. *E.I.*, XXI, pp. 204-06.
2. *E.I.*, XXXV, pp. 105-14.
3. *Ibid.*, pp. 85-88.
4. *E.I.*, XXXIV.
5. *E.I.*, XXIII.
6. *Panorama of Maharashtra*, Bombay, p. 71.
7. *Ibid.*
8. K.V. Ramesh, *A History of South Kanara*, Dharwar, 1970, pp. 57-58.
9. K.K. Handiqui, *op. cit.*, p. 23.
10. A.M. Annigeri, *The Paṭṭadakal Temple*, Dharwar, 1961.
11. *E.I.*, XXII, p. 181.
12. Vijayendra Kumar Mathur, *Aitihasik Sthānāvalī*, Delhi, 1969.
13. In 988 A.D. a bookseller of Baghdad, named Abdul Faraj Muhammad b. Ishaque al-Nadim, the warraq (copyist), compiled, possbily for the use of his customers, which could be truly described as a classified and annotated bibliography of books of all nations. This is *Fihrist*. It was more about the authors, their classes, together with their genealogies, dates of birth, length of their times, time of their death, places to which they belonged, their merits and faults.

is placed on a throne of gold in the centre of a golden cupola, the whole of which is set with jewels like white pearl, ruby, sapphire, blue and emerald stone."[1]

This description requires no explanatory note to indicate the good economic condition of the kingdom.

1. Deviprasad Chattopadhyay (ed.), *History and Society: Essays in Honour of Professor Niharranjan Ray*, Calcutta, 1978, p. 435.

7

Means of Transport

Means of transport is the back-bone of social and economic life. Communications and transportation played an important role in the highly centralised administrative set-up of the Rāshṭrakūṭas. Again, in trade and commerce, briskly carried out within India as well as outside as discussed in the previous chapter, called for a variety of conveyances. The history of the Rāshṭrakūṭas is characterised by internecine warfare for several centuries. The wars were fought at far-off places. Therefore, the society of this period had naturally devised different types of conveyances for administrative, military, agricultural and commercial purposes. The main source to find the mode of transport prevalent in the society in those days is the sculptures of the great Kailāsa temple at Elūra.

The conveyances illustrated in the sculptures of the Kailāsa temple are of two categories :

(A) those used for transportation on land :

(a) horses,
(b) chariots,
(c) elephants,
(d) bullock carts,
(e) palanquins;

(B) those employed for water transportation : boats.

(A) LAND TRANSPORT

(a) *Horses*

The horse has undoubtedly revolutionised the ancient Indian transport system and the mode of warfare. Though the existence of the horse was known to Indians from times immemorial, the exact use to which it was put is not known prior to the Vedic period. The Vedic literature is replete with references regarding the fast-moving horse-drawn chariots employed in warfare. It may be, however, admitted that in India the employment of horses in larger numbers in warfare began a few centuries before the Christian era. Indians were probably influenced by the foreign hordes such as the Scythians and the Kushāṇas who ruled in the north-western region of this country. Gradually, the Indian rulers developed a cavalry wing in their armies.

The Elūra sculptures depicting horses show that the animals were used both for riding as well as for dragging the chariots. The twin functions of the horse, *i.e.*, carrying the royal personages and the soldiers and pulling the carriages, remained constant whether it was a ceremonial procession or warfare. The frequent representation of the horses in the reliefs suggests that it was one of the most important conveyances among the people during the period of the study. However, the horse may not have been a common man's conveyance as it is always shown ridden either by the royal personages or the soldiers. The horse-riding scenes are depicted at three places in the Kailāsa temple. They are on the architrave of the outer screen wall, the *Mahābhārata* panel and the *Rāmāyaṇa* panel in this temple. The horses are shown usually highly caparisoned.

As the horse riders happened to be either royal personages or soldiers, the horses seem to have been provided with elaborate trappings. But the details are not clearly seen in the sculptural representations. It may be, however, inferred that the galloping horses as seen in the reliefs were equipped with saddles, bridles and breast bands. The saddle may have been a stuffed cushion secured by means of a girth band around the horse. Sometimes the saddle borders were decorated with colour designs. The bridles comprised the leather straps, forehead band, check, pieces, etc. The breast bands appear to have been provided in order to prevent the horse from rearing on its hind legs. The horses used in wars and for ceremonial processions were probably of a good breed and in all likelihood imported from the Arab countries.

Use of horses is testified to from Arab accounts also. The Rāshṭrakūṭa kings, probably, had encouraged the Arab merchants not only for the growth of trade, but also for importing horses of good breeds.[1] The Rāshṭrakūṭas could succeed in their campaigns against the Pālas of Bengal and the Pratīhāras of Kanauj by travelling a very long distance with the horse power.

(b) *Chariots*

The chariots have been invariably depicted in war scenes. Thus it is evident that charioteering was an important aspect of the ancient Indian warfare. Besides the visual representation of chariots in sculptures and terracottas, the *Mahābhārata* and the *Arthaśāstra* have also described in greater details about the chariots.[2]

The Elūra sculptures reveal two types of chariots, namely, (i) Those drawn by four horses and (ii) those by two horses.

The panel depicting the Tripurāsura-vadhamūrti in the Kailāsa temple reveals an interesting chariot drawn by four horses. It consists of a rectangular frame mounted on two solid wheels. The sides of the chariot have been artistically designed and were possibly made of wood. In the panel of Rāvaṇa fighting against the Jaṭāyu bird carved on the southern wall of the Kailāsa temple is illustrated another variety of the

1. Devising Chauhan, 'Arab Horses in India', *ABORI*, XLVIII-XLIX, pp. 391-94; and also *RATT*, p. 359.
2. *Journal of American Oriental Society*, XIII, p. 235.

chariot.[1] Here the oblong frame of the chariot seems to have been covered and drawn by two horses. Its wheels have well decorated spokes with the hub and the axle prominently highlighted.

(c) *Elephants*

The elephant symbolised sovereignty in ancient India. The regal pomp and pageantry were displayed by the royal personages riding on elephant back in ceremonial processions and military expeditions. In fact, the elephant corps is said to have existed in the Indian army much earlier than cavalry. Nearchus refers to the elephants in the army of Porus, while he is silent about horse chariots and cavalry.

The elephants in the reliefs are shown elaborately decorated. Their necks and heads are bejewelled. Sometimes a decorated saddle is placed on the back of the elephant and secured by means of a rope. At some places the elephant is shown with a *howdah*. The *howdah* is a simple seat secured by means of a rope. The *Mahābhārata* scene, depicted on the exterior wall of the Kailāsa temple, illustrates both the types described above.[2] The elephants are found in the reliefs with *māhūts*. In such cases the prince or the royal dignitary is shown seated on a *howdah* with a bodyguard behind him. The frequent depiction of elephants in war scenes suggests that the elephant corps played an important role in the royal conquests.

Elephant's importance can be judged from the following evidence as well. In a defeat, the Pallava king of Kāñchī paid a tribute with a large number of elephants to the Rāshṭrakūṭa king Dhruva.[3] In an Arab account about Mānyakheṭa it is stated that in the city there are for the ordinary people one million elephants which carry the merchandise; in the king's stable there are sixty thousand

1. T.V. Pathy, *op. cit.*, Plate XXV.
2. T.V. Pathy, *op. cit.*, Plate XLIII.
3. R.G. Bhandarkar, *Early History of the Deccan and Miscellaneous Historical Essays*, Poona, 1983, pp. 89-90.

elephants, and for the defence of the fortress there are one hundred sixty thousand elephants.[1] In the *Yaśastilaka*, the king himself is shown taking part in the training and arming of elephants.[2] There were committees of experts appointed to examine and select elephants.[3]

Karnataka is even today rich in elephants. The use of elephants and their availability can also be seen in the temple of Kailāsa where quite a large number of elephants are standing on the plinth of the temple.[4]

(d) *Bullock Carts*

The principal means of transport in our period for the general public was the bullock cart. Al-Idrisi states that there was no other means of travelling in Gujarat, except chariots drawn by oxen under the control of a driver.[5] A.S. Altekar is of the opinion that the same was probably the case in our period. Horses were fairly dear and were therefore not available for general transport purposes. The bullockcarts were, however, fairly comfortable. Besides the bullock cart, the oxen and pack horses of an inferior breed must have been used for transport, especially in the hilly tract, or when it was desired to have a speedy transport.[6]

We have no contemporary records which throw light upon the condition of the roads. *The Periplus of the Erythraean Sea*[7] informs that goods from Paithan, Tagara and other places in the Deccan had to be brought to Bharoach in wagons through great tracts without roads, but the military necessities of the empire must have compelled the Rāshṭrakūṭas to keep the roads in a fairly good condition.

1. Debiprasad Chattopadhyaya (ed.), *History and Society: Essays in Honour of Professor Niharranjan Ray*, Calcutta, 1978, p 435.
2. K.K. Handiqui, *op. cit.*, p. 90.
3. *Ibid.*, p. 54.
4. Percy Brown, *Indian Architecture (Buddhist and Hindu Period)*, Bombay, Sixth reprint, 1971, Plate LVII.
5. Elliot, *History of India*, I, London, 1870, p. 87.
6. *RATT*, p. 360.
7. Schoff. *The Periplus of the Erythraean Sea*, London, 1912, p. 30.

(e) *Palanquins*

A palanquin (śibikā) is depicted in the ceiling paintings of the Kailāsa temple, which is shown carrying a prince accompanied by the armed soldiers. The other painted representation of a palanquin in cave No. 32 of Elūra is shown carrying a Jain bhikku. Palanquins are shown being carried by men. Both the specimens appear to be a flat square bottom with vaulted roof and mounted on a curved pole.

(B) WATER TRANSPORT : BOATS

There is a solitary example of a boat depicted in the *Rāmāyaṇa* panel of the Kailāsa temple. It is a simple boat consisting of a high stern or prow and devoid of sails. It may be, however, mentioned here that the non-representation of different varieties of ships cannot in any way lead us to the conclusion that there was less advancement in water transportation. It has been shown in the preceding chapter on trade and commerce that India had maintained overseas commercial contacts with distant countries. Some of the ships illustrated in the paintings at Ajantā suggest that they could have as well been used for carrying huge cargo.[1]

It is interesting to note that from the earliest times, all civilizations and empires flourished on river banks, as water is the main source of nourishment. Later it proved to be a good path for transport. Masudi has described in his work the rivers of India in detail. In his description one unique feature we come across is that in his time the ships were given names after their master or their relations (as is done today like 'and sons' and 'and brothers').[2]

Masudi also informs us of the time of ocean journey, which was based on the time of high tides or neaps. From the Arab side ships towards India seldom go and if they do

1. T.V. Pathy, *op. cit*, p. 125.
2. S.S. Nadvi, *op. cit.*, p. 32.

at all they are very light and with little load. In the rainy season Indians do not sail their boats, and they engage themselves in cultivation.[1]

As an evidence of ship transport the latest discovery is a wall painting at Tiruppudaimarudar in Ambasamudram taluk which throws light on the Indo-Arab contacts. It shows an Arab ship carrying horses.

Sea voyages were usually performed in the hope of earning money; but they were very difficult too, and so required a lot of courage. There was risk of life as well. On many occasions ships were damaged completely.[2]

1. *Ibid.*, p. 52; also *HCIP*, IV, p. 402.
2. Prem Suman Jain, *op. cit.*, p. 209.

8

Important Rashtrakuta Towns

It has been well said that God made the country and man made the town. Towns grew up on the basis of their geographical situations and mainly due to human factors. Towns are main centres of all human activities such as administrative, commercial, cultural, educational or other activities. They may be treated as a link between social and economic developments in the society. When we talk of urbanization, we talk of towns. Decline of towns is termed as decline of trade. We have seen earlier that trade was at its zenith during the time of the Rāshṭrakūṭas, and so there would not be any dearth of towns. But here we are restricting ourselves to more important towns of the empire.

Towns being the centres of all human activities, we are tempted to give here details of some important towns. We take up the capitals first.

CAPITALS

(a) *The early capital or capitals*

Latūr

Latūr or Laṭṭalūra is identified with Latur in Osmanabad district of Maharashtra. It is considered to be the original home of the Rāshṭrakūṭas. A number of Rāshṭrakūṭa records describe the rulers by the epithet *Laṭṭalūrapuravarādhīśa* 'lord of Laṭṭalūra, the best of towns.'[1] This epithet is changed into *Laṭṭalūrapura-vinirgata* 'emigrants from the town of Laṭṭalūra', in some of the Raṭṭas of Saundatti.[2] Earlier, the original home was suggested by Fleet as Ratanpnr in Bilaspur district of Madhya Pradesh. Later, he himself rejected his own view after getting information from a twelfth-century inscription of the place, that the original name here was Ratnapura. He then identified it with modern Latur[3] which Altekar considered to be 'hitting the truth.'[4] The change of Laṭṭalūra into Latur is phonetically quite natural. The letter '*la*' from the original name might have been dropped by hypology to obtain its Prakrit form Laṭṭaūra. This form would have later changed into Lāṭūra, and the loss of the double consonant *ṭṭa* would have been compensated by the doubling of the preceding vowels, and thus the modern form. Moreover, this is a place in a clear-cut manner within the boundary of the Rāshṭrakūṭa empire whereas others are not. Near Elūra in a village called Nandrabad Rāshṭrakūṭa habitation has been explored by T.V. Pathy.[5]

Elichpur

Scholars have suggested several places to have been the pre-Mānyakheṭa capital of the Imperial Rāshṭrakūṭas. They are identified with places such as Elichpur, Morkhanda and Elūra. Elichpur, also called Achalpur, in Berar and situated in the north of Amaravati was probably the capital

1. *I.A.*, XII, p. 218 and *E.I.*, VI, p. 102. These include Sirur and Nilgund Inscriptions of Amoghavarsha I.
2. *J.B.B.R.A.S.*, X, pp. 167ff.
3. *E.I.*, VII, pp. 186ff.
4. *R.A.T.T.*, p. 23.
5. I owe this information to Dr. Amarendra Narayan of Archaeological Survey of India, Western Circle, Aurangabad.

from where the ancestors of Dantidurga were ruling[1] and it might have been shifted to some other central place in Maharashtra when Dantidurga conquered the entire Maharashtra. It was a famous centre of Jain learning. Jain scholar Dhanapāla completed his *Dhamma-Parikkhā* here. Āchārya Jayasiṁha Sūri of the ninth century A.D. has mentioned this town in his *Dharmopadeśamālā*. It was in a flourishing condition till the twelfth century A.D.[2]

Mayurakhindi

Five records[3] of Govinda III and as many as eight other Rāshṭrakūṭa epigraphs dated before 814 A.D. *i.e.*, in the pre-Mānyakheṭa period explicitly state Mayurakhindi as a place of royal residence.[4] This place has been variously identified. Some identify it with the modern fort of Morkhand in the Nasik district of Maharashtra. But some other scholars do not agree with this identification. Their argument is that Nasik being the seat of the provincial viceroyalty, a place less known than Nasik could not have been the capital of the Rāshṭrakūṭas. They identify Mayurakhindi with the present-day Morkhandi village in the Bidar district which is situated near Kalyāṇī, the capital city of the later Chālukyas. Morkhandi has little phonetic similarity with Mayurkhindi. Archaeological explorations of the village have brought to light two inscriptions which are datable to the eighth century A D. Some potsherds and brickbats have also been discovered.[5] It is also reported that there was a fortified wall but now it does not exist as the village is completely under occupation

1. A.S. Altekar, *Rāshṭrakūṭas and Their Times*, Poona, 1934, p. 48.
2. V.K. Mathur, *Aitihāsik Sthānāvalī*, New Delhi, 1969, p. 11.
3. *I.A.*, XI, p. 159; *I.A.*, VI, p. 245; *Sources of the Medieval History of the Deccan*, published by Bhārat Itihāsa Saṁsodhaka Mandala, pp. 27f; *E I.*, XXIII, pp. 8-18 etc.
4. G. Yazdani (ed), *The Early History of the Deccan*, Oxford, 1960, p. 257; A.V. Naik, 'Inscriptions of the Deccan: An Epigraphical Survey', *BDCRI*, IX, pp. 1-160.
5. T.V. Pathy, *op. cit.*, pp. 12-13.

and cultivation. From the defence point of view, the modern Morkhandi seems to be well protected due to the undulating laterite deposits with huge tanks on all sides. V.V. Mirashi and L.R. Kulkarni, however, have tried to associate this place with Markaṇḍi on the bank of the river Naingaṅgā, 88 km south-east of Chandā or Chandrapur in Maharashtra.[1]

Elūra

Cousens was of the view that the Rāshṭrakūṭa capital may have been located somewhere in the vicinity of the Elūra caves in the time of Dantidurga.[2] For this he suggests Sooloobunjun (Soolibhanjan) which is just above the plateau near the Elūra caves. Altekar has accepted this suggestion conditionally saying it is possible only if archaeological evidences support this.[3]

T.V. Pathy[4] is strongly of the opinion that the early Rāshṭrakūṭa capital was at Elūra. For this he advances the following argument : "The Rāshṭrakūṭa phase of art at Elūra was as extensively undertaken as it is exuberant which has no parallels elsewhere. Even the monuments in its later capital city, Malkheḍ, are not worthy of comparison with those of Elūra. Their temple building activities elsewhere in their kingdom were equally insignificant. The question would naturally arise as to why the Rāshṭrakūṭa rulers chose Elūra as the venue of excavating activities of such magnitude and high-artistic excellence. This factor coupled by the fact of the existence of a large township overlooking the cave temples have prompted several scholars to speculate on the possibility that Elūra was probably the early capital city of the Rāshṭrakūṭas."[5]

1. *E.I.*, XXIII, pp. 8-18.
2. Cousens, *The Chalukyan Architecture*, p. 1.
3. A.S. Altekar, *op. cit.*, p. 48.
4. T.V. Pathy, *Elūra: Art and Culture*, New Delhi, 1980, pp. 10-13; also H.S. Thosar and T.V. Pathy, 'Bhindhon Plates of Mahārāshṭrakūṭa Karkarāja', *MUJ*, XVII-XVIII, pp. 111-15.
5. T.V. Pathy, *op. cit.*, p. 11.

Elūra was either an administrative centre or a religious centre during the Rāshṭrakūṭa period. As a religious centre it was well-known for Buddhists and the Hindus and a cluster of rock-cut temples had already come into existence during the Chālukya period. One of the earliest records of the Rāshṭrakūṭas is the Elūra Copper Plates of Dantidurga which refers to Guheśvara Tīrtha at Elūra.[1] Another inscription is engraved in Cave XV (Daśāvatāra) and it eulogised Dantidurga's military exploits and his performance of several *dānas*.[2] The Baroda Copper Plates of Karkarāja describe graphically the excavation of a unique Śivālaya in the hills of Elāpura by Kṛshṇa I, *i.e.*, Kailāsa temple, and this Elāpura is identified with Elūra.[3] T.V. Pathy says that it is possible that the ancient township of Elūra was very extensive and included the present-day Khuldabad.[4] The invading Muslims who captured Daulatabad must have noticed the ruined city and the vestiges of them could still be seen in the mosques and the mausoleums at Khuldabad. The existence of a township above the Elūra hills is further substantiated by the presence of a huge masonry tank or reservoir with well-dressed stone steps on all sides. Subsequent Rāshṭrakūṭa records after the reign of Kṛshṇarāja are completely silent.

In a manuscript entitled *Verul Śivālaya Māhātmya* of the late medieval period and written in old Marathi language, Elāpura figures throughout the narrative of the MS.[5] The importance of the MS. lies in its recording of the oral tradition pertaining to Elūra, especially the Kailāsa temple. A thirteenth century work, *Līlācharitra*, also refers to the township of Elāpura which was spread extensively in front of the Caves.[6] Thus the importance of Elūra was not reduced,

1. A.V. Naik, *op. cit.*, pp. 87-88.
2. G. Yazdani (ed.), *op. cit.*, p. 122.
3. *I A.*, XII, p. 156.
4. T.V. Pathy, *op cit.*, p. 12.
5. T.V. Pathy, 'Verul Śivālayamāhātmya MS. and some more facts about Ellora' in *Studies in Indian History & Culture*, Dharwar, 1971, p. 106.
6. Vijayendra Kumar Mathur, *Aitihasik Sthanavali*, New Delhi, 1969, p. 734.

at least as a temple town, even after Mānyakheṭa was made the capital city of the Rāshṭrakūṭas.

Mānpur

It is also in Maharashtra. Some scholars consider it to be the first capital of the Rāshṭrakūṭas.

(*b*) *The later or final capital*

Mānyakheṭa

It is a small village, identified with Malkheḍ (Lat. 17°15′ and Long. 77°7′) now situated on the left bank of the Kāginā, a tributary of the Bhīmā river in the Sedam taluk of the Gulbarga district (Karnataka State).

A certain amount of uncertainty is still experienced in regard to the location of the capital of the early Rāshṭrakūṭa period as we have seen above. But Dantidurga seems to have made Elūra his royal headquarters, which might have continued this status during the reigns of his successors. With the rise of their political ambitions and in order to exercise effective control over their southern dominions inherited from the Chālukyas of Bādāmi, the Rāshṭrakūṭa rulers must have felt the necessity of establishing their capital in a southern and centrally situated region. Growth of empires from small nuclei had always necessiated the founding of a second capital in more central localities wherefrom it could be easy to watch the counter-movements of the new enemies at whose cost the empire had grown. The Pallavas, the Western Chālukyas and the Western Gaṅgas, who had been dealt severe blows by the predecessors of Govinda III, having been in a state of constant revolt, and Govinda himself having had to make them acquiesce in the Rāshṭrakūṭa overlordship, and further risings of a similar nature and coalition of the subdued powers being expected at any moment, might have prompted Govinda III to found the new city. Besides, the Rāshṭrakūṭas had now to meet a more formidable foe in the person of the Eastern Chālukya Vijayāditya II (A.D. 799-843), the son of

Vishṇuvardhana IV, who had suffered defeat at the hands of Govinda II in the reign of Kṛshṇa I and who was one among the hostile kings taken by Dhruva to the Rāshṭrakūṭa country. All these must have strongly urged the necessity of having a city in a more central place and close to the Veṅgī country, leave alone any ambition on his own part to acquire any fresh territory. The move in this direction must certainly have been taken to bring under complete subjection all the conquered powers and to maintain the supremacy over them.[1] The choice ultimately fell on Mānyakheṭa or Malkheḍ, and the decision was taken in the time of Govinda III to develop this rural township into an imperial capital.

This project was accomplished during the long and relatively peaceful reign of his successor Nṛpatuṅga Amoghavarsha I.[2] Mānyakheṭa remained the central capital city of the Rāshṭrakuṭa empire until their last days. Further on, the Chālukyas who supplanted the Rāshṭrakūṭas also preferred this city as capital for a period of about half a century from the reign of Taila II to that of Jayasiṁha II, wherefrom they shifted to Kalyāṇa. With the rise of its rulers, Mānyakheṭa attained dimensions, splendour and vast reputation in the nations of the world. It is extolled in contemporary literature and admired in the accounts of foreign visitors.

The planner who selected this site for making the new capital must be given credit for its geographical situation from the military point of view. The whole area is a plain land with thick black cotton soil cover overlying the laminated sedimentary rock beds consisting of lime stones etc. of the Bhīmā series. Comparatively speaking, the whole region where Malkheḍ is located is surrounded by waters on three sides and thus it has considerably the natural defensive character. Probably it is this aspect of the site that had made

1. K.V. Subrahmanya Aiyar, *Three Lectures*, second edition, Dharwar, 1978, pp. 95-96. This book is concerned with (1) The Method of Historical Research and (2-3) Some Dark Spots in the History of the Rāshṭrakūṭas.
2. *JBBRAS*, X, p. 31.

the Imperial Rāshṭrakūṭas select it for founding their capital.

The fort has been raised in an area closely surrounded by the rivulet on the east and south and the river Kāginā on the west. The river Kāginā flows southwards. Away from the left bank of the river, there is another small rivulet flowing westwards and then takes suddenly a turn southwards and south-westwards and joins another longer rivulet. The latter flows westwards and then joins the river Kāginā. On the northern side nearly half the length of the eastern side from the north-east corner, there is no natural channel or rivulet, hence a moat was dug immediately by the side of the fort on the northern and eastern sides connecting the river Kāginā to the rivulet on the eastern side. The river water flows through the moat into the rivulet. Thus, the whole of the fort has natural defensive rivers and the rivulets and the moat fulfils the need of the remaining sides. What is particularly noteworthy, here, is exploitation of the natural resources of the water, with minimum effort for providing moats round the fort. The width of the moat is 20 metres and the depth is 7.5 metres which are almost equal to the rivulet, which it joins. The river Kāginā on the west, which is right at the foot of the fort, is wide.

Today the place is nothing but a small village with mounds of ruins with two forts. There is not a single monument of the Rāshṭrakūṭas of any type worth the name excepting a Jain Basādi (Neminātha temple) of the usual type and style of the period. People as well as scholars, who have some ideas about the glory of Mānyakheṭa, visit the place, find themselves in a state of utter disillusion and deep disappointment. This is a hard fact. P.B. Desai[1] who explored the site thus writes : "I have explored this place carefully during my visits, with a view to securing confirmatory evidence in support of this identification. But I was rather disappointed with my feelings which are as follows. Firstly, this place is poor in

1. P.B. Desai, *Jainism in South India and Some Jain Epigraphs*, Sholapur, 1957, p. 192.

antiquities, most of which are of a late period. Secondly, there is no trace whatsoever of either the monuments or inscriptions of the Rāshṭrakūṭas' times. In the neighbouring villages, which are said to have constituted the suburbs of the great metropolis, I discovered some inscriptions of the later Chālukyas; but no single inscription was found anywhere. Its first mention is found in the Mudhol Plates of Pūgavarman[1]... The glaring dearth of early relics may probably be ascribed to the close proximity of the river Kāginā which might have swept them away or submerged them by its overflowing operations. Excavation may reveal some of them. This suggestion is justified by the reported vestiges of old temples and other structures noticed by the residents of this place in course of digging wells or the foundations of new houses."

The local traditions[2] are also important in this connection. A tradition which unmistakably identifies this place with the illustrious capital of the Rāshṭrakūṭas, is prevalent among the common folk of this region. It is believed that this was a very big city extending as far as Sedam, 16 km to the east, and up to Daṇḍoti, 6.4 km to the west, and including among its suburbs the modern twin villages of Nīlhalli and Konkanalli between Sedam and Malkheḍ. Malkheḍ, as the report goes, was the seat of the royal palace; the imperial secretariat was housed in Sedam; the army was stationed at Daṇḍoti; and the treasury was deposited at Nīlhalli-Konkanalli. In support of this contention the name Daṇḍoti[3] is said to have been derived from the word '*daṇḍa*' meaning 'an army', which has thus retained its old association to the present day.

This belief is in conformity with the memories cherished by the Jain community of this region also. These reminiscences, which may be characterised as peculiarly Jain traditions,

1. *Progress of Kannada Research in Bombay Province from 1941-46*, p. 71.
2. P.B. Desai, *op. cit.*, p. 193.
3. Its name in a twelfth-century record from Tengali occurs as Daṇḍahaṭṭi. Here *haṭṭi* may be of Kannada origin meaning 'a settlement' or *pati* in Tamil meaning 'an abode', *e.g.*, Tirupati.

emphasise in their own way the two-interlinked aspects of the problem; to wit, one, Malkheḍ was the headquarters of the Rāshṭrakūṭas of the Deccan who were great patrons of Jainism, and two, it was an important ecclesiastical centre of the faith. We cannot, in this context, rule out the possibility that some of these traditions might have been influenced by the statements contained in the earlier works of the Jain religious literature.[1]

Malkheḍ was of course subjected to series of unspeakable destructions by the Cholas, and later by the Muslims during the Sultanate and Mughal periods. Within the fort is at present a Jain temple and a few sculptures, door frames, pillars of some temples of the period scattered here and there or used as building material in the fort wall.[2] But there must have been structural stone temples of the Rāshṭrakūṭa period. Inside the fort there is a Nemināthа Basādi of the ninth century. Its exterior is not original and had undergone renovations.

The earliest reference to this place is available in an inscription, Mudhol Plates of Pūgavarman, dated *c.* 560 A.D.[3] It is referred to as Mānyakheḍa in a record[4] of 993 A.D. In the inscriptions of the locality as well as of the villages near about Mānyakheṭa (mod. Malkheḍ), ranging from the eleventh to the sixteenth centuries, the place is spoken of as Malikeḍa and Maleyekheḍa.[5] This shows the continuity of the place even after its destruction. This is also evidenced through the presence of the vestiges of the medieval fort.

Pushpadanta also confirms the identity of Mānyakheṭa when he says that it was surrounded by water so that it could not be accessed easily. He describes high and white houses of Mānyakheṭa.[6] On the destruction of this royal city he says

1. P.B. Desai, *op. cit.*, p. 193.
2. Other antiquities here including the forts are of the Muslim period.
3. *E.I.*, XXXII, p. 296.
4. *B K. Coll.*, No 170 of 1933-34.
5. P.B. Desai, *Jainism in South India and Some Jain Epigraphs*, Sholapur, 1957, pp. 192ff.
6. *Mahā.*, 1.1.11-12 and 1.3.2-3.

with a sense of lamentation that it was the solace even for the poor and the helplesss and always full of many people.[1]

RELIGIOUS AND OTHER TOWNS

Religious towns, which in turn served the purpose of trade too, were centres of many social activities. Elūra, which we have discussed earlier, typifies a rare example of the harmonious existence of three religious sects—Buddhism. Hinduism and Jainism. In addition to this, there were so many religious, commercial and educational towns flourishing during the Rāshṭrakūṭa period. There are quite a number of temples existing in Maharashtra and Karnataka which have been identified as Rāshṭrakūṭa temples on the basis of their architectural features. We have already covered the educational towns Sālotgi and Kalas in the chapter on education. And also, we have dealt with the port towns such as Cambay, Thana, Suparā etc. in the chapter dealing with trade and commerce. Other important towns are discussed below.

Aihole

Aihole is an ancient place near Bādāmi in the Bijapur district of Karnataka. Its history is very old and an inscription dated 634 A.D. had been obtained from this place.[2] The stone temple at this place is unique. The architectural features of the temple indicate its condition during the period of the Rāshṭrakūṭas.

Pillars without carvings occur at the closing stages of the early Chālukya period and the beginning of the Rāshṭrakūṭa period. In fact, they become popular under the Rāshṭrakūṭas. Pillars with 45° profile brackets were popular

1. धारानाथ धनं सदाबहुजनं प्रोत्फुल्लवल्लीवनं ।
मान्यखेटपुरं पुरंदरपुरीलीलाहरं सुन्दरम् ॥
धारानाथ नरेन्द्र कोपशिखिना दग्धं विदग्धप्रियं ।
केदानीं वर्सात करिष्यति पुनः श्रीपुष्पदन्तः कविः ॥

—*Mahā.*, Praśasti 50.

2. V.K. Mathur, *op. cit.*, p. 114.

in the Rāshṭrakūṭa and later Chālukya periods and not in the early Chālukya period. There are a number of features which fall in line with the Rāshṭrakūṭa phase of architecture at Aihole. The base is well developed. It is different from the early Chālukya base. The presence of projected dentils in the top moulding of the base is a late feature.

In addition to these architectural features, there is an inscription which states that one Sānta-gāvuṇḍa built the temple and made a gift of *gosahasra* in A.D. 971 during the reign of Koṭṭiga.[1]

Thus, on the basis of the above-mentioned two grounds and its location being in the heartland of the Rāshṭrakūṭa empire, we may presume that Aihole had an important place among the towns that flourished during the Rāshṭrakūṭa period.

Ajantā

Ajantā[2] (Lat. 20°32′ N and Long. 75°45′ E) is located in the Aurangabad district of Maharashtra. Its name itself is enchanting for the lovers of ancient monuments.

> "Ajantā takes us back into some distant, dream-like but a very real world."
>
> —Pt. Jawahar Lal Nehru

Ajantā was flourishing in the Vākāṭaka period, but a fragmentary Rāshṭrakūṭa record of some uncertain purpose, inscribed on the right wall of the landing to the left of the Court of Cave 26, proves the use of the caves even during the eighth-ninth centuries.[3] The location of this cave which is almost in the row of caves, because there are only 29 caves there, also gives a clear hint that the total area was humming with human activities.

1. *S.I.I.*, XI, Pt. I, No. 44.
2. G. Yazdani, *Ajantā*, Vols. I-IV, Texts and Plates, Oxford, 1930-55 and also M.K. Dhavalikar, *Ajantā*: *A Cultural Study*, Poona, 1973 speak all about this town
3. Debala Mitra, *Ajantā*, New Delhi, Eighth ed., 1980, p. 8.

Aland

This town is situated in the north-west direction of Gulbarga at a distance of 43 km. Although not many antiquities were discovered here, there are sufficient indications to vouchsafe the importance of the place. Most of the Jain relics seem to have been destroyed or submerged under the impact of times. This place is referred to as Alande in the inscriptions. It was the headquarters of a district styled Alande-1000, evidently comprising villages. This town was also known as Alakāvatī in the hey-day of its glory. Another tradition credits this place with the honour of a visit by Jinasena Bhaṭṭāraka, the reputed preceptor of the Rāshṭrakūṭa monarch Amoghavarsha I. The belief is prevalent that a pontifical seat was founded at Mānyakheṭa by this divine and that this tract came under the ecclesiastical jurisdiction of the preceptors of his time. The members of the local Jain community still pay their homage to the pontifical throne of the Mānyakheṭa *Gurus.*[1]

Aṇṇigeri

Aṇṇigeri (or more correctly Aṇṇigere) is a village in the Navalgund Taluk of Dharwar District in Karnataka on the Hubli-Guntakal section of the Southern Railway line. Though at present a small village, Aṇṇigeri appears to have been an important town from the early Chālukya times down to the Muhammadan period. In the ninth century it was the chief town of the Belvola-300 district administered by Devaṇṇaya, an officer of the Rāshṭrakūṭa king Amoghavarsha I.[2] Under the Chālukayas of Kalyāṇī and the Hoysalas it continued to be known as the rājadhānī-paṭṭana or the capital town.[3] Several other inscriptions of successive periods prove the importance of the place down to the time of Sultan Muhammad Shah of Bijapur. In Sanskrit records the place is called

1. P.B. Dehai, *Jainism in South India and Some Jain Epigraphs*, Sholapur, 1957, pp. 180-81.
2. *E.I.*, VI, p. 100 and VII, p. 204.
3. *E.I.*, XXI, p. 204.

Anyālaṭāka, obviously in the Sanskritized form of the Kanarese name Aṇṇigere.

Bankāpur

Bankāpur in Shiggaon Taluk of Dharwar district has an old fort which encloses a very wide area and has a number of mounds. Some of these are under cultivation. They have yielded pottery also. There are remains of square and rectangular houses too. The presence of the Nagareśvara temple of the times of the Chālukyas of Kalyāṇī and later Muslim buildings shows that it was inhabited during the days of the Rāshṭrakūṭas. The reference to Baṅkeyarasa also hints at Bankāpur.[1] Excavation only would be able to throw some light regarding the habitation and the life of the Rāshṭrakūṭa period.

Bhokardan

Bhokardan is situated on the bank of the Kelalnā river in Jalana district of Maharashtra where Vaishnava temples are built in underground caves. The time of the excavation of these temples is also assigned to the eighth-ninth centuries A.D. which is indicated in an inscripation available in the verandah of the temple.[2] This establishes the association of the Rāshṭrakūṭas with this temple in an unmistakable manner.

Jogeśvarī

About 32 km south of Goregaon railway station in Maharashtra there is a small village Amboli. Near it the huge cave temple of Jogeśvarī or Yogeśvarī is located which is next to the Kailāsa temple of Elūra in India in its size and shape. It was excavated during the seventh-eighth centuries A.D.[3]

1. *Progress of Kannada Research in Bombay State, 1953-57*, Dharwar, 1958, p. 25.
2. V.K. Mathur, *op. cit.*, p. 678.
3. *Ibid.*, p. 372.

which must have been in a flourishing condition during the period of the Rāshṭrakūṭas. The maximum part of the cave is underground. The stone of this temple is brittle in nature; so it could not withstand the time and is in ruins now. There were the Śiva idol and other Hindu deities which are now in a dilapidated condition. The arrangement for drainage of water in this temple was remarkable.

Kandahār

Kandahār, also called Kandhār, is the headquarters of the Taluk of that name and situated 51 km south-west of its district headquarters Nānded in Maharashtra. It was a flourishing city during the Rāshṭrakūṭa period and probably a provincial capital. From the description of the city in the inscription[1] it becomes clear that Kandhār had developed as the religious centre with a cluster of temples, constructed by kings and officials in the royal personages. It was a trade centre as well with different markets. A number of civic amenities were provided to the people, especially those coming from outside.[2]

The city had become famous even a century earlier as indicated by the inscription itself. It mentions the temples of Baṅkeśvara and Challeśvara which obviously were named after Bankeśa, the famous general of Amoghavarsha I and Challaketana, the name of the family of this general. Apart from the temples of Kālapriya and Vīranārāyaṇa, temples were built here in the name of Kṛshṇa II and Gojjiga Somanātha in the name of Govinda III, Gojjiga being a familiar Kannada term for Govinda. *Jaggattuṅga Samudra* also must have been a tank built in the name of Jagattuṅga Govinda III.

The city must have been a vast one where people from outside came in regularly for religious or trade purposes. A rest-house, meaningfully called *Sarvalokāśrayamaṇḍapa*, was

1. *E.I.*, XXXV, pp. 105-14.
2. G.C. Shelke, *A History of Marathwada Region* (unpublished Thesis), Aurangabad, 1979, p. 87.

built where even bedsheets and coverings were supplied for travellers. Watersheds were installed in various places in the city in summer while fire-places were installed in winter. Arrangement was made for the supply of fodder and water to the bullocks which brought mercantile goods into the market of Kandhār. These activities only go to show that this region during the days of the Rāshṭrakūṭas was active politically and culturally.

The inscribed stone slab lies near an old well called 'the Khas Bag Well' in the locality called Bahādurpur nearly 1.5 km from the present town of Kandhār. The place abounds in ruined structures noticed around the well. The most notable existing structure at Kandhār is the fort just outside the town. There is no doubt that the fort was built before the advent of the Muhammadans there.[1] The present Dargah and the mosque inside the fort have pillars of old Hindu temples. But there is no record of the Hindu rulers anywhere inside the fort. The town of Kandhār also abounds in many ruined structures as well as Hindu, Buddhist and Jain images. Even now old images and Śivaliṅgas come out here and there while people dig for the foundation of a house.

Kanheri

Kanheri is situated in the Kṛshṇagiri hills in north Konkan of Maharashtra. There are three ancient Śaiva cave temples about 1.5 km from Borivali railway station. Kanheri is 8 km from Borivali which is part of Kṛshṇagiri. It is understood that Kanheri is the *apabhraṁśa* of Kṛshṇagiri. There are one hundred and nine caves of the ninth century here which may be assigned to the Rāshṭrakūṭa period.[2] Out of these, only one is worth being mentioned here where a beautiful image of the Buddha is present. Here also, on the walls of the caves, paintings had been made in the Ajantā style, but now they are lost.

1 *E.I.*, XXXV, p. 105.

2. V.K. Mathur, *op. cit.*, p. 132.

Karahāṭa

Karahāṭa or Karhāḍ is situated on the confluence of the Kṛshṇā and the Koinā (Koyanā) rivers in Satārā District of Maharashtra. Somadeva describes Karahāṭa as a prosperous country and gives an interesting picture of a large dairy farm of the locality.[1] More interesting is the description of the mart owned and run by the trusted priest Śrībhūti. The mart was furnished with tents containing many compartments and large stores of merchandise, with stalls for cattle nearby. Water, fodder and fire-wood were easily available, and the establishment covered an area of about 6 km. It was closely guarded by troops, and protected by moats, gates, walls and ramparts, and had avenues with arrangements for water-supply, eating houses, assembly halls, and warehouses for different classes of commodities. Gamblers, whoremongers, jesters and dancing masters were excluded from the precincts of the mart. Here merchants from many countries were allowed to carry on their business, the rates of toll and rent being extremely moderate. The granting of proper facilities and protection to merchants was the chief aim of these marts; highway robbers were a source of fear to travellers.

The Bhor State Museum Plates[2] would show that Karahāṭa was a centre of scholarship where Vedic exegesis was also given attention to. Karhāḍ was undoubtedly a famous centre of education in the Rāshṭrakūṭa period, for we find many of the donees of Rāshṭrakūṭa grants having come from that town. This, for instance, is the case with the donees of the Samangad plates of Dantidurga,[3] and the Sanjan Charter of Amoghavarsha I[4] also.

Kolhapur

Kolhapur is a well-known place and district town in

1. K.K. Handiqui, *op. cit.*, pp. 119-20.
2. *E.I.*, XXII, p. 181.
3. *I.A.*, XI, pp. 111ff.
4. *I.A.*, XVIII, pp. 235ff.

Maharashtra. The present Mahālakshmī (Ambābāī) temple dates back only to the seventeenth century A.D. The older parts of this temple might belong to the tenth century A.D. The earliest known inscriptional reference is from a copper-plate grant made by Amoghavarsha I in 817 A.D. It was found at Sanjan and states that this Amoghavarsha cut off one of his fingers as an offering to the goddess for bringing peace to the people of his place. Although the relevant verses do not mention Kolhapur by name, scholars are agreed that the Mahālakshmī mentioned in the plate is none other than that of Kolhapur. As a religious centre, it is known as Dakshiṇa-Kāśī or the Kāśī of the South.

Mangalore

Mangalore is an important sea-port in the Karnataka state. The author of Valvikkuḍi Copper-Plate grant[1] of Pāṇḍya Neḍuñjaḍaiyan (A.D 756-815), describes Mangalore, *i.e.*, Mangalapura as the great city where the peacock danced with the cuckoo near tanks perfumed with opening flowers. From this record we can also conclude that as early as in the seventh-eighth centuries, the Tulu region had made great strides in the economic fields and that Mangalore was even in those times a flourishing and populous township well-known to be called a *mahā-nagara* (great city) in the records.[2]

Melapāti

Kṛshṇa III was camping at Melapāti after his southern campaign which is testified to by Somadeva and Karhāḍ Plates.[3] It is mentioned in the *Yaśastilaka* of Somadeva and the *Mahāpurāṇa* of Pushpadanta.

Pushpadanta in his *Mahāpurāṇa* (1.3) says that Kṛishṇa III was camping in the city of Mepādi,[4] *i.e.*, Melapāti in North

1. *E.I*, XVII, pp. 301 & 307.
2. K.V. Ramesh, *A History of South Kanara*. Dharwar, 1970, p. 271.
3. *E I.*, IV, p. 278.
4. *H.K.*, p. 141.

Arcort District after having severed the Chola prince's head 'with the hair tied up'. This is obviously a reference to Rājāditya's death in the battle of Takkolam, the memory of which was still fresh in 959 A.D. Pushpadanta describes the town of Melapāti as 'rolling in festivities', and as a place where presents of money and gold had been given to the poor. It is natural to surmise that Kṛshṇa III was celebrating his southern victory at Melapāti that year, and the town was in a gay mood on account of the celebrations. The year 959 A.D. was indubitably a year of political and cultural importance in the history of the Deccan as it not only was the culmination of the Rāshṭrakūṭa hegemony in the south, but the commencement and completion respectively of two monumental works of Indian literature, *i.e.*, the *Mahāpurāṇa* and the *Yaśastilaka*.

Panahala

Panahala in Kolhapur district of Maharashtra is well laid out. With its red soil and salubrious climate it had several ancient ruins and monuments including the Tīna Darwājā, which has an inscription dating back to 954 A.D.[1] From this inscription we feel tempted to presume that it was a town during the Rāshṭrakūṭa period.

Paṇḍharpur

Inscriptional reference to Viṭṭhal and Paṇḍharpur during the last thousand years are mostly records of grants made by various rulers and commoners to the shrine. The earliest known reference to Paṇḍharpur comes from the sixth century A.D. This is a Copper-Plate grant of the Rāshṭrakūṭas and although it mentions Paṇḍharangapalli, that is, Paṇḍharpur, it does not make any mention of Viṭṭhal at all.[2]

1. *Panorama of Maharashtra*, p. 71.
2. M.S. Mate, *Temples and Legends of Maharashtra*, Bombay, Second Edition, 1970, p. 196.

Paṭṭadakal

Paṭṭadakal (Lat. 17°57′ and Long. 75°52′ E) stands on the left bank of the river Malaprabhā in the Bādāmi Taluk of the Bijapur district in Karnataka. A look at the temple and the several *liṅgas* standing or lying here and there at the village of Paṭṭadakal, impresses upon the historians that it was a great centre of Śiva worship in our days. The inscribed salab of A.D.1162 standing in the temple of Vijayeśvara (mod. Saṅgameśvara) mentions Kisuvolal as the Kāśī of the south and considers Vijayeśvara as identical with Viśveśvara (of Kāśī).[1] These episodes add to the sanctity of Paṭṭadakal.

During the times of the Rāshṭrakūṭa it was known as Kisuvolal, the chief town of Kisukādu-70. Kisuvolal (*i.e.*, Paṭṭadakal) was one of the chief outposts of the pure Kannada speaking tract (*Tirulgannadanādu*) as described in the Kannada work the *Kavirājamārga* written during the time of Nṛpatuṅga I (A.D. 814-878). According to this work the other important outposts of this tract were Okkunda (Belgaum district), Puligere (Dharwar district) and Kopaṇa (Kopbal in the Raichur district).

An inscription[2] of Indra III (A.D. 782-84) has been found here in northern porch of the Virūpāksha temple. Besides this, scholars are of the opinion that the old Jain temple of Paṭṭadakal was built during the times of Amoghavarsha I or Kṛshṇa I. This is a mere conjecture based upon literary, architectural, religious and historical grounds.

The Malaprabhā river, on which Paṭṭadakal stands, flows here northwards which adds grace and sanctity to the village. Owing to this reason only, nine out of the ten existing temples are built at this place by the side of the river. People fervently believe that the spots where the rivers flow northwards are quite sacred.[3] Comparisons for this are not

1. A M. Annigeri, *The Paṭṭadakal Temples*, Dharwar, 1961, pp. 1-4.
2. *Ibid.*, p. 9.
3. Cf. Vārāṇasī and Sultanganj (in Bhagalpur district of Bihar) where due to the geographical situation the Ganges flows northwards and river waters at these places are taken to be quite suitable for worship.

far to seek. Rivers in North India like the Sindhu, the Yamunā, the Ganges and the Brahmaputra originate from the Himalayan ranges and empty themselves either in the Arabian Sea or the Bay of Bengal. As rivers flowing northwards are rare and North India is considered to be quite holy, being the abode of gods, such of the rivers or spots where the river takes a northward course are taken to be quite sacred. At such holy spots Indians have built temples, installed images of gods in them and worshipped them. As already stated, Paṭṭadakal enjoys the privilege of standing on such a spot. Similar reasons can be assigned to some of the temples at Aihole, Kolhapur and other towns. It was customary in the Deccan to enshrine the *liṅga* of Uttareśvara at such spots by erecting temples.

The ten temples referred to above are dedicated to gods Pāpanātha, Virūpāksha, Mallikārjuna, Kāśiviśveśvara, Saṅgameśvara, Chandraśekhara, Jaṁbuliṅga, Galaganātha, Kāḍasiddheśvara and to a Jina. All these temples except the last one are situated in this very order on the left bank of the river as one goes from the south to the north. The Jain temple stands about 200 m away from the village of Paṭṭadakal by the side of the Bādāmi-Paṭṭadakal road.

Poona

The names of villages mentioned in the grants[1] are situated in the Poona district. It seems that the original name was Pūnā or Pūrṇā, which was Sanskritized partially into Puṅaka in the first grant and fully in the second as in modern times into Pūrṇa. This Poona was known as early as the second half of the eighth century A.D. when the Rāshṭrakūṭas were asserting their supremacy over south India. What is noteworthy is that not only a town but also the headquarters of a district named after it.

1. *E.I.*, XIII, p. 275 and XIX, pp. 165ff.

Pratishṭhāna

Pratishṭhāna[1] is identified with modern Paithan, 56 km south of Aurangabad situated on the northern bank of the river Godāvarī. It was one of the well-established *tīrthas* of the ancient times and its glory continued up to the fourteenth century A.D. when the Mahānubhāva sect was born here. Hence this place cannot be denied its existence during the period of the Rāshṭrakūṭas. It was a good river port and supposed to be a centre of trade. It served as a link in the trade being carried on from the extreme north to the extreme south.

Rohaṇkheḍ

Rohaṇkheḍ is situated at a distance of 13 km from Khamgaon in Berar of Maharashtra State. It was a famous town during the time of the Rāshṭrakūṭas.[2] Here ruins of ancient temples are still present. The temple of Lord Śiva is important among them. Its roof is flat, pillars are rectangular or hexagonal in shape and the *garbhagṛha* is quite large. Near the temple there is a fragmentary inscription on a broken piece of rock in which '*Tadanvaye Bhūpatiḥ Kūṭaḥ*' is readable which testifies that this temple is of the time of the Rāshṭrakūtas. This temple has great similarity with the Kailāsa temple of Elūra. Here in this temple copper rods have been used for the stability of the rock wall of the temple. In the verandah of the temple the idol of the Lord Vishṇu has been installed which is a unique art piece. Some Jain images of the medieval times have been discovered from here. The great poet Pushpadanta is supposed to be the inhabitant of this place.

Sanjan

This is a small town right on the western seacoast at

1. V.K. Mathur, *op. cit.*, pp. 581-83.
2. *Ibid.*, p. 804.

present in the Dahanu taluk of the Thana district. But two thousand years ago, it was an important place, mentioned as it is in one of the Nasik inscriptions of the first century A.D. as "Chechijna".[1]

Sanjan was reputed to be the earliest Parsi Colony. Here come the Parsis in the eighth century A.D. when they had left Iran, because of their persecution by the new Muslim rulers. But it is little known that this Colony and the surrounding region—the present Thana district which formed a province under the Rāshṭrakūṭas, were placed under an Arab governor, called Madhumati (*i.e.* Mohammad), though he was a Muslim. He had not only patronised Hindu temples, but invited Brāhmaṇas from north India to settle in Sanjan. Thus a unique instance of communal harmony 1200 years ago was supplied by the discovery of five copper-plates at Chinchini.[2]

Saundatti

This ancient town, the early name of which was Sugandhavatī, developed as a powerful centre of Jain religion from the period of ninth century A.D. It was the capital of the feudatory governors of the Rāshṭrakūṭas. An epigraph[3] found in the Ankaleśvara or Ankeśvara temple at Saundatti furnishes many details in regard to the religious leanings of the early rulers of the Rāshṭrakūṭa house and their activities that promoted the spread of Jain doctrines in this region.

Śrīpura

The Manor Plates[4] of Dantidurga dated Śaka 671 (A.D.

1. H.D. Sankalia, 'When the Adivasi was King', *TOI*, September 19, 1982.
2. *E.I.*, XXXII, pp. 45-76.
3. *JBBRAS*, X, pp. 194ff.
4. V.V. Mirashi, *Studies in Indology*, II, p. 13. Also *P.I.H.C.*, Twenty-first Session, Trivandrum, p. 51.

749) is important in several ways. It clearly shows that at Śrīpura in Konkan there was a Brahmā temple which is a rare one. Generally the images of Brahmā are seen on the outer walls of the temples dedicated to other gods like Vishṇu or Śiva. This temple testifies to the cult of that god flourishing there in the eighth century A.D.

Another interesting feature of this record is that the grant was made not by a king or a royal personage but by the Mahājanas of the city of Śrīpura. These Mahājanas evidently consisted of the representatives of the city and managed the civic affairs including charitable endowments of the city.

Vātāpi

Vātāpi is identified with modern Bādāmi in Bijapur district of Karnataka which is situated about 225 km away from Sholapur on the Sholapur-Gadag railway line. Before the advent of the Rāshṭrakūṭas it was the capital of the Chālukya dynasty. In about 750 A.D. this city came under the direct control of the Rāshṭrakūṭas.

In addition to the administrative purpose which it served, it was a great religious centre. Temples and sculptures connected with the Hindus, Buddhists and Jains added much to its beauty and importance.[1]

In addition to these towns, there may be several other towns which have not been discovered so far. Scholars have tried to identify the habitation of the Rāshṭrakūṭa period on the basis of surface finds. There have been traced many Rāshṭrakūṭa temples throughout the Deccan and there are many which have been identified as Rāshṭrakūṭa temples both in Maharashtra ond Karnataka States. Many of the towns must still be there awaiting further exploration and excavation.

1. V.K. Mathur, *op. cit.*, p. 840.

Bibliography

A. ORIGINAL SOURCES

(i) Literature

Āpastamba Dharmasūtra, Ed. & Pub. by Halasyanath Śāstrin, Kumbakonam, 1895.

Āpastamba Gṛhyasūtra, Ed. with commentary by Sudarśanāchārya, Mysore Govt. Central Library Series.

Baudhāyana Dharmasūtra, Ed. by Srinivasacharya, Mysore, 1907,

Elliot, Sir H.M. and John Dowson, *History of India as told by its own Historians*, 8 Vols., London, 1866-77. Vol. II Reprinted with Introduction by Mohammad Habib, commentary by S.H. Hodiwala, and supplement by Khaliq Ahmad Nizami, Aligarh, 1952 and later reprinted by Kitab Mahal also.

Indranandi, *Jvālini-Kalpa*, An unpublished MS. preserved in the Deva Kumar Oriental Jain Library, Arrah (Bihar).

Janna, *Anantanāthapurāṇam*, Edited by H. Deveerappa and P.C.M. Sharma, Mysore, 1972.

Jinasena, *Ādipurāṇa*, Ed. by Pannalal Jain, Part I, 2nd Ed., Kasi, 1963 and Part II, Kasi, 1951.

Kalhaṇa, *Rājataraṅgiṇī*, Eng. Tr. by M.A. Stein, Westminster, 1900.

Mahāvīrāchārya, *Gaṇitasāra-Saṁgraha*, Ed. by L.C. Jain, Sholapur, 1963.

——— *Gaṇitasārasaṁgraha*, Ed. by M. Rangacharya, Madras, 1912.

Maulvi Mahesh Prasad Sadhu, *Sulaiman Saudagar*, Hindi Tr. published by the Nagari Pracharini Sabha, Banaras, 1922.

Nāgavarmā, *Karṇāṭakabhāshābhusaṇa*, Ed. by L. Rice, Bangalore, 1884.

Nṛpatuṅga, *Kavirājamārga*, Ed. by K.B. Pathak.

Pampa, *Ādipurāṇa*, Ed. by K.G. Kundangar and A.P. Chauguler, Belgaum, 1953.

———, *Vikramārjunavijaya*, Ed. by Venkatanarayanappa Belleve, Bangalore, 1931.

———, *Vikramārjunavijaya*, Ed. by K.V. Puttapa, Mysore, 1973.

Purāṇa, Agni Purāṇa, Eng. Tr. M.N. Dutta, Vols. I-II, Calcutta, 1903-04.

Liṅga Purāṇa, Ed. by Jīvānanda Vidyāsāgara, Calcutta, 1905.

Matsya Purāṇa, Ed. and Pub. by Hari Narayan Apte, Poona, 1907.

Pushpadanta, *Jasahara-chariu*, critically edited with intr., glossary, and notes by P.L. Vaidya, Karanja, 1931.

———, *Jasahara-chariu* of Pushpadanta, ed. by H.L. Jain, New Delhi, 1972.

———, *Mahāpurāṇa*, critically ed. by P.L. Vaidya, 3 Vols., Bombay, 1937-41.

———, *Nāyakumāra-chariu*, critically ed. with intr., glossary, indices, and notes by H.L. Jain, Karanja, 1933.

———, *Nāyakumāra-chariu* of Pushpadanta, ed. by H.L. Jain, New Delhi, 1972.

Rājaśekhara, *Karpūramañjarī*, ed. by Durga Prasad and Kashinath Pandurang Parab.

Ranna, *Ajit-Tirthakara-Purāṇa-Tilakam.*

Smṛtis, *Bṛhaspati-Smṛti*, tr. into English by J. Jolly, *SBE*, 1889. Reconstructed by K.V. Rangaswami Aiyangar, *GOS*, Baroda, 1941.

Kātyāyana-Smṛti, Ed. by N.C. Bandyopadhyaya, Calcutta, 1927.

Manusmṛti, tr. into English by W. Jones, Calcutta, 1794; also tr. by G. Buhler, *SBE*, Vol. 25.

Nārada-Smṛti, tr. into English by J. Jolly, *SBE*, 53, Oxford, 1889,

Vasishṭha Smṛti, Smṛti-Samdarbha, Vols. I-IV, Calcutta.

Yājñavalkya-Smṛti, tr. into English by J.R. Charpure, Bombay, 1936.

Somadeva, *Nītivākyāmṛta*, Pub.: Manikchand Granthamala Series No. 22.

———, *Yaśastilaka*, ed. by Sivadatta & K.M. Parab, Bombay, 1901-03.

———, *Yaśastilakachampū*, ed. by Kedar Nath Sharma, Nirnaya Sagar Press, Bombay.

———, *Yaśastilakachampū*, tr. into Hindi by Sundarlal Shastri, Varanasi, 1960.

Trivikramabhattṭa, *Nalachampū* or *Damayantīkathā*, ed. with Comm. by N.K. Sharma, Banaras, 1932; ed. with Comm., Bombay, 1885.

Uddyotanasūri, *Kuvalayamālākahā*, tr. into Sanskrit by Ratnaprabha Sūri, Bhavanagar, 1916.

———, *Kuvalayamālākahā Saṁkshepa*, ed. by A.N. Upadhye, Bombay, 1961.

———, *Kuvalayamālā*, Notes and Introduction by A.N. Upadhye, Singhi Jain Granthamala, Bombay, 1970.

Ugrādityāchārya, *Kalyāṇakāraka*, ed. by V.P. Shastri, Sholapur, 1940.

(ii) Monuments and Inscriptions

Archaeological Remains, Monuments and Museums, Parts I & II, ASI, New Delhi, 1964.

Aiyer, K.V.S., *South Indian Inscriptions* (ASI New Imperial Series), Vols. 52 & 53, Madras, 1928, 1933.

Annigeri, A.M. and B.R. Joshi, *The Descriptive List of Stone and Copper-plate Inscriptions Examined by the Kannada Research Institute During the years 1940-41 to 1942-43*, Dharwar, 1961.

Archaeological Survey of Western India.

Bhandarkar, D.R., 'List of Inscriptions of Northern India', Appendix to *EI*, XIX-XXIII.

Burgess, Jas. and Bhagwanlal Indraji, *Inscriptions from the Cave Temples of Western India*, Delhi, First Reprint, 1976.

Desai, P.B., (Ed.), *A Corpus of Inscriptions in the Kannada Districts of Hyderabad State*, Hyderabad, 1958.

Dikshit, M.G., *Selected Inscriptions from Maharashtra (5th to 12th century A.D.)*, Poona, 1947.

Epigraphia Carnatica, Vols. I-XVII, VII and VIII (Suppl.), Bangalore, 1898 onwards; Revised Vols., Mysore, 1973 onwards.

Hiralal, R.B., *Inscriptions in the Central Provinces and Berar*, 2nd Ed., Nagpur, 1932.

Hultzsch, E., *South Indian Inscriptions*, 3 Vols. (ASI, NIS, Vols. 9, 10 & 29), Madras, 1890-1929.

Karnataka Inscriptions, Vols. I-III, Ed. by R.S. Panchamukhi, Dharwar, 1941-53.

———, Vol. IV, Ed. by A.M. Annigeri, with a foreword of B.A. Saletore, Dharwar, 1961.

———, Vol. V, Ed. by B.R. Gopal, Gen. Ed. P.B. Desai, Dharwar, 1969.

———, Vol. VI, Ed. by B.R. Gopal, Gen. Ed. Shrinivas Ritti, Dharwar, 1973.

Krishnamacharlu, C.R., *Bombay Karnataka Inscriptions*, Madras, 1940.

Mirashi, V.V., *Corpus Inscriptionum Indicarum*, Vol. V.

Mittal, A.C., *The Inscriptions of the Imperial Paramāras* (800 A.D. to 1320 A.D.), Ahmedabad, 1979.

Naik, A.V., 'Inscriptions of the Deccan : An Epigraphical Survey (*circa* 300 B.C.-1300 A.D.)', *BDCRI*, Vol. IX, pp. 1-160.

Rice, Lewis, *Mysore and Coorg from Inscriptions*, London, 1909.

Ritti, S. and G.C. Shelke, *Inscriptions from Nanded District*, Nanded, 1968.

South Indian Inscriptions, Vols. I-XX, Madras, 1890 onwards.

Subramaniam, T.N., *South Indian Temple Inscriptions*, 3 Vols , Madras, 1953-55.

Summaries of Inscriptions (1943-44 to 1949-50), Gen. Ed. P.B. Desai, and Prepared by B.R. Gopal and Shrinivas Ritti, Dharwar, 1966.

(iii) Important Published Rashtrakuta Inscriptions

Elura Plates, A.D. 741 : *EI*, XXV, p. 25; *JBBRAS*, XXVI, p. 163; *AIOC, Session XV* (*Summary*), p. 97; *SI*, II, p. 3.

Manor Plates, A.D. 749 : *PIHC*, 1958, p. 49; *IHQ*, XXXV, p. 183; *SI*, II, p. 10.

Baroda Inscription, A.D. 753 : *IA*, XII, p. 228.

Samangad Plates, A.D. 753-4 : *IA*, XI, p. 108; *List*, No. 53.

Antrol-chharoli Plates, A.D. 757 : *JBBRAS*, XVI, p. 106; *IA*, XXXI, 329.

Poona Plates, A.D. 758 : *QBISM*, VIII, p. 165.

Elura Dasavatara Cave Inscription, *ASWI*, V, p. 42.

Hatti-Mattur Inscription (A.D. 765): *EI*, VI, 160; *List*, No. 55.

Talegaon Plates, A.D. 768 : *EI*, XIII, p. 275.

Alas Plates, A.D. 770 : *EI*, VI, p. 208; VII, p. 230; *List*, No. 56.

Bhāndak Plates, A.D. 772 : *EI*, XIV, p. 121.

Pimpri Plates, A.D. 775 : *EI*, X, p. 81.

Pattadakal Temple Inscription, A.D. 778 : *IA*, X, p. 167; XI, p. 124.

Dhulia Plates, A.D. 779 : *EI*, VIII, p. 182.

Bhor State Museum Plates, A.D. 780 : *EI*, XXII, p. 176; *ASI*, 1934-35, p. 61.

Naregal Inscription (A.D. 780) : *EI*, VI, p. 162; *List*, No. 58.

Uttaramallur Inscription, A.D. 782 : *EI*, XXIV, p. 28.

Kasarsirsi Plates, A.D. 783 : *JASB*, XLIII-XLIV (N.S.).

Jethwai Plates, A.D. 786 : *EI*, XXII, p. 98.

Hilol Inscription, A.D. 788 : *EI*, XXXIV, p. 213.

Kachavi Inscription (Dhruva) : *KRI*, 1953-57, p. 65.

Lakshmesvara Temple Inscription (Dhruva) : *EC*, VI, p. 166; *List*, No. 60.

Daulatabad Plates, A.D. 793 : *EI*, IX, p. 98.

Paithan Plates, A.D. 794 : *EI*, III, p. 105; *IA*, XXX, p. 515; *List*, No. 61.

Anjanvati Plates, A.D. 800 : *EI*, XXIII, p. 101.

Mane Inscription, A.D. 802 : *EC*, IX, No. 61.

Jharika Grant, A.D. 803 : *EI*, XXXII, p. 157.

British Museum Plates, A.D. 804: *IA*, XI, p. 104: *EI*, XXXIII, p. 327.

Ramesvar Tirtha Plates, A.D. 804 : *IA*, p. 126; *List*, No. 62.

Nesarikā Plates, A.D. 805 : *EI*, XXXIV, p. 123; *JAS*, XXIV, p. 18; XXVI, p. 133; *SMHD*, I, p. 15.

Dharur Plates, A.D. 806 : *EI*, XXXVI, p. 290.

Sisvai Plates, A.D. 807 : *EI*, XXIII, p. 204.

Wani Plates, A.D. 808 : *IA*, XI, p. 156; XXXI, p. 217; *List*, No. 63.

Radhanpur Plates, A.D. 808 : *EI*, VI, p. 249; *IA*, VI, p. 59; *List*, No. 64.

Prince of Wales Museum Plates, A.D. 810 : *EI*, XXVI, p. 248.

BISM Plates, A.D. 810 : *QBISM*, XVI, p. 27; *SMHD*, II, p. 27.

Bahulavad Plates, A.D. 810 : *SMHD*, II, p. 13.

Mayurakhandi Plates, A.D. 811 : *JBBRAS* (NS), III, p. 187.

Sirso (Lohara) Plates, A.D. 812 : *EI*, XXIII, p. 212.

Baroda Grant, A.D. 812-13 : *IA*, XII, p. 156.

Torkhed Plates, A.D. 812-13 : *EI*, III, p. 54; *List*, No. 67.

Kadaba Plates, A.D. 813 : *EI*, IV, p. 332; *IA*, XII, p. 11; *List*, No. 66.

Lakshmesvar Inscription (Govinda III) : *EI*, VI, p. 163; *IA*, XI, p. 156; *List*, No. 59.

Gundagatti Inscriptions (Govinda III) : *KRI*, 1953-57, pp. 66-68.

Nulageri Inscription (Govinda III) : *KRI*, 1953-57, p. 68.

Sivagambi Inscription (Govinda III) : *KRI*, 1953-57, p. 69.

Medur Inscription (Govinda III) : *KRI*, 1953-57, p. 70.

Khanda-Bagur (Govinda III) : *KRI*, 1953-57, p. 71.

Navasari Plates, A.D. 816 : *JBBRAS*, XX, p. 135.

Anastu Inscription, A.D. 817 : *Important Inscriptions from the Baroda State*, I, p. 55.

Javakhed Plates, A.D. 820 : *EI*, XXXII, p. 129; *JBRS*, XLV, p. 13; *PIHC*, 1968, p. 31; *SI*, II, p. 207.

Surat Plates, A.D. 821 : *EI*, XXI, p. 133.

Brahmanpalli Grant, A.D. 824 : *EI*, XXII, p. 77.

Kavi Plates, A.D. 827-8 : *IA*, V, pp. 113, 144.

Baroda Plates, A.D. 835-6 : *IA*, XIV, p. 196.

Gudimall Temple Inscription, A.D. 843 : *IA*, XL, p. 111.

Kanheri Inscription, A.D. 843 : *IA*, XIII, p. 136; *List*, No. 72.

Kanheri Inscription, A.D. 851 : *IA*, XIII, p. 134; *List*, No. 73.

Ranibennur Inscription, A.D. 859 : *ASI*, 1930-34, p. 209; *KI*, II, p. 14.

Arishinaguppi Inscription, A.D. 859 : *KRI*, 1953-57, p. 72.

Konnur Inscription, A.D. 860 : *EI*, VI, p. 29; *List*, No. 74.

Pathari Pillar Inscription, A.D. 861 : *EI*, XI, p. 252; *IA*, XL, p. 239.

Mantrawadi Inscription, A.D. 865 : *EI*, VII, p. 198.

Shiggaon Inscriptions, A.D. 865 : *EI*, VII, p. 201; XXXV, 85 *KI*, I, No. 14.

Nilgund Inscription, A.D. 866 : *EI*, VI, p. 98; *List*, No. 75.

Sirur Inscription, A.D. 866 : *EI*, VII, p. 202; *IA*, XII, p. 218; *List*, No. 76.

Begumra Grant, A.D. 867 : *IA*, XII, p. 179.

Soratur Inscription, A.D. 869 : *EI*, XI, p. 179.

Sanjan Plates, A.D. 871 : *EI*, XVIII, p. 235, *SI*, II, p. 210.

Kazipet Inscription, A.D. 872 : *IAP*, 1974, p. 1, No. 1.

Ron Inscription, A.D. 874 : *EI*, XI, p. 183.

Nilagundi Inscription, A.D. 874-5 : *EI*, VII, p. 208.

Saundatti Inscription, A.D. 875 : *JBBRAS*, X, p. 194; *List*, No. 79.

Kanheri Inscription, A.D. 877 : *IA*, XIII, p. 135; XX, p. 421; *List*, No. 80.

Hirbidri Inscription, A.D. 878 : *ASI*, 1935-36, p. 103.

Siramja Inscription, A.D. 883 : *EI*, XXI, p. 208.

Soratur Inscription, A.D. 883 : *EI*, XXI, p. 208.

Batageri Inscription, A.D. 888 : *EI*, X, p. 187; XI, p. 189.

Begumra Grant, A.D. 888 : *IA*, XIII, p. 65.

Mantralaya Inscription, A.D. 893 : *SII*, IX, No. 55; *KI*, V, No. 2.

Kunimellihalli Inscription, A.D. 896 : *EI*, XVI, p. 277.

Nandivadige Inscription, A.D. 900 : *IA*, XII, p. 221; *List*, No. 82.

Siyamangalam Inscription, A.D. 900 : *SII*, VII.

Mulgund Inscription, A.D. 902-3 : *EI*, XI, p. 190; *JBBRAS*, X, p. 190; *List*, No. 83.

Venkatapur Inscription, A.D. 906 : *EI*, XXVI, p. 59.

Kapadvanaj Plates, A.D. 910 : *EI*, I, p. 52; *List*, No. 84.

Aihole Temple Inscription, A.D. 911-12 : *IA*, XII, p. 222.

Jambgaon Plates, A.D. 914 : *EI*, XXXVI, p. 223; *MUJ*, I, No. 1.

Begumra Plates, A.D. 914 : *EI*, IX, p. 24; *JBBRAS*, XVIII, p. 257; *List*, No. 86.

Vajirkhed Grants, A.D. 914 : *EI*, XXXVIII, p. 5; *NUJ*, XVII, p. 117.

Punganur (Puriganur) Inscriptions (Krishna II) : *ASI*, 1930-34, p. 240.

Siragambi Inscription (Krishna II) : *KRI*, 1953-57, p. 73.

Nulageri Inscription (Krishna II) : *Ibid.*

Galpoji Inscription (Krishna II) : *KRI*, 1953-57, p. 74.

Anaji Inscription (Krishna II) : *Ibid*, p. 75.

Navasari Plates, A.D. 915 : *EI*, IX, p. 26.

Ranibennur Inscription, A.D. 915 : *ASI*, 1934-35, p. 67.

Hatti-Mattur Inscription, A.D. 916 : *IA*, XII, p. 224; *List*, No. 88.

Gadag Inscription, A.D. 918 : *ASI*, 1930-34, p. 235.

Dandapur Well Inscription, A.D. 918 : *IA*, XII, p. 222; *List*, No. 89; *KI*, II, p. 11; *Digest of Annual Report on Kannada Research in Bombay Province, 1940-41*, p. 11.

Shiggaon Inscription, A.D. 919 : *KI*, p. 18.

Kandebagur Inscription, A.D. 924 : *KRI*, 1955-57, p. 76.

Chinchini Plates, A.D. 926 : *EI*, XXXII, p. 45.

Haveri Inscription, A.D. 928 : *ASI*, 1930-34 p. 244.

Kalas Inscription, A.D. 929 ; *EI*, XIII, p. 326; *IA*, XII, p. 211; *List*, No. 90.

Gaonri Plates, A.D. 929 : *EI*, XXIII, p. 106.

Andhra Plates, A.D. 929 : *EI*, XXXVI, p. 259.

Cambay Plates, A.D. 930 : *EI*, VII, p. 26; *List*, No. 91.

Devanagera Inscription, A.D. 930 : *EC*, XI, Dg. 119.

Doddamakala Inscription, A.D. 930 : *SII*, IX, Pt. I.

Tirunamandallur Inscription, A.D. 931 : *EI*, VII, p. 135.

Halaharavi Inscription, A.D. 932 : *SII*, IX, No. 62.

Sangali Plates, A.D. 933-4 : *IA*, XII, p. 247; XXXI, p 219; *List*, No. 91; *SI*, II, p. 207.

Tirukkovalur Inscriptions, A.D. 935, 936 & 938 : *EI*, VII, pp. 142-43.

Deoli Plates, A.D. 940 : *EI*, V, p. 190; *EHD*, p. 306, *List*, No. 93.

Salotgi Inscription, A.D. 945 : *EI*, II, p. 58; *List*, No. 94.

Tuppad-kurhatti Inscription, A.D. 946 : *EI*, XIV, p. 364.

Kyasanur Inscription, A.D. 946 : *EI*, XVI, p. 280.

Tiruvorriyur Inscription, A.D. 949 : *EI*, XXVII, p. 292.

\takur Inscription, A.D. 950 : *EI*, II, p. 167; VI, p. 50; *List*, No. 95.

Soratur Inscription, A.D. 951 : *IA*, XII, p. 257; *List*, No. 96.

Chinchi Inscription, A.D. 954 : *EI*, VI, p. 180; *List*, No. 97.

Vellur Rock Inscription, A.D. 955 : *EI*, IV, p. 81.

Ukkal Inscription, A.D. 955 : *SII*, III, No. 7, p. 12; *List*, No. 100.

Tirukkalukkunram Inscription, A.D. 956 : *EI*, III, p. 284; *List*, No. 101.

Karjol Inscription, A.D. 957 : *ASI*, 1930-34, p. 241.

Tirukkalukkunram Inscription, A.D. 958 : *EI*, III, p. 285; *List*, No. 102.

Bhavaji Rock Inscription, A.D. 959 : *EI*, IV, p. 82; *List*, No. 103.

Karhad Plates, A.D. 959 : *EI*, IV, p. 278; *EHD*, p. 275; *List*, No. 98.

Kolhapur Plates, A.D. 960 : *JBBRAS* (NS), X, p. 21.

Devi Hosur Inscription, A.D. 962 : *EI*, VI, p. 180; XVI, p. 285; *List*, No. 99.

Uppinabetagiri Inscription, A.D. 964 : *Jainism in South India*, Ins. No. 46.

Uttaramallur Inscription, A.D. 964 : *EI*, XXIV, p. 28.

Embadi Inscription, A.D. 965 : *ASI*, 1930-34, p. 223.

Khakurdi Inscription, A.D. 966 ; *QBISM*, XXI, No. 4.

Kolagallur Inscription, A.D. 967 : *EI*, XXI, p. 260.

Chinichini Plates (Krishna III) : *EI*, XXXII, p. 55; XXXVII, p. 277.

Saundatti Records (Krishna III) : *IA*, XXXII, 215.

Kandhar Inscription (Krishna III) : *EI*, XXXV, p. 105.

Jura Prasasti of Krishna III (Undated) : *EI*, XIX, p. 289.

Bahadurpur Pillar Inscription (Krishna III) : *EI*, XXXV, p. 10.

Sudambi Inscription (Krishna III) : *KRI*, 1953-57, p. 77.

Halgur Inscription, A.D. 971 : *EI*, XXXIV, p. 56.

Adaragunchi Inscription, A.D. 971-72 : *IA*, XII, p. 255; *List*, No. 104.

Kyasanur Inscription (Khottiga) : *EI*, XVI, p. 284.

Kharda Plates, A.D. 972-73 : *IA*, XII, p. 263; XXXI, p. 220; *List*, No. 105.

Navasari Grant (Karkaraja) : *IA*, XXXI, p. 363.

Gandur Inscription, A.D. 973-74 : *IA*, XII, p. 270; *List*, No. 105.

Sravana Belagola Inscription (Undated) : *EC*, II, p. 6; *List*, No. 60.

Sravana Belagola Inscription, A.D. 982 : *EC*, II, p. 65 (No. 133); *List*, No. 107; *Inscriptions at Sravana Belgola*, 53, No. 57.

B. SECONDARY SOURCES

(i) General Works

Adhya, G.L., *Early Indian Economics*, Bombay, 1966.

Ahmad, Nafis, *Muslim Contribution to Geography*, Lahore, 1947.

Ahmad, Qeyamuddin, *India by Alberuni* (Abridged Edition), National Book Trust, 1983.

Aiyangar, K.V.R., *Aspects of Ancient Indian Economic Thought*, Varanasi, 1934.

Aiyangar, S. Krishnasvami, *Ancient India and South Indian History & Culture*, Poona, 1941.

Aiyar, K.V. Subrahmanya, *Historical Sketches of Ancient Dekkan*, Coimbatore, 1969.

———, *Three Lectures*, 2nd ed., Dharwar, 1978.

Altekar, A.S., *A History of the Important Ancient Towns and Cities in Gujarat*, Bombay, 1925.

———, *Village Communities in Western India*, Bombay, 1927.

———, *Rashtrakutas and Their Times*, First published in 1934, 2nd Revised ed., Poona, 1967.

———, *Education in Ancient India*, Varanasi, 1943.

———, *State and Government in Ancient India*, Delhi, 1958.

———, *The Position of Women in Ancient Hindu Civilization*, Delhi, 3rd ed., 1962.

Annigeri, A.M., *A Guide to the Kannada Research Institute Museum*, Dharwar, 1958.

———, *A Guide to the Pattadakal Temples*, Dharwar, 1961.

Appadorai, A., *Economic Conditions in Southern India, 1000-1500 A.D.*, Vols. 1-2, Madras, 1936.

Awasthi, A.B.L., *Studies in Skanda Purana*, Lucknow, 1966.

Ayyangar, P.T. Srinivasa, *Bhoja Raja*, Madras, 1931.

Bajpai, K.D., *Indian Numismatic Studies*, New Delhi, 1976.

———, *Prachina Bharatiya Vyapara Ka Itihasa* (in Hindi).

Bandyopadhyaya, N.C., *Economic Life and Progress in Ancient India*, Calcutta, 1945.

Barnett, L.D., *Antiquities of India*, London, 1913.

Barrett, Douglas, *Ter*, Bombay, 1960.

Basham, A.L., *The Wonder that was India*, London, 1954. Translated into Hindi as *Adbhut Bharat*, Agra, 3rd ed., 1978.

———, *Studies in Indian History and Culture*, Calcutta, 1964.

Belvalkar, *System of Sanskrit Grammars*, Poona, 1934.

Bhandarkar, R.G., *Early History of the Deccan*, Calcutta, 1928.

———, *Early History of the Deccan and Miscellaneous Historical Essays*, Poona, 1983.

Bhattacharya, Sachchidanand, *Bharatiya Itihasa Kosa*, Hindi Translation of *A Dictionary of Indian History*, Lucknow, 1967.

Birdwood, Sir George, *Industrial Art of India*, London, 1915.

Bose, A.N., *Social and Rural Economy of Northern India*, 2 Vols., Calcutta, 1942-45.

Bose, Nemai Sadhan, *History of the Chandellas of Jejakabhukti*, Calcutta, 1956.

Brown, Percy, *Indian Architecture (Buddhist and Hindu Period)*, 6th Reprint, Bombay, 1971.

Chakladar, H.G., *Social Life in Ancient India*, Calcutta, 1954.

Chakraborty, Haripada, *Trade and Commerce in India (200 B.C.—c. 650 A.D.)*, Calcutta, 1966.

Chanana, Dev Raj, *Slavery in Ancient India*, Delhi, 1960.

Chattopadhyaya, Brajadulal, *Coins and Currency System in South India (c. A.D. 225-1300)*, New Delhi, 1977.

Cordier, *Yule's Travels of Marco Polo*, London, 1926.

Cousens, H., *Architectural Antiquities of Western India*, London, 1920.

Cunningham, A., *Coins of Medieval India from the Seventh Century down to the Muhammadan Conquests*, London, 1894.

Dange, S.A., *India from Primitive Communism to Slavery*, Bombay, 1949.

Dalal, C.D. and R.A.K. Shastri (eds.), *Rajasekhara : Kavyamimamsa*.

Das, Dipakranjan, *Economic History of the Deccan (From the first to the sixth century A.D*), Delhi, 1969.

Datta, Swati, *Migrant Brahmanas in Northern India, c. A.D. 475-1013*, Delhi, 1989.

Das, S.K., *Economic History of Ancient India*, Calcutta, 1925.

Davis, C. Collin, *An Historical Atlas of the Indian Peninsula*, Oxford University Press, 1959.

Deglurkar, G.B., *Cultural History of Marathwada*, Ph. D. Thesis, Marathwada University, Aurangabad.

Deo, Prabhakar R., *Temples of Marathwada*, Ph. D. Thesis, Marathwada University, 1972.

Deo, S.B., *History of Jain Monachism*, Poona, 1953.

———, *Excavations at Bhokardan*, Nagpur, 1974.

Desai, Devangana, *Erotic Sculptures in India : A Socio-cultural Study*, New Delhi, 1975.

Desai, P.B., *Jainism in South India and Some Jain Epigraphs*, Sholapur, 1957.

———, *Basavesvara and His Times*, Dharwar, 1968.

———, (Ed.), *A History of Karnataka* (*From Pre-History to Unification*), Dharwar, 2nd ed., 1981.

Dey, N.L., *Geographical Dictionary of Ancient and Medieval India*, London, 1927.

Dhavalikar, M.K., *Ajanta : A Cultural Study*, Poona, 1973.

Dikshit, R.K., *The Chandellas of Jejakabhukti*, New Delhi, 1977.

Diwakar, R.R. (Ed.), *Karnataka Through the Ages*, Mysore, 1968.

D'Souza, Victor S., *The Navayats of Kanara*, Dharwar, 1955.

Dutta, B.B., *Town Planning in Ancient India*, Calcutta, 1925.

Edwards, Michael, *Everyday Life in Early India*, London, 1969.

Fariq, K.A., *Ancient India in Arabic Literature* (in Urdu), New Delhi, 1973.

Fleet, J.F., *The Dynasties of the Canarese Districts of the Bombay Presidency*, Bombay, 1896.

Gangoly, O.C., *The Art of the Rashtrakutas*, Calcutta, 1958.

Ganguly, D.C., *Eastern Chalukyas*, Banaras, 1937.

Ghatapanadi, S.G., *Taxation in Ancient and Medieval Karnataka*, Ph.D. Thesis, Karnataka University, 1977.

Ghosh, A. (Ed.), *Ajanta Murals*, Calcutta, 1967.

Ghosh, P.C., *India as Known to Ancient and Medieval Europe*, Calcutta, 1978.

Ghoshal, U.N., *Contributions to the History of the Hindu Revenue System*, Calcutta, 1929.

———, *The Agrarian System in Ancient India*, Calcutta, 1930.

———, *Studies in Indian History and Culture*, Calcutta, 1957.

Gode, P.K., *Studies in Indian Cultural History*, Vol.III, Poona, 1969.

Gopal, Lallanji, *The Economic Life of Northern India (c. A.D. 700-1200)*, Delhi, 1965.

———, *Aspects of History of Agriculture in Ancient India*, Varanasi, 1980.

Gupta, K.M., *The Land System in South India between c. 800 A.D. and 1200 A.D.*, Lahore, 1933.

Gupte, R.S., *Ajanta, Ellora and Aurangabad Caves*. Bombay, 1962.

———, *The Iconography of the Buddhist Sculptures (Caves) at Ellora*, Aurangabad, 1964.

———, *The Art and Architecture of Aihole*, Bombay, 1967.

Gururajachar, S., *Studies in Indian Place Names*, Vol. I, Mysore, 1980.

Habibullah, A.B.M., *Foundation of Muslim Rule in India*, Lahore, 1945.

Haig, Sir Wolseley, *The Cambridge History of India*, Vol. III, Cambridge, 1928.

Handiqui, K.K., *Yaśastilaka and Indian Culture*, Sholapur, 1949.

Harle, James C., *Temple Gateways in South India*, Oxford, 1963.

Hirematha, R.C. (ed.), *Sakala-Puratanara-Vacanyalu*, Dharwar, 1972.

Hitti, P.K., *History of the Arabs*, London, 1956.

Hodivala, S.H., *Studies in Indo-Muslim History*, Bombay, 1939; Supplement Volume, Bombay, 1957.

Hourani, G.F., *Arab Seafaring in the Indian Ocean in Ancient and Early Medieval Times*, Princeton, 1951.

Husaini, S.A.Q., *The Economic History of India*, Vol. I (From the earliest times to the foundation of feudalism), Calcutta, 1962.

Jain, Dinesh Chandra, *Economic Life in Ancient India as depicted in Jain Canonical Literature*, Vaishali, 1980.

Jain, Jagadish Chandra, *Life in Ancient India as Depicted in the Jain Canons*, Bombay, 1947.

Jain, Mahendra Kumar, *Introduction to Siddiviniśchaya*, Kashi, 1959.

Jain, P.C., *Socio-economic Exploration of Medieval India, (From 800-1200 A.D.)*, Delhi, 1976.

Jain, Prem Suman, *Kuvalayamalakaha Ka Samskritika Adhyayana* (A cultural study of the Kuvalayamalakaha) (in Hindi), Vaishali, 1975.

Joshi, S.K, *Defence Architecture : Early North Karnataka*, Ph.D. Thesis, Karnataka University, 1981.

Jung Bahadur, Nawab Aziz, *Tarikh-un-Nawayat*, Hyderabad, 1904.

Kalghatgi, T.G., *Jainism and Karnataka Culture*, Dharwar, 1977.

Kamath, Jyotsna, *Studies in Social Life in Karnataka (10th-14th Centuries A.D.)*, Ph.D. Thesis, Karnataka University, 1972.

Kapre, K.R., *Archaeology of the Ancient Place Names in the Deccan*, Ph.D. Thesis, Poona University, 1961.

Karmakar, A.P., *Cultural Heritage of Karnataka*, Dharwar, 1947.

Kane, P.V., *History of Dharmasastra*, 5 Vols., Poona, 1930ff.

— —, *Dharmasastra Ka Itihasa*, in Hindi, 2 Vols., Lucknow, 1965.

Khare, G.H., *Sources of the Medieval History of the Dekkan*, I, Poona, 1930.

Kosambi, D.D., *An Introduction to the study of Indian History* Bombay, 1956.

———, *Myth and Reality*, Bombay, 1962.

———, *The Culture and Civilization of Ancient India*, London, 1965.

———, *Indian Numismatics*, Orient Longman, 1981.

Kulkarni, B.S. (Ed.), *Indian Chronological Tables*, Dharwar, 1977.

Kuppuswamy, G.R., *Economic Conditions in Karnataka* (*A.D. 973-A.D. 1336*), Dharwar, 1975.

Liceria, M., *Social and Economic History of Karnataka* (*c. A.D. 300-1300*), Ph.D. unpublished Thesis, Patna University, 1972.

Mahalingam, T.V., *The South Indian Temple Complex*, Dharwar, 1970.

Maity, Sachindra Kumar, *Economic Life of Northern India in the Gupta Period cir. A.D. 300-500*, Calcutta, 1957.

Majumdar, R.C., *Corporate Life in Ancient India*, 2nd ed., Calcutta, 1922.

———, *History of Bengal*, Vol. I, Dhaka, 1943. Also reprinted, Patna, 1971.

Majumdar, R.C. and A.D. Pusalker (Eds.), *The History and Culture of the Indian People*, Vol. IV: *The Age of Imperial Kanauj*, Bombay, 1955; Vol. V: *The Struggle for Empire*, Bombay, 1957.

Majumdar, R.C. and K.K. Dasgupta (Eds.), *A Comprehensive History of India*, Vol. III, Pt. I, 1981; Pt. II, 1982. People's Publishing House.

Mate, M.S., *Temples and Legends of Maharashtra*, Bombay, 1970.

Mathur, Vijayendra Kumar, *Aitihasika Sthanavali* (in Hindi), New Delhi, 1969.

Mazumdar, Bhakat Prasad, *Socio-Economic History of Northern India (1030-1194 A.D.)*, Calcutta, 1960.

McCrindle, J.W., *India as Described by Megasthenes and Arrian*, London, 1877.

Minakshi, C. *Administrative and Social Life under the Pallavas*, Madras, 1938.

Mirashi, Vasudev Vishnu, *Studies in Indology*, Vol. I, Nagpur, 1960; Vol. II, Sholapur, 1961; Vols. III & IV, Varanasi, 1966.

Mishra, B.B., *Polity in the Agni Purana*, Calcutta, 1965.

Mishra, Sudarshan, *Mahākavi Pushpadanta aur unkā Mahāpurāṇa* (in Hindi), Vaishali, 1987.

Mishra, Vibhuti Bhushan, *The Gurjara Pratiharas and Their Times*, Delhi, 1966.

Mishra, Yogendra, *Megasthenes Ka Bharata Vivarana* (in Hindi), Patna, 1951.

———, *Bharat Ka Aitihasik Atlas* (in Hindi), Patna, 1952.

———, 'Prachina Bharatiya Vyapara evam Samudrayatra' (in Hindi), *JBRS*, 1961 (Patna, 1964). Also published as a separate book (Patna, 1964).

Mitra, Debala, *Ajanta*, New Delhi, 8th Ed., 1980.

Mitra, R.L., *A History of Indian Shipping*, London, 1957.

Mookerji, R.K., *A History of Indian Shipping and Maritime Activity*, London, 1912.

———, *Ancient India*, Allahabad, 1956.

Motichandra, *Sarthavaha* (in Hindi), Patna, 1953.

———, *Costumes, Textiles, Cosmetics and Coiffure in Acient and Medieval India*, Delhi, 1973.

Moreland, *From Akbar to Aurangzeb*, London, 1923.

Mugali, R.S., *Heritage of Karnataka*, Mysore, 1953.

Murthy, A.V.N., *The Coins of Karnataka*, Mysore, 1975.

Murthy, A.V. Narasimha (Ed.), *Archaeology of Karnataka*, Mysore, 1978.

Murthy, H.V. Sreenivas and R. Ramakrishna, *A History of Karnataka*, Delhi, 1977.

Murthy, N.S. Ramchandra, *Forts in Ancient and Medieval Andhra : A study (Up to 1600 A.D.)*, Ph.D. Thesis, Karnataka University, Dharwar, 1975.

Nadvi Saiyad Suleman, *Arab aur Bharata Ke Sambandha*, Hindi Tr. by Ramchandra Varma, Allahabad, 1930. Also in Urdu as *Arab wa Hind-ke-Ta'lqat*, Allahabad, 1930.

Nainar, S.M.H., *Arab Geographers' Knowledge of South India*, Madras, 1942.

Nandi, Ramendra Nath, *Religious Institutions and Cults in the Deccan (c. A.D. 600-A.D. 1000)*, Delhi, 1973.

Nath, Pran, *A Study in the Economic Condition of Ancient India*, London, 1924.

Nizami, A.K., *India in the Early Arabic Travelogues*, Ph.D. Thesis, Bombay University, 1978.

Niyogi, Pushpa, *Contribution to the Economic History of Northern India (from the tenth to the twelfth century A.D.)*, Calcutta, 1962.

Ojha, Gaurishankar Hirachand, *Madhyakalin Bhartiya Samskriti* (in Hindi), Allahabad, 1951.

Panchamukhi, R.S., *Annual Report on Kannada Research in Bombay Province, For the Year 1939-40*, Dharwar, 1941.

———, *Digest of Annual Report on Kannada Research in Bombay Province, For the Year 1940-41*, Bombay, 1945.

———, *Progress of Kannada Research in Bombay Province, From 1941-45*, Pts. I & II, Dharwar, 1948.

———, *Twelve Years of Kannada Research (in Bombay State)*, Dharwar, 1951.

———, *Progress of Kannada Research in Bombay Province (1947-52)*, Dharwar, 1953.

———, *An Outline of Karnataka Structure*, Dharwar, 1956.

A Panorama of Maharashtra, Published by the Directorate of Tourism, Bombay, 3rd Ed., 1964.

Pandey, Ayodhya Prasad, *Chandelakalinu Bundelakhanda Ka Itihasa*, Prayag, 1968.

Pandey, Raj Bali, *Hindu Samskaras, a Socio-religious Study of the Hindu Sacraments*, Banaras, 1949.

Pandey, Rajnarain, *Mahakavi Pushpadanta* (in Hindi), Jaipur, 1972.

Patankar, B., *Kailasa : A Cultural Study*, Ph.D. Thesis, Nagpur University, 1973.

Pathy, T.V., *Elura : Art and Culture*, New Delhi, 1980.

Pathy, T.V., & V.R.N. Prasad, *Ajanta, Ellora and Aurangabad Caves : An Appreciation*, Bombay, 1972.

Portam, M.M., *Medieval Trade and Finance*, Cambridge, 1973.

Prakash, Buddha, *Aspects of Indian History and Civilization*, Agra, 1965.

Prakash, Om, *Food and Drinks in Ancient India*, Delhi, 1966.

Premi, Nathu Ram, *Jain Sahitya Ka Itihasa*, Bombay, 1956.

Puri, B.N., *The History of the Gurjara-Pratiharas*, Bombay, 1957.

Qadri, H.S. Shamsulla, *Malabar* (in Urdu), Aligarh, 1928.

Raghavan, V., *Yantras or Mechanical Contrivances in Ancient India*, Bangalore, 1952.

Rai, Jaimal, *The Rural-Urban Economy and Social Changes in Ancient India*, Varanasi, 1974.

Rajan, K.V. Soundara, *Early Temple Architecture in Karnataka and its Ramifications*, Dharwar, 1969.

———, *Art af South India*, Delhi, 1980.

Rajasekhara, S., *Study of Aihole Temples*, Ph.D. Thesis, Karnataka University, 1975.

Ramesh, K.V., *A History of South Kanara*, Dharwar, 1970.

Rao, B.S.L. Hanumantha, *Religion in Andhra : Survey of the Religious Developments from Early Times up to A.D. 1300*, Ph.D. Thesis, Karnataka University, 1969.

Rao, M. Rama, *Andhra Through the Ages*, Guntur, 1957.

———, *Karnataka-Andhra Relations (220 A.D.-1323 A.D.)*, Dharwar, 1974.

Ray, H.C., *Dynastic History of Northern India*, 2 Vols., Calcutta, 1931, 1936.

Rice, Edward P., *A History of Kanarese Literature*, Calcutta, 1921.

Ritti Shrinivas (ed.), *A Decade of Epigraphical Studies in South India*, Dharwar, 1985.

Rowland, Benjamin, *The Art and Architecture of India*, Penguin, 1970.

Rowlinson, H.G., *Intercourse between India and the Western World*, Cambridge, 1916.

Roy, S.N., *Historical and Cultural Studies in the Puranas*, Allahabad, 1978.

Roy, U.N., *Prachina Bharata Men Nagara Tatha Nagara Jivana* (in Hindi), Allahabad, 1965.

———, *Hamare Purane Nagar* (in Hindi), Allahabad, 1968.

Sachau, E.C., *Alberuni's India*, 2 Vols., London, 1914, First Indian reprint, Delhi, 1964.

Sadyojata (Swamiji), *Saiva and Virasaiva Mathas in Karnataka*, Ph D. Thesis, Karnataka University, 1974.

Sah, Ayodhya Prasad, *Life in Medieval Orissa (circa A.D. 600-1200)*, Varanasi, 1976.

Saletore, B.A., *Ancient Karnataka*, Vol. I, Poona, 1936.

———, *Karnataka's Trans-Oceanic Contacts*, Dharwar, 1956

———, *Ancient Indian History and Culture*, Dharwar, 1957.

———, *Progress Reports of the Kannada Institute for 1953-57*, Dharwar, 1958.

Saletore, R.N., *Early Indian Economic History*, Bombay, 1973.

Sampath, M.D., *Chittor Through the Ages*, Ph.D. Thesis, Karnataka University, 1975.

Sankalia, H.D., *Indian Archaeology Today*, Bombay, 1962.

Sankalia, H.D. & M.S. Mate, *Maharashtratila Puratattava* (in Marathi), Pune, 1976.

Sankalia, H.D. & S.B. Deo, *Report on the Excavations at Nasik and Jorwe*, Poona, 1955.

———, *From History to Pre-History at Nevasa*, Poona.

Sastri, K.A. Nilakanta, *The Colas*, 2 Vols., Madras, 1935, 1937.

———, *Foreign Notices of South India*, Madras, 1939.

———, *South Indian Influences in the Far East*, 1944.

———, *A History of South India*, 2nd ed., Oxford University Press, 1958. Also in Hindi as Dakshina Bharata Ka Itihasa, Patna, 2nd Ed., 1978.

———, *Sources of Indian History with special reference to South India*, Bombay, 1961.

———, *Development of Religion in South India*, Madras, 1963.

Sastri, S. Srikantha, *Sources of Karnataka History*, Mysore, 1940.

Schoff, W.H., *The Periplus of the Erythraean Sea*, Londan, 1912.

Settar, S., *Sravana Belgola Monuments*, Dharwar, 1967.

———, *Archaeological Survey of Mysore : Annual Reports : 1911-1911 : A Study*, Vol. III, Dharwar, 1976.

Settar, S. & Gunthar D. Sontheimer (Eds.), *Memorial Stones*, Dharwar, 1982.

Seely, J.B., *The Wonders of Ellora*, London, 1824.

Shah, K.T., *Ancient Foundations of Economics*, 1954.

Shanthakumari, S. Leela, *History of the Agraharas in Karnataka, 400-1300* Madras, 1986.

Sharma, Brijanandan, *Social Life in Northern India*, Delhi, 1966.

Sharma, Brijendra Nath, *Social and Cultural History of Northern India*, Delhi, 1972.

Sharma, R.S., *Sudras in Ancient India*, Delhi, 1958.

———, *Indian Feudalism (c. 300-1200)*, Calcutta, 1965.

———, *Light on Early Indian Society and Economy*, Bombay, 1966. Revised and substantially enlarged as *Perspectives in Social and Economic History of Early India*, New Delhi, 1983.

———, *Material Culture and Social Formations in Ancient India*, Macmillan, 1983.

———(ed.), *Indian Society : Historical Probings*, Delhi, 1974.

Sharma, S.R., *Jainism and Karnataka Culture*, Dharwar, 1940.

Shelke, G.C., *A History of Marathwada Region*, Ph.D. Thesis, Marathwada University, Aurangabad, 1979.

Shriyan, Ratna Nagesh, *A Critical Study of Mahapurana of Pushpadanta*, Ahmedabad, 1969.

Singh, Ram Bhushan Prasad, *Jainism in Early Medieval Karnataka*, Delhi, 1975.

Singh, Yogyendra Bahadur, *Social Life in Ancient India*, New Delhi, 1980.

Sircar, D.C., *Indian Epigraphicai Glossory*, Delhi, 1965.

———, *Studies in the Society and Administration of Ancient and Medieval India*, Vol. I, Calcutta, 1966.

Sircar, D.C., *Studies in Indian Coins*, Delhi, 1968.

———, *Landlordism and Tenancy in Ancient and Medieval India as revealed by Epigraphical Records*, Lucknow, 1969.

———, *Studies in the Geography of Ancient and Medieval India*, Delhi, 1971.

Sitaramaiah, V., *Mahakavi Pampa*, Bombay, 1967.

Sivaramamurti, C., *Royal Conquests and Cultural Migrations in South India and the Deccan*, Calcutta, 1955.

———, *Indian Bronzes*, New Delhi, 1963.

———, *Expressive Quality of Literary Flavour in Art*, Dharwar, 1974.

Smith, W. Robertson, *Kinship and Marriage in Early Arabia*, London, 1907.

Srinivasan, K.R., *Temples of South India*, New Delhi, 3rd ed., 1985.

Srivastava, B., *Trade and Commerce in Ancient India*, Varanasi, 1968.

Sundaram, K., *A Study of Economic and Social Conditions in Medieval Andhra*, Masulipatnam, 1968.

Tavernier, *Travels in India*, Calcutta, 1905.

Thapar, Romila, *Ancient Indian Social History : Some Interpretations*, Longman, 1978.

Thaplyal, K.K. *Studies in Ancient Indian Seals*, Lucknow, 1972.

Tiwary, Marutinandan Prasad, *Jain Pratima Vijnana*, Varanasi, 1981.

Tripathi, R.S. *History of Kanauj*, Banaras, 1937.

Tulpule, S.G., *Prachina Marathi Koriv Lekha* (in Marathi), Pune, 1964-67.

——— (ed.), *Lilacharitra*, Nagpur, 1964.

Upadhyay, Bhagwat Sharan, *Prachin Pashchim Asia aur Bharat*, Publication Division, Delhi, 1977.

Upadhyaya, R., *Sanskrit and Prakrit Mahakavyas*, Varanasi, 1935.

Upadhyaya, B., *The Socio-Religious Condition of Northern India*, Varanasi, 1964.

Upadhye, A.N. (ed.), *Atmanusasana*.

Vaidya, C.V., *History of Hindi Mediaeval India*, 3 Vols., Poona, 1921-26.

Vincent, W.D.D., *The Commerce and Navigation in the Ancient Indian Ocean*, London, 1807.

Wadia, A.R. (ed.), *Social Work in Ancient and Medieval India*.

Warmigton, E.H., *The Commerce between the Roman Empire and India*, Cambridge, 1928.

Winternitz, M., *History of Indian Literature*, Vol. 2, New Delhi, 1977 & Vol. 3, Pt. I tr. into English by Subhadra Jha, Delhi, 1963.

Yadav, B.N.S., *Society and Culture in Northern India*, Allahabad, 1973.

Yadava, Ganga Prasad, *Dhanapala and His Times* (A Socio-Cultural Study based upon his Works), New Delhi, 1982.

Yazdani, G., *Ajanta*, 4 Vols., Vol. I, Oxford, 1930; Vol. II, 1933; Vol. III, 1946 and Vol., 1955.

———(ed.), *The Early History of the Deccan*, 2 Vols., London, 1960. Also in Hindi as *Dakan Ka Prachin Itihas*, Macmillan, 1977.

(ii) *Miscellaneous Works*

a. Dictionaries

Apte, V.S., *Sanskrit-Hindi Kosa*, Delhi, 1966.

Kittel, Rev. F., *Kannada-English Dictionary*, Mangalore, 1884.

Monier Williams, *Sanskrit-English Dictionary*, Oxford, 1951.

———, *English-Sanskrit Dictionary*, Varanasi, 1969.

b. Gazetteers

Bombay District Gazetteers.

Gazetteer of India, Maharashtra State, History, Part I, 1967.

Imperial Gazetteer of India.

Mysore Gazetteer, Bangalore, 1930.

c. Indexes

Anstey, Lavinia Mary, *Subject Index, IA, Vols. I-L (1872-1921)* Bombay.

Index, JBRS, Patna.

Index to the JIH (up to 1972), Delhi, 1973.

Lahiri, A.N., *Index, EI, Vols. I-XXXIV (1888-1962).*

Ram, Sadhu, *Index, IHQ*: New Delhi, 1970.

Sen, S.P. (Ed.), *Silver Jublee Souvenir Volume (Index), Indian History Congress*, 1963.

Shrigondekar, G.N., *Index, ABORI, Vols. I-XXI (1919-1940)*, Poona, 1941.

d. Special Volumes

Acharya Pushpanjali Volume, Calcutta, 1940.

Bhandarkar Commemoration Volume, Poona, 1917.

Dr. C. Kunha Raja Presentation Volume, Madras, 1041.

Commemorative Essays Presented to Professor Kashinath Bapuji Pathak, Poona, 1934.

History and Society: Essays in Honour of Professor Niharranjan Ray, Calcutta, 1976.

The Homage of Indology, Dr. Lakhman Sarup Memorial Volume, Hosiarpur, 1954.

Professor K.V. Rangaswami Aiyangar Commemoration Volume, Madras, 1940.

L.N. Mishra Commemoration Volume, Bodh Gaya, 1978.

P.B. Desai Commemoration Volume, Dharwar, 1971.

S.R. Rao Felicitation Volume (Recent Researches in Indology), Delhi, 1983.

V.V. Mirashi Felicitation Volume, Nagpur, 1965.

Yazdani Commemoration Volume, Hyderabad, 1966.

C. SELECTED ARTICLES IN PERIODICALS

Altekar. A.S., 'Was there a Rāshṭrakūṭa Empire in the Sixth Century A.D.?, *ABORI*, XXIV, pp. 149-55.

———, 'The chronology of the companions of Govinda III of the Rāshṭrakūṭa Dynasty', *Āchārya Puspāñjali Volume*, Calcutta, 1940, pp. 153-58.

———, 'The Home and Nationality of the Rāshṭrakūṭas of Malkhed', *AIOC, Session 6* pp. 65-73.

———, 'New Light on the History of the Gujarat Rāshṭrakūṭa,' *G.H. Ojha Filicit. Vol.*, III, pp. 3-7.

———, 'Society in the Deccan during 200 B.C. to 500 A.D., *JIH*, XXX, pp. 57-66.

Ayyar, A.S. Ramanatha, 'A note on the Dates of three Rāshṭrakūṭa Kings', *EI*, XXVI, pp. 161-64.

Banerjee, R.D., 'The Northern Conquests of Kṛshṇa III', *JBORS*, XIV, pp. 476-88.

Bhandarkar, D.R.,'Antiquities of the Poona District', *JBBRAS*, VI, 1930, pp. 131-38.

Bharadwaj, D.D., 'The Rāshṭrakūṭas and the Gahadwalas', *PIHC*, 1936, pp. 24-29.

Chauhan, Devising, 'Arab Horses in India', *ABORI*, XLVIII-XLIX, pp. 391-94.

Dasgupta, K.K., 'Sources of History of Karnataka Monumental Remains' in *Sources of History of India*, Vol. I, ad. by S.P. Sen, Calcutta. 1976.

Das Gupta, N.N., 'On the reign of Kṛshṇa II, the Rāshṭrakūṭas', *IA*, LXII, pp.134-6.

Deoras, V.R., 'Fresh Light on the Southern Campaign of the Rāshṭrakūṭa Emperor Kṛshṇa III', *PIHC*, 1957, pp. 133-40.

———, 'Govinda III—A Forgotten Emperor of Madhya Pradesh', *Annual Bulletin of the Nagpur Historical Society*, No. 6, 1951, pp. 60-75.

Dhavalikar, M.K., 'Evolution of the Buddhist Rock-cut shrines of Western India', *JASB*, Vols. 45-46 (New Series), pp. 50-61.

Dikshit, G.S., 'Some Aspects of Administration in the ninth and tenth centuries as illustrated by contemporary Kannada works', *PIHC*, 1950, pp. 121-25.

Fleet, J.F., 'The Appellations of the Rāshṭrakūṭas of Malkheḍa', *EI*, VI, p. 167.

———, 'Some Special features in the use of the Apoellation', *Ibid*, p. 882.

———. 'The Appellation by which the earlier members of the family were remembered in later times', *Ibid.*, p. 122.

———, 'The use of the birude Śrivallabha in the Rāshṭrakūṭa Records', *Ibid.*, p. 193.

———, 'The Date of Dhrava', *Ibid*, p. 195.

———, 'The family name of the Rāshṭrakūṭas of Malkheḍ', *EI*, VII, p. 214.

———, 'The Original Home of the Rāshṭrakūṭas of Malkheḍ, *Ibid.*, p. 223.

———, 'The Banners and Crests of the Rāshṭrakūṭas of Malkheḍ and the Raṭṭas of Saundatti, *Ibid.*, p. 227.

Gai, G.S., 'On the Date of the Ellora Plates of Dantidurga', *IHQ*, XXVIII, pp. 79-82.

Ganguly, D.C., 'The Guajaras in the Rāshṭrakūṭa Inscriptions', *PIHC*, 1939.

Gode, P.K., 'Some References to Persian Horses in Indian Literature from A.D. 500-1800', *Poona Orientalist*, XI, Nos. I & II.

Gopal, Lallanji, 'On Some Problems of Feudalism in Ancient India', *ABORI*, XLIV, pp. 1-32.

Gupte, R.S., 'Dancing Panel of Aurangabad Caves', *ABORI*, XLII. pp. 81-86.

Habibullah, A.B.M., 'An Early Arab Report on Indian Religious Sects', *History and Society*, Calcutta, 1978, pp. 433-44.

Indraji, Pt. Bhagwanlal, 'The Undikatika grant of the Rāshṭrakūṭa King Abhimanyu', *JBBRAS*, XVI, pp. 88ff.

Jha, Vivekananda, 'Status of the Rāshṭrakūṭas in Early Indian History', *PIHC*, 1973.

Khare, Ganesh Hari, 'A note on a Copper Plate grant of Rāshṭrakūṭa Govinda III', *AIOC, Session 20*, Vol. I, p. LXXVII.

Krishna, M.H., 'The Early Rāshṭrakūṭas of Maharashtra', *Rangaswami Commemoration Vol.*, Madras, 1940, pp. 55-63.

———, 'The Early Rāshṭrakūṭas of the Sixth Century', *PIHC*, 1944.

———, 'The Rāshṭrakūṭa Empire of the fifth and sixth Centuries A.D.' '*AIOC*, Session 18, pp. 71-72.

Maity, S.K., 'Forced Labour in Ancient India, '*PIHC*', 1978, pp. 147-55.

Mathur, M.L., 'Rāshṭrakūṭas of Kanyakubja and their migration to Marwar', *IHQ*, XX, pp. 153-66.

Mazumdar, B.P., 'Merchants and Landed Aristocracy in the Feudal Economy of Northern India (8th to 12th century A.D.)', *Land System and Feudalism in Ancient India*, Calcutta, 1966.

Mirashi, V.V., 'Chandragupta II Vikramāditya and Govinda IV', *SI*, I, pp. 158-64; also in *IHQ*, X, pp. 48f.

———, 'The Rāshṭrakūṭas of Mānapura', *SI*, I, pp. 177-88; also in *ABORI*, XXV, pp. 25f.

———, 'Dantidurga, the Founder of Rāshṭrakūṭa Imperial Power', *SI*, II, pp. 1 -24; also *Journal of Maharaja Sayajirao Gaikwar University* also in *JOI*, I, pp. 31-8.

———'Riddle in the History of the Rāshṭrakūṭas', *SI*, TV pp. 145-52.

———, 'Were Dramma Coins issued in Gold?', *SI*, IV, pp. 213-15; *JNSI*, XXV, pp. 238f.

———, 'The Indragadh Stone Inscription of Rāshṭrakūṭa Naṇṇa', *IHQ*, XXXI, pp. 99-104.

———, 'Minor Plates of Rāshṭrakūṭa Dantidurga', *IHQ*, XXXV, pp. 183-88.

———, 'The date of Ellora Plates of Dantidurga', *AIOC, Session 15*, pp. 97-98.

———'The Javakheda Plates of Amoghavarsha I (Śaka 742)', *PIHC*, 1960, pp. 31-6.

Mihra, V.B., 'The Tripartite Struggle', *ABORI*, XL, pp. 231-40.

Modi, P.M., 'Discovery of a Copper Plate Evidence of the Rāshṭrakūṭas ruling over some parts of Kathiwar in the ninth century A.D.', *AIOC, Session 13*.

Nandi, R.N., 'Social Life in the Agraharas of the Deccan,' *PIHC*, 1966, p. 97.

Nadvi, Syed Sulaiman, 'The Early Relation between Arabia and India', *Islamic Culture*, XI, 1937.

———, 'Arab Navigation', *Islamic Culture*, XV, 1941.

Neogi, (Miss) Roma, 'The Rāshṭrakūṭas of Kanauj', *PIHC*, 1949, pp. 138-43.

Pathy, T.V., 'Verul Sivalayamahatmya MS and some more facts above Ellora', *Studies in Indian History and Culture*, Dharwar, 1971, pp. 105-09.

Prakash, Buddha, 'A new approach to Kalachuri-Rāshṭrakūṭa Relation', *V.V. Mirashi Felicitation Volume*, pp. 406-23.

Ramchandran, T.N., 'The Kailāsa Temple, Ellora', *JAHRS*, XIX, pp. 88-90.

Ramswami, N.S., 'A portrait of Kṛshṇa III', *S.R, Rao Fel. Vol.*, pp. 228-232.

Rangaswamiah, G.R., 'The Ganga King Marasimha, '*PIHC*, 1972, pp. 65-70.

Raychaudhuri, G.C., 'The Rāshṭrakūṭa Invasions of Northern India in the tenth century A.D.', *PIHC*, 1952, pp. 131-35.

———, 'Fall of the Rāshṭrakūṭas', *PIHC*, 1954, pp. 191-93.

Reu, Bisheshwar Nath, 'Rāshṭrakūṭa and Gaharvalas', *AIOC, Session 5*, p. 133.

———, 'The Early Rāshṭrakūṭas and the present Mysore State', *JIH*, XVI, pp. 253-8.

———, 'The Early Rāshṭrakūṭas of the Deccan and the Nizam's Dominions', *AIOC, Session 10*, pp. 411-18.

Sastri, K.A. Nilakanta, 'Amoghavarsha I and Karka Suvarṇa-varsha of Lāṭa', *PIHC*, 1947, pp. 210-14.

———, 'Did Dhruva abdicate?' *JOR*, XV, pp. 9-12.

———, 'Kṛshṇa III and the Chedis', *JOR*, XVI, pp. 155-8.

———, 'The achievements of Rāshṭrakūṭa Indra III as Yuvarāja', *AIOC, Session 24*, pp. 93-94. Also in *Sarup-Bharati, The Homage of Indology, Dr. Lakhman Sarup Memorial Volume*, Hosiarpur, 1954, pp. 55-63.

Seshadri, C., 'Kṛshṇa III (Rāshṭrakūṭa King of the tenth century A.D.)', *AICO, Session 8*, p. 83.

Sharma, R.S., 'Feudal Elements in Rāshṭrakūṭa Polity', *JBRS*, XLVI, pp. 241ff.

Shastri, Ajay Mitra, 'Kalchuri-Rāshṭrakūṭa Relation in *Viddhasalabhanjika*' *L.N. Mishra Comm. Vol.*, pp. 266-74.

Shastri, H.G., 'Rise of the Rāshṭrakūṭa Rule in Gujarat', *PIHC*, 1954, pp. 391-2.

Shivann, K.S., 'Farm labourers of Karnataka,' *PHIC*, 1978. pp. 142-46.

———, 'Rāshṭrakūṭa Kṛshṇa I and Gangavadi (758-774 A.D.)', *PIHC*, 1977, pp. 65-70.

Sircar, D.C., 'A Rāshṭrakūṭa Ruling Family in Orissa', *JAHRS*, XIX, pp. 131-33.

———, 'Alleged Inscription of Rāshṭrakūṭa Kṛshṇa III, *AIOC, Session 21*, p. 120.

Srivastava, O.P., 'Slave Trade in Ancient and Early Medieval India', *PHIC*, 1978, pp. 124-36.

Subramaniam, K.R., 'The rclation between the Rāshṭrakūṭas and the Eastern Chālukyas from 747 to 925 A.D.', *PIHC*, 1938.

Subrahmanyam, R. (Ed.), *Sri Mallampalli Somasekhara Sarma Commemoration Volume, JAHRS*, Hyderabad, 1976.

Thosar, H.S., 'The Early Capitals of the Imperial Rāshṭrakūṭas', *PIHC*, 1979, pp. 68ff.

Tripathy, Snigdha, 'Rāshṭrakūṭa Ruling Family in Orissa', *S.R. Rao Fel. Vol.*, pp. 189-94.

Trivedi, H.V., 'New light on the Early Rāshṭrakūṭa House', *IHQ*, XXX, pp. 193ff.

Vaidya, P.L., 'A missing chapter in the history of the Rāshṭrakūṭas', *AIOC, Session 8*, pp. 414-18.

Venkataramanayya, N., 'Rāshṭrakūṭa Conquest of Sapadalaksa', *Dr. Kunha Raja Presentation Volume*, Madras, pp. 113-23.

———, 'The Rāshṭrakūṭa King Kṛshṇa II and Gurjara-Pratīhāras of Kanauj', *PIHC*, 1943.

———, 'An unknown incident in the history of the Rāshṭrakūṭas of Malkhaḍ', *PIHC*, 1945, pp. 85-90.

Warmington, E.H., 'Roman Coins found in India', *JRAS*, 1904.

Yazdani, G., 'Wall Paintings of Ajanta', *JBORS*, XXVII, pt. I. p. 12.

D. JOURNALS AND PERIODICALS

Annals of the Bhandarkar Oriental Research Institute

Annual Reports of Indian Epigraphy, 1946 onwards

Annual Report of the Mysore Archaeological Department

Annual Report on the South Indian Epigraphy

Archaeological Survey of India Annual Report

Bulletin of the Deccan College Research Institute

Bulletin of the Institute of Traditional Culture, Madras

Epigraphia Indica, 1892 onwards

Illustrated Weekly of India

Indian Antiquary

Indian Arehaeological Review

Indian Historical Review

Islamic Culture

The Jain Antiquary, Arrah

Journal of the Andhra Historical Research Society

Journal of the Asiatic Society of Bengal

Journal of the Bihar Research Society

Journal of Bombay Branch of Royal Asiatic Society

Journal of Historical Research (Ranchi University)

Journal of Indian History

Journal of Karnatak University (Humanities and Social Sciences)

Journal of the Numismatic Society of India

Journal of American Oriental Society

Journal of the Royal Asiatic Society

Journal of the University of Bombay

Marathwada University Journal

Marga (Pathyway), A magazine of Arts, Vol. IX, No. 2, March 1956

The Mirror, a monthly Magazine from Bombay

Ouarterly Journal of Mythic Society, Bangalore

Poona Orientalist

Proceedings of All-India Oriental Conference

Proceedings of Indian History Congress

Times of India (a daily from New Delhi).

[illegible] Indica, 1891 onwards.

[illegible] of India

[illegible]

[illegible] Historical Review

[illegible]

[illegible] Culture

Indian Antiquary, Annals

Journal of [illegible] Oriental Society

Journal of the [illegible] Society

[illegible] University, Bangalore

[illegible]

[illegible] from New Delhi.

Index

Abbasid, Khalifa 164
Abhidhanaratnamālā 146
Adulterous adventures 106
Abu Zaid 23
Agnisthitkā (fire place) 101
Agrahāra, 110, 111, 112, 113, 114
Al-Beruni 23, 27, 28, 30, 34, 36, 38, 40, 66, 91
Al-Istikhri 23, 41
Al-Masudi 41, 80
Altekar, A.S. 1, 34, 35, 49, 60, 150, 151, 184
Agriculture 140
—types of land 140
—ownership 141
Amoghavarsha I 6, 10, 18, 57, 113, 117, 147, 185
—II 10
—III 10
—Nṛpatuṅga 13
—monastery named 108
Antiquities 20
Appadorai, A. 2
Apbhraṁśa 128
Appadorai 151, 164
Arab, writers 41, 184
—merchant, contemporary 163
—relation 164
—horse 171
—Indo, contacts 198
Aryanisation 13
Ascendancy, Brāhmaṇas 26
Astronomy 98
Astrology 98, 99
Avatāras 19
—Shiva 19
—Vishṇu 19
Assessment, village 150

Balhara, greatest king 165
Ballah-ray (Balahara) 23
Bāṇa 122
Bandopadhyaya, N.C. 3
Banking system 188
Banura 23
Bharat 129
Bhāravi 122
Bhartṛhari 122
Bhāsa 122
Bhaṭṭa, Muñjārya 124
Bhavabhūti 122
Bombay Gazetteer 18
Brahmadeya grants 34
Brāhmaṇas, Karhatak 33
—exemption from taxation 34
Brāhmaṇas 26, 39
liberty 30
—characteristic names 27
—gotras and pravars 27
—life I 28

—II 29, III 29, IV 30
—universal duties 30
—lived in their own Agraharas 31
—freely migrating 32
—list of Gotra 32
—migration of 33
Brahmanic surnames 27
—values 66
Brothers and sisters, sacred relation 61
Buddha Prakash, Dr. 175
Buddhist, reference to 38

Capitals 199
—Latūr 199
—Elichpur 200
—Mayurkhindi
—Elūra 202
Mānyakheṭa (Malkheḍ) 204
Cattle, love for 153
—sheer love for 154
Cave, Daśāvatāra 6
—Ellūra 20
Caste, system 26
Chakraborti, Haripada 2
Champū, style 22
Chālukyas of Bādāmi 11, 15
Chariots 194
Chastity, signal proof 96
Chinese emperor 163
Coins, and currency system 178
—list of 180
—Gādhiyā 186
Coins 20
Corruption 104
Commercial taxes 188
Courtesans 62
Cousens 202
Crime and punishment 105
Crops 146
—main 146

Dantidurga 6, 9, 13
—Conquered Maharashtra 201
Das, Deepak Ranjan 2
Dasgupta, K.K. 2
Das, S.K. 3
Desai, P.B. 2, 206
Deshmukhs 3
Deshpandes 3
Dhruva 4, 5, 9
Dikshit, G S. 184
Drachma, Greek word 185

Education, higher, arrangements for 109, 110
Egypt 147
Elliot, H.M. 24
Elliot, Sir Walter 17
Ellura, Daśāvatāra Cave inscription 23
—sculpture 193, 194
—administrative centre 203
Empire, collapse of 16
Epigraphia Carnatica 148
Epigraphia Indica 18
Ereyanga 57
Experience, narrated 174
Export, articles 172
Extent of empire 12

Family
—system 50
—joint 51
Festivals 82
—Durga pooja 83
—Kaumudi 83
—Dīpotsava 83
—Sankranti 84
—Sarasvati 84
—Raṭṭabandha 85
Fihrist, account of Indian religious sects 190
Fleet, J.F. 17, 18, 49
Flowers, had important place 72
Food and drinks 79
Food and drinks of the time 81
Food, different for seasons 81
Founder, the 6
Flesh, Brāhmaṇas abstained 80

Forest 147
Fruits 147

Games and pastimes 85
Gaṇapati, image of 12
Garden 147
Garuḍa, vehicle of Vishṇu 11, 12
Genealogy 7, 8
Gode, Dr. 171
Grant, Lohārā 145
Gokhale, Shobhana 145
Govinda, II 9
—III 9, 11, 145
—IV 12
Guṇabhadra 126
Gunāḍhya 122
Gurjar-Pratihāras 15
Gurjar rulers, as doorkeepers 6
Guilds, played important part 176
Gupte, R.S. 178

Habib, Mohammad 24
Hair style 73
Halāyudha 118
Hattimattur record 19
Hauqal, Ibn 146
Hauqal Maqdisi 23
Hinduisation 13
Hindu, society, early medieval 26
—abstained from drinking wine 80
Hiraṇyagarbha, sacrifice 6
Hodiwala, S.H. 24
Hourani, G.F. 164
Household, articles 73
—jars 77
—basins 77,
—pots 77
—baskets 77
—trays 78
—pans 78
—mirror 78
—jewel boxes 79
Hunting 86

Idrisi-Al, Moroccan traveller 165
Indian, ports and coasts 165
India, gateway 165
—goods 170, 171
Indra II 4, 6
—III 10, 15
Industries 154
—mineral resources connected with 155
—textile 157
—leather 158
—sugarcane 159
—boat 160
—coir 160
—oil 161
—bangle making 161
—others 161
Inscription, density of 17
—deciphered 18
—divided 20
—Kanheri 185
—Chincholi 102
—Kandahār 153
—Karnataka 102, 103
—Māvali 107
—Ātakūr 106
—Parbhani 123
Jurā 133
—Daṇḍāpur 141, 151
—Shiggaon 189
Irrigation works 148

Jain, reference to 38
Jaina, literature 125
Jainism, patronised 95
Jinasen 125, 126
Jagatuṅga 6
Jain, D.C. 3
Jewels, Three 39

Kālidās 122
Kandahār, records 100
Kailāsa, temple 189
Karka I 9, 16

Kavirājamārga 6, 132, 133
Kalchuri Dynasty 54
Kalyana, natural port 166
Kanbaya 167
Khalifa 163
Khoṭṭiga 10, 129
Kurdadbeh 23, 80, 97
Kārtvīrya 145
Kīrtivarman II 6
Kṛshṇa (Lord) 74
—Kaliyamardan panel 74
Krishṇa, M.H. 186
Kṛshṇa I 9, 11
—II 10
—III 10
Kuppuswamy, G.R. 2
Kshatriya 30, 35, 38, 39, 92
Khurdādba, Ibn 38
Kshetrapāl 101
Kunti 62
Kannad literature, enriched 134
Kuppuswamy, G.R. 148
Kushāṇas 193

Labour, forced 102, 103
Land, measurement 144
—ownership 141
Lattur or Lattalur 5
Lemulvāḍa (Vemulavāḍa) 150
Life, different stages of 46
Liṅga Purāṇa 100
Levies 149
—Brāhmaṇa marriage 149
—Śūdra marriage 149
Literature, indigenous 21
—Smṛti 21
Literature 115
—Sanskrit 115, 116

Madālsāchampū 117
Mahānubhāva sect 137
Madhumati, Sugatipa 41
Madhyadesha 15
Madri 62, 63
Madridatta 122

Mahābhārat 21
Mahādāna 95
Mahājanas 48, 49, 50
Mahālakshmī goddess 97
Mahāpurāṇa 22, 46, 51
Mahmud bin Sabuktagin 40
Malkheḍa, subjected to destruction 208
Maity, S.K. 3
Majumdar, R.C. 2
Mānyakheṭa 16, 21
Manners and customs 91
Marriage, muta 43, 44
—saṁskār 51
—form of 52
—Svayambar 52
—different acts 53
—anuloma 53
—pratiloma 53
—intercaste 54
—alliance 54
—early 54
Marsiṁha 15
Masudi 23, 197
Material, paucity of 1
Mānpur 204
Mazumdar, B.P. 2
Means of livelihood 46
Medhātithi 37
Mesopotamia 147
Mineral resources 155, 156
Ministers, misappropriate funds 105
—as monsters 105
Mirashi, V.V. 36, 50, 185
Miśra, Maṇḍan 119
Monuments 20
Moplas of Malabar 45
Morality, taught 118
Motichandra, Dr. 69
Mugali, R.S. 116
Muhammad or Muhammadi 41
Munshi, K.M. 15
Muslims

—infiltration 40
—Konkani 45
—Conquered Daulatabad 203

Nadvi, Sayed Sulaiman 24, 164
Nāgabhaṭa I 13, 15
Nālchampū 117
Naik, A.V. 18
Nair Polyandry 43
Navayats 42, 44
Niyogi, Pushpa 2
Nizami, Khaliq Ahmad 24
Nṛpatuṅga 6

Origin 4
Ornaments 73, 75

Pampa Bhārata 135
Parameśvar, temple 21
Pathy, T.V. 202
Pārvati, goddess 12, 74
Periplus of the Erythraean Sea 196
Perfume dealers (Saugandhika) 72
Place names 106
Plates
—Baroda 5
—Deoli 31
—Nausari 5
—Chinchani 37, 184
—Radhānpur 49
—Samangad 6
—Manor 50
—Dhulia 110
—Bahur 113
—Wani-Dindori 32
—Maṇṇe 127
—Bandora 141
—Silhara 177
—Cambay 184
Political background 3
Ponna, poet 137
Pran Nath 3
Precious and semi-precious stones 156
Pre-Islamic 42
Pṛthvivallabha 6
Purāṇa
—Ādi 125, 129
—Uttar 125, 126
—Samasyā 126
Pulkeshin II 13
Purdah system 67
Pushpadanta 22, 51, 129, 208
—wrote *Mahāpurāṇa* 22

Qazi 41
Qāmus 44

Rājataraṅgiṇi 68
Rāmāyaṇa 21, 197
Ranna, poet 136
Rāvaṇa 71
Regnal years, importance of 99
Religious and social change 25
Religious towns 209
—Aihole 209
—Ajantā 210
—Alande 211
—Aṇṇegeri 111
—Bankāpur 212
—Bhokardan 212
—Jogeśvari 212
—Kandahār 213
—Kanheri 214
—Karhata 215
—Kolhapur 215
—Mangalore 216
—Melpāti 216
—Panahala 217
—Paṇḍharpur 217
—Paṭṭadakal 218
—Poona 218
—Pratishṭhāna 220
—Rohaṇkheḍ 220
—Sanjan 220
—Saundatti 221
—Sripur 221
—Valapi 222
Royal emblem 11

Sābkufria 38

Śaivas 39
Sah, A.P. 3
Sāhasatuṅga 5
Saints in society, status 47
Saletore, R.N. 3
Sallekhanā (fasting unto death) 17, 94
Samangad, grant 19, 23
Sanskrit works 21
Sankalia 161
Sati, system 62, 66, 67
Sarvajñatman 120
Serpent catching alive 98
Shiva, Lord 176
Sircar, D.C. 163
Siyaka, King 16
Siddiqui, W.H. 164
Scientific works 127
Scythians 193
Saundatti 143
Smṛti literature 21
—writers 118
Social values, nourished 65
Somadeva 22, 39, 47, 57, 82, 83, 85, 96, 104, 106, 121 (passim)
Sports and games 85
—Hunting 86
—Animal fights 87
—Amusement with birds 87
—Wrestling 87
—Dice 88
—others 89
—Jalkrida 89
—dance, music 90
Śubhatuṅga 5
Śūdras (untouchables) 36, 37, 92
Sulaiman 23, 41, 66
Sundaram, K. 3
Superstitious belief 96
Supremacy 13

Taila II 16
Tarikh-un-Navayat 45
Tax, on clarified butter 189
Taxes, agricultural 149
—formidable 151
—time of 152
—exemption from 152
Temple, Kailāsa 20, 75
—Jain 21
—Parameśvara 21
Textile industry 157
Theological field 125
Temple, Kailāsa 189
Times of India, The 17
Tipu Sultan 45
Transport, means of 192
Traders, position of 176
Trade routes 167, 169
—internal 173
—slave 172
Travellers, Arab and Muslim 23
Trivikrambhaṭṭa 117
Tuṅga 5
Transport 193
—Horses 193
—Chariots 194
—elephants 195
—bullock carts 196
—palanquins 197
—boats 197

Uddyotanasūri 22, 83
Utbi-Al, foreign authority 177

Vaishnavite deities 36
Vaiśyas 35, 36
Varṇasl four 26
Vikramāditya Vijaya 102
Varma, Ramchandra 24
Vatsarāja 15
Vedic, interpretation 124
—period 193
Veṅgī, ruler of 12
Vijayāditya 19
Vikramāditya II 6
Vikramārjuna Vijaya 135
Vishṇu Purāṇa 29

Vyāsa 122
Voyages, nature of 43

Weights and measures 186
Widow remarriage 60
—virgin 60
Wife-husband, relation 67
Wilks 45
Womanhood 70
Women, using stitched cloth 71
Women, position of 57
—held in high position 58
—religious independence 58
—higher education 59
—enjoyed good position 62
Work, charitable, 100
—meritorious 100

Yadav kings, of Devagiri 138
Yaduvaṁśa, Sātyaki branch 5
Yajnopovita 37
Yakshī, image 75
Yamunā and Gaṅgā, images of 11
Yaqubi 23
Yaśastilaka 21, 70, 72, 75, 81, 105, 175
Yazdani, G. 2

Zaid, Abu 23, 41, 68, 95, 160